One Life, Three Cultures

An Iranian-Armenian Odyssey

by

Elma Hovanessian

Taderon Press
London

Printed in association with the Gomidas Institute.

ISBN 978-1-903656-38-9

For further details please contact:
Garod Books Ltd.
42 Blythe Rd.
London, W14 0HA
England
Email: *info@garodbooks.com*

Dedication

To the memory of my parents who live not only in my heart, but also in the pages of this book.

To my husband for his support, valuable guidance, and for helping me make it this far in life. To our son, daughter, and their spouses for their gracious assistance, and to our four wonderful grandchildren, who have inspired and enriched our lives.

And

Thanks to my good friend, Cathleen McCann, a retired UCLA professor, who was the first to encourage me in this task.

Remember the flight
– The bird is mortal.

Forough Farrokhzad
Iranian poetess

CHAPTERS

Part I

The Pre-WWII Years

1936 – 1939

Chapter 1

Our Home in Tehran

On a hot July night, I'm lying in my bed, trying to sleep. Suddenly, I hear a popular Iranian melody coming in through the open sliding door of our bedroom. I hear someone playing a mellow love song on a flute. In this neighborhood, where a few Iranian families live, the music drifts out of a window, filling the peaceful atmosphere with its richness. That tune swiftly takes me back to Tehran, to its hot summer days and breezy starry nights some sixty years ago, when we lay down on our folding beds on our balcony, trying to sleep as we listened to someone in the street pouring his heart out through a primitive reed-pipe. And the reed-pipe reminds me of the opening poem of Molana Jalal-eddin Rumi's collection of mystical poems, *Masnavie Maanavi*:

> *Listen to the reed-pipe how it tells tales,*
> *When it complains of the agony of separation:*
> *Ever since they cut me from my reed bed,*
> *My mournful notes have moved men and women to tears...*

It is amazing how time passes so quickly. I'm a grandmother now, once a child, then a teenager, next an adult, then married with children. Now that I have two grown up children and four grandchildren, it seems that time passes much more quickly than before. It is like a handful of sand that gradually and continuously runs out of my clenched fist no matter how hard I try to squeeze it. This is why I have kept a journal to keep track of that slithering time.

I don't exactly know when my childhood ended and adulthood began, when motherhood started then was put on hold (by no means ended) and my position as a grandmother was established. When I think of my childhood, it seems like a remote shimmering mirage, a dream which, after it ends and you wake up in adulthood you don't find a trace of. No matter how much hardship or disappointment that childhood contains, you still can't help dreaming and longing to turn the hands of the clock back, returning to the past, trying to solve some unsolved mysteries and seeking answers to lingering questions. On the other hand, sometimes when people ask me, "Would you like to be young again?" I say, "No. I'm comfortable and happy right where I am. This is the place and time for which I have fought and struggled throughout my life. This is the end of a track-and-field race, during which I have run, jumped over hurdles, fallen numerous times, and finally made it to my destination."

It seems like yesterday when my first granddaughter, Taleen, was born, a ball of blood-and-tissue-covered flesh, and was put on my daughter's bosom to "bond" as the nurses advised. That picture had an immediate impact on my emotions – a shock first, then a sense of relief, and yes, a deeper bond with the two of them.

Ten days later the pattern was repeated, with another girl, Christine, my son's daughter, then eighteen months later, the two boys, Ara and Eric arrived, two months apart, and before I knew it, they were in school.

When I close my eyes I like to visualize our old home in Tehran into which my parents moved when I was six months old. It was a place that would be home for me for the next twenty-five years, until I got married and moved out.

It was a second floor rented apartment on Naderi Avenue, where residences mixed with businesses, and everything we needed could be found within walking distance. The building was an imitation of neo-classical architecture, with two off-white identical apartments and a balcony with balustrades facing the noisy avenue. Our apartment was perched above a confectioner's shop, from which the heavenly aromas of cookies, chocolate and vanilla wafted, filling our rooms in the mornings.

The other apartment, occupied by a Jewish family, was situated above a pharmacy which also sold medical supplies. Each apartment had three large rooms, a kitchen, a narrow, small storage area and one washroom and toilet, with a long corridor connecting them. We didn't have a bathroom, but we used the bathhouse across the street by taking a shower in one of its private stalls after disinfecting the place with potassium permanganate and water. We also had another balcony in front of the kitchen that faced a vacant lot where its owner raised chickens, apparently waiting for the right time to sell his property when the real estate prices picked up. We hung our laundry to dry on that balcony and occasionally kept a goose, a turkey, and even a piglet until a designated date when the creature was slaughtered, cooked and eaten. We kept our potted plants in the corridor, behind a window overlooking the vacant lot. Since we didn't have a yard, those balconies served like front and back yards.

We spent most of our evenings on the front balcony for five months of the year, from June to October. My brother, Emil, and I sat there with our mother and relaxed in the cool air as we drank tea with home-made strawberry, sour-cherry or blackberry jam, enjoying the life that passed us down below. That small pleasure was more satisfying then than watching the big-screen TV in our den today. By spending our time there, we felt good about ourselves. It gave us even more satisfaction when a friend or relative passed by and was invited up by mother to join us for a cup of tea.

We slept on folding beds there on hot summer nights. I especially liked to sleep there when there was a dinner dance in the garden of the nearby Armenian Club, from where I could hear the romantic French, Italian, Spanish or American songs played by the band. *Strangers in the Night, I'll Be Seeing You, Isn't it Romance? Perhaps, There Was a Boy, Besa Me Mucho;* and dances like *Tango Jealousy* and *La Comparsita* still enjoy universal appeal after all these years. I liked to listen to an Armenian male vocalist who did his best to imitate Frank Sinatra, Dean Martin, or other singers, as I imagined a handsome man asking an elegantly-dressed pretty woman for a tango then whirling her around under the starry sky. That balcony, as you will see, would become a witness to some turning points in my personal life in years to come, as well as to events in the history of Iran.

The Hashemi family in the identical apartment was a Jewish émigré from Soviet Georgia. The middle-aged couple had a daughter and four sons. The eldest son was married and lived there with his wife and baby girl, and how they fitted in that small space was a wonder. The father, whom everybody called, Agha (Sir), was a graduate of the prestigious Nersessian Armenian High School in Tbilisi, who spoke Armenian fluently and had taught it to his three elder sons. Their excellent knowledge of Armenian was amazing to me then and even now, because I haven't heard any other non-Armenian speak our difficult language with such ease and grace. Armenian, an Indo-European language, with its thirty-eight letters (thirty-one consonants and seven vowels) is not very easy to speak for a person who has not been brought up with it. As for his wife (his second, and an Iranian Jew) and his Iranian-born daughter and youngest son, they only spoke Farsi.

We shared a steep staircase with that family. It had a polished wooden banister, over which Emil and I liked to slide when no one was looking. The staircase ran down to a huge oak-wood gate which was normally left open during the day and closed during the night. However, when there were riots and police clashes with political dissidents or students (which happened frequently and for various reasons), we two neighbors helped each other to shut the gate by wedging a thick log between the last step of the staircase and the gate. We did it to strengthen the gate for extra security and our peace of mind. We were two families from two religious minorities: one Christian, the other Jewish. Still, we lived side by side, sharing each other's happy and sad days.

I can't recall if the Hashemis lived there when my father died. I was four and a half years old. But I still remember them showing me love and sympathy, especially their daughter, Anichka, who gave me her big doll to play with. I didn't know about my father's death of course. My mother had told me he had gone to America whenever I asked her about him. I believed her, because he had been in America as a student.

I had a china doll myself that my father had bought for me. It was either made in Germany or France. It was fragile and *expensive*, and was kept on the top shelf of our wardrobe. I was only permitted to play with it on certain occasions, like when I had a fever and had to swallow a spoonful of castor oil. I complied because of the prospect of hugging the doll and playing with it for a few hours. I adored that doll whom I had named Henriette. She had blond hair and closed her blue eyes when I laid her down. I adored her because it reminded me of my father. But over the years, I began to detest her because she also reminded me of the horrible thick oil that, even after repeated attempts at swallowing, stuck to my throat and refused to go down. Every time I took the oil in my mouth, I retched and brought it up, but my mother found a way to prevent it from happening. She made me lie down on my back and stretch my arms above my head.

I don't really know what happened to that doll. I must have broken it at some point. Now, sometimes watching the *Antique Road Show* on TV and seeing people bringing old European dolls for appraisal, I wish I still had mine. I even wish I had a Raggedy Ann instead of a china doll, which would have survived and would sell for thousands of dollars today.

I loved playing with any kind of doll, but neither my daughter nor my two granddaughters have been interested in them. I have bought a variety of dolls for them only to satisfy my own ego. When I gave one to my granddaughter, Taleen, on her first birthday, she hit it on the head and pushed it away.

Other than the Hashemis, we had another neighbor who lived across the street. She was a divorced mother who lived with her ten- year-old daughter and seven-year-old son, who were about the same ages as Emil and me. Their residence was not a house or an apartment, but a boarding house called "European Pension", where a number of families lived on a long-term basis and were served meals from its general kitchen. The brother and sister didn't go to school and didn't have any friends. Their mother, a distant relative, preferred to tutor them at home, as she had been a teacher in the past. Sometimes Emil and I went to their courtyard and played ball, jumped rope, or just sat on a bench under the shadow of pine trees. They didn't talk much, except for asking questions about our schools and friends, listening wistfully to our answers.

I didn't like the courtyard. It was kind of gloomy with all those densely planted tall pine trees, with their dark-green needles, casting too much shadow on the ground, turning the place dreary and dull in the bright light of day. However, with my mother's encouragement we kept them company whenever we could. We didn't see their mother. Neighbors said she rarely left the premises. Now when I think about those visits, I remember we were never invited to play inside their home, or offered a glass of water in the heat of summer, or a cup of tea in the cold of winter.

Then a few years later, the boarding house was closed, the families moved out, the building was renovated and converted into the Russian Hospital, with its wide metallic gates always open to the general public. As for the quiet sister and brother, they *did* make it in life – and they did it in a big way. The sister became a successful fashion designer who also tailored for the Iranian royal family and celebrities at her *maison*, then relocated to Paris after the Islamic Revolution. The brother studied medicine in the United States, became a pediatrician and practiced in California.

Chapter 2

My Father

In its quest to penetrate the Iranian auto market in the mid-1920s, the Ford Motor Company offered grants to twelve young men, enticing them to travel to America to learn auto mechanics, auto painting and design at the Ford Trade School in Detroit, Michigan.

My father, Mac (shortened in the U.S. from Mkrtich), a graduate of the American College of Isfahan (an elite high school) was selected from hundreds of qualified candidates, with two other Armenians and nine Persians from distinguished families. A trip to America in those days, under the existing hard circumstances was not only an education in the trade and learning the English language, but also helped the students build strong characters and get acquainted with Western culture. In those days few Iranians traveled abroad, especially to the other end of the globe, to far away America, and returned to Iran to tell their families and friends about their experiences.

That was in 1926. The students had been sent to Beirut by bus via Baghdad in Iraq and Damascus in Syria. In Beirut, they boarded a ship, sailed to Alexandria in Egypt where they stayed overnight, then crossed the Mediterranean Sea towards the Atlantic Ocean, passing through the Strait of Gibraltar, traveling to New York, from where they boarded a train for Detroit.

In a letter that my father had written to his parents on the back of a postcard-sized photograph, taken of him and a couple of other students, he indicated that the group had boarded a ship on January 14th for Alexandria, arriving there the next day. Unfortunately, because of lack of an Egyptian visa, they were not allowed to leave the ship. However, the position of the ship was such that the whole town was visible from its deck and one glance at that gorgeous view was enough to wet my father's appetite to see it on his way back to Iran. The ship sailed on January 16 to New York, from where he sent his family a telegram, assuring them of his wellbeing.

In that year America was celebrating the 150th anniversary of its independence. Calvin Coolidge was its president. The Ford Motor Company had just set a forty-hour week, over a 5 day schedule at $6.00 pay per day. The Model T was its best selling car, with Model A on its way to the market. Those were the days of Mae West, Greta Garbo, Rudolph Valentino, Mary Pickford and Paula Negri. Those were also the historic days of a courageous pilot, named Charles Lindberg, who flew his monoplane,

My father's trip to America (second from left, 1926).

The Spirit of St. Louis, over the Atlantic Ocean, the distance of 3600 miles from New York to Paris in thirty three and a half hours. It was unbelievable for my father and his co-travelers, whose trip to America from Iran had taken more than two months.

During his years of training, my father became acquainted with the American culture of the roaring twenties. He listened to the music of Duke Ellington and his band, and George Gershwin's popular *Rhapsody in Blue* on the radio. He learned to dance the Charleston, with flying legs and arms. He read Earnest Hemingway's newly-published *The Sun Also Rises*. He even went as far as deciding to marry an American girlfriend, but one threatening, angry letter from his mother was enough for him to give up the idea.

He witnessed the landslide election of Herbert C. Hoover in 1928, the man who had promised the American public "A chicken in every pot and a car in every garage", then the Black Tuesday, the collapse of Wall Street, the chaos of the stock market crash in 1929 and the era of the Depression that followed. He had lived in America long enough to see its opposing sides: the pretty and the ugly. On returning to Iran, he brought gifts for his mother and three sisters – long streams of pearls and dresses in the flowing flapper fashion of the twenties, some with a drop waist, and some with no waist at all. He had thought about buying a cloche hat for each, but had given up the idea because of their bulkiness. However, the fashion had already arrived in Iran and even in his home town of New Julfa – an old Armenian quarter, south of city of Isfahan.

Of the small group of the students, a few decided to remain in the United States. The majority returned to Tehran via Alexandria, with which my father had fallen in love on first sight and dreamed of relocating to and settling there. "The city of memory", which later a writer would call, was a city that boasted a blend of rich British and French cultures, with a sizeable Armenian community at the time. Although his dream never became reality, the wish to visit Alexandria became an obsession for his daughter in the years to come. However, after returning to Tehran, starting a family, and discussing it with my mother, they applied to join the immigration quota (for a permanent visa) at the American embassy and had to wait for many years for their turn to immigrate to the United States.

Back in Tehran, except for my father and another Armenian student who preferred to use their training, the rest, who belonged to upscale, influential Persian families, chose careers in politics, working their way into leadership positions and keeping strong ties with the United States.

Among those who stayed behind was one of the three Armenians who later served in the U.S. army, fought in WWII, attended a U.S. university and became a professor and an award-winning novelist. His name was Emanuel Varandian. I learned about this man from an obituary in an Armenian weekly in the late eighties. He had been living in Detroit all those years, hadn't married and had no relatives to contact with. A year before his death, when I was visiting my son, a medical student in Chicago, we decided to drive to Detroit to see the city where my father had spent a short part of his life. Had I known about this old man then, I would have found him and learned many details about their student lives. He might have told me about their moonlighting and holiday trips to Chicago, the hub of night clubs in the era of prohibition.

My aunts told me much later that my father had taught my mother the fast popular Charleston, which they danced at their wedding. No wonder I'm so crazy about that dance, which is still popular eighty years later and was exquisitely represented in the Broadway musical show and the film, *Chicago.* Looking at his photos, I can say he was a combination of Hugh Beaumont and Montgomery Clift, a dashing handsome bachelor, who attracted pretty young girls like a magnet. However, it was my mother who was the lucky one to be chosen by him. Or was she?

After establishing a successful career – a workshop named "Detroit" – the first car painting factory in Iran, and having a daughter and a son, my father was not fortunate enough to enjoy them for long. He died of pneumonia at the age of thirty-four, leaving my twenty-four-year-old mother with the responsibility of our fledgling family and business, with no one to help out.

My father's untimely death was one of the ironies of fate. He had put his life in jeopardy, enduring months of uncomfortable trips on the dirt roads of Iran and the Middle East, crossing treacherous stormy seas to the New World, working hard to get a degree and to create a semblance of an American dream in Iran: a good permanent job, a prosperous family, and a respectable life in his community, which was realized, but didn't last. He succumbed to a disease that was a killer then, but curable today.

During his short-lived career, my father had achieved a few seemingly unattainable goals. He was the special painter of the royal court's automobiles – an honor for an Iranian citizen, especially for an Armenian. That was during the reign of Reza Shah the Great, the father of Mohammad Reza Shah Pahlavi, an imposing, powerful monarch whose decree was law for his people.

One morning, the Shah's driver brought the Shah's purple-colored automobile into the workshop. (The egg-plant dark-purple paint was my father's creation, his trademark, a color he was not allowed to use on other people's cars.) The driver got out of the car and pointing to the rear window, told my father that the Shah wanted him to reduce it to a smaller size. It was too large, exposed the interior, and the Shah didn't like it. (In those days tinted glass didn't exist in the market.) The Shah wanted it done within a month. The Shah was meticulous, hard to please, and didn't take no for an answer.

My father had no other choice but to try. He hadn't done such a risky project before. What if he completely ruined the window? There surely would be repercussions. Anxious and scared, he went home earlier than usual and told my mother about it. Mother, on the other hand, saw opportunity in the project. She provided encouragement by assuring him that with his expertise and resourcefulness, he would succeed if he tried hard. She suggested that he start immediately. She brought him pencils and sheets of brown paper, and he started drawing a smaller version of the existing window with the measurements he had brought along. He sat at the dining table every evening after dinner, under the sputtering light of an oil lamp and made sketch after sketch, piling crumpled papers in the waste basket until he approved one of them, then completed the design and worked on it for a whole week. That was the easy part. The hard part was still ahead.

Having finished the drawing, he started dismantling the designated window with the help of two employees: one step at a time, piece by piece, working carefully so as not to damage anything in the process. They finished the job in a few days. Then the time came to build a new window with sheets of metal – which they cut with their machine tools – and a smaller piece of glass that an expert glass-cutter had cut for them. Then they carefully installed the combination of metal and glass in place of the old window. When that part of the job was done successfully, they breathed a sigh of relief and began painting the entire automobile.

Two days before the deadline, he took my excited mother – who was initially the driving force behind his efforts – to the shop and, in the presence of his employees, unveiled the monarch's gleaming purple automobile with its newly-down-sized window.

For his creativity, punctuality, and the state-of-the-art work, my father was given a trophy and was paid generously, a part of which he shared with those who had helped him in the task. The next thing he knew, his name was in the papers, and the Armenian community talked respectfully of Mac Hovsepian and the top honor he had garnered for himself and the Armenians of Tehran.

*****

It was late in December 1936. The coal stove was spreading heat around our dining room where my mother and my father's three sisters were sitting, clad in black. They were speaking softly, occasionally opening the tiny door of the cast-iron heater, rattling the burning red coals with a poker and feeding the fire with black charcoal, while my brother, Emil, and I were quietly playing on the other side of the room, under our Christmas tree. Hating all those black clothes and sensing that something unusual had happened, I went to my mother and asked, "Where is my daddy?" She said, "He is in America, dear. Go play with your toys."

"I don't want the toys. I want my daddy," I yelled, and burst into tears, hiding my head in her lap. Only God knew how desperately I wanted to trust and believe her. But then, how could I ignore the kids in the kindergarten who kept reminding me of my father's death, no matter how hard I tried to convince them, in my own childish way, that he was *not* dead but had gone to America.

In those days it was not common to talk to children about death, much less about the death of a parent or a loved one. The issue was taboo. In the same way, it seemed to be taboo to talk about a person's achievements because it would be considered arrogance or vanity. Even when we had grown up, Emil and I didn't dare talk or ask questions about my father's life in the past. I had no idea until after mother's death about his being chosen among hundreds of students to be sent to America, when I heard it by chance from a distant relative. I also learned much later that he used to play the violin. That was when Emil found the dusty musical instrument in our attic.

When I grew up I didn't have the chance to ask mother about my father, because she remarried, and whenever I attempted to bring up the question, she somehow evaded it. Apparently the past was too painful for her to be reminded of. However, she too died early and left me with unanswered questions. Later when I felt obsessed with my father's life and decided to ask relatives or friends, they either had died or were unable to recall the past. Fortunately, two of my female cousins who are much older than me but have brilliant memories shared them with me.

I don't know how they had the heart to decorate a tree in those tragic days that had coincided with Christmas and New Year, but I suppose mother had done it to prove to all of us that everything was normal. She might also have done it to cheer up father, whose bed had been moved to the dining room to keep him warm.

That Christmas tree was the last one we saw in our home until I married and moved to my own house. Even then, mother made me promise not to decorate a tree before I had my first child. However, in the years that followed she took us to Christmas parties at relatives' and friends' homes where we admired the trees which were decorated with handmade ornaments and fragrant white candles, and were given candies and dried fruit and nuts wrapped in colorful crepe paper.

My mother was neither superstitious, nor stubborn, but she was adamant in her refusal to decorate a pine tree in our house. She was convinced that Christmas trees brought bad luck to our family, and she clung to her beliefs for the rest of her life. I didn't blame her for that. You wouldn't believe it if I told you that three deaths occurred in my father's family within two weeks of the holidays. Other than my father, his sixty-two-year-old mother died shortly after she was diagnosed with yellow fever, and his thirty-eight-year-old brother of kidney failure. I don't remember my uncle, but they say he was a tall, handsome man with blue eyes and light brown hair who earned a top salary working for the government as an English/French/Farsi translator. However, he had a major vice: he was a heavy drinker who had failed to maintain a family and his health.

Besides that year's tragedies, mother hadn't forgotten the death of our young male servant, Manouk, which had happened the year before. (I'm surprised that I can remember his name.) One day in late December, he had gone to my paternal grandfather's house to cut a pine tree in their courtyard. On his way back home, he had been attacked and bitten by a stray dog which later was diagnosed with rabies. A few days later Manouk died in the hospital. In those days there was no cure for that fatal viral disease.

Parallel to that misfortune, another strange thing happened in those days. We had a little yellow canary in a cage hanging from a hook on the wall of our corridor. Every morning, Manouk took down the cage, opened its tiny door, cleaned it, and put new seed and water in it. And the happy bird sang his heart out all

My picture taken at the age of two or three.

day long, until the day when he accidentally left the cage door open and the canary escaped. Unable to fly (canaries are bred as cage birds), our kitten grabbed it in its paw and started playing with it. Luckily, Manouk saw them in time, saved the frightened bird, put it in its place and shut the door, but from that day on, the yellow-feathered tiny creature didn't sing a single note. It kept silent for some time until it fell dead on the same day that Manouk died. It surely was a coincidence, but it had a strong impact on my mother's emotions.

Now one can see why mother didn't enjoy having a Christmas tree in our house. I too learned throughout my life to be indifferent toward it. When I grew up and thought about it, I could only sympathize with the poor pine tree which was cut from its roots, taken into a heated room, away from its natural environment and loaded with burning candles that would expedite its demise.

Years later in Los Angeles, I was flicking through TV channels when a movie featuring Jason Robards caught my attention. It was called *The House*

Without a Christmas Tree. It was a similar story to ours, but with a moral conclusion and a much happier ending. It was the story of a young man who had lost his wife to pneumonia during the previous Christmas holidays and refused to decorate a Christmas tree for his little girl. However, the little girl was so eager to have a Christmas tree that despite her father's refusal, she somehow found an abandoned pine tree in the neighborhood, dragged it home, and decorated it. The astonished father, who was faced with an accomplished fact, couldn't do anything but to accept it. Thus, the little girl, by her strong will and determination, not only fulfilled her own wishes, but also played a great role in changing her father's mood and way of thinking.

Chapter 3

My Mother

My mother, Lusik, after losing her husband and the short glorious time she had shared with him, suddenly found herself a widow at the age of twenty-four, all alone with two children, confronting the difficulties of life with no marketable skills or any knowledge of business.

She was a tall woman with a self-confident posture. With her brown eyes and short brown hair, usually combed back from her wide forehead, I found her the prettiest woman in the world. She had graduated from the junior high school of her home town, New Julfa, and like other girls of her age hadn't stood a chance of continuing her education at a high school in the nearby city of Isfahan. There was no public transportation and people used horse-drawn carriages for going to the *city* for business. As for the boys, some of them were sent at an early age to India to a prestigious Armenian boarding school in Calcutta to later continue their higher education at a British university – as my grandparents did with my elder uncle, Hovik. The other boys who remained in New Julfa just rode their bicycles to the American College, pedaling across the Sio-se-pole Bridge over the Zayandeh-Rood River that connected New Julfa with Isfahan. Not that the girls couldn't ride a bicycle, but the Julfan community restricted them from doing so. Thus, the girls' schooling came to an abrupt halt in that small town.

After my father's death, however, my mother had enough presence of mind not to sell the factory, but to hire Uncle Johnny (one of her three younger brothers) to manage it. Uncle Johnny, a graduate of the American College in Isfahan had just completed military service and was looking for a job. He had no experience and training but with the help and supervision of the head technician my father had trained, Johnny, a smart, curious young man, learned the details and finesse of the business, and in no time took control of the factory. After a couple of years he became a partner.

When I think about that whole situation now, I simply marvel at the strength and determination that my mother found in herself to handle those challenges. At a time when most wives of her level stayed at home, being supported by their husbands, my mother had to rear a family *and* take care of the business. She became a frugal housewife and made everything from scratch, sometimes from nothing. She sewed our clothes, including the underwear from the best fabrics she could find. When it came to heavy jackets and coats, she bought the fabrics and gave them to a tailor to make them for us. She produced vinegar from left-over grapes, liquors from sour cherries, peaches and coffee with alcohol, leaving them in bottles under the scorching summer sun for weeks, to later distil them with a cheese-cloth and pour them into decanters. She made jams from seasonal fruit: luscious black-berries, fragrant strawberries, apples and green figs; and preserves from walnuts, watermelon skins and tiny slender eggplants, making them brittle by leaving them overnight in a solution of water and limestone.

She made sacrifices and dedicated her time, energy and money to give her two children a better life. In our lives, there was no place like home. We were attached to the security of routine, especially doing homework and playing with our friends. Maybe that is why I'm a creature of habit and enjoy routine in my life. I loved to listen to her bedtime stories which she either told or read from an Armenian children's book. For me, she was the best storyteller in the world. When she told a story, she simply brought it to life by the changes of expression on her face and eyes and the nuances in the tone of her voice, like when she shifted from the piping voice of the Little Red Riding Hood to the gruff voice of the wolf. By listening to her, I always felt secure and good about myself.

Speaking of routine, since we didn't have an electric refrigerator, my mother did the grocery shopping on a daily basis. A refrigerator was considered a luxury item. A few families who owned one placed it in their living rooms to show it off to their guests. When mother went shopping, she sometimes took me along. At the butcher's shop, she would usually buy half a kilo of lamb shanks, ribs or filet, depending on what she was intending to cook for the day. I liked to watch the butcher, who talked and cracked jokes, as he sharpened a cleaver by pulling it against another, then disjointing and cutting up a freshly-slaughtered whole lamb hanging from the ceiling by an iron hook. My mother was on the alert as she listened to him, lest he tried to cheat her by throwing into the package a piece of goat meat which was much cheaper and harder to cook. At the grocery shop, she would sort out parsley, cilantro, dill, chives, and some vegetables, then select some seasonal fruit and give them to the grocer, who would weigh them on a brass scale and put them in a paper bag in exchange for a few *rials*.

My mother was a great cook who had a large range of recipes, not only of Armenian and Persian meals of pilaf and vegetable stews; stuffed vine-leaves, cabbage or pumpkin, but also those of other nationalities. She also prepared French chateaubriand steak, Italian pastas, Russian beef-stroganoff, borsch and *piroshki*, even hot Indian dishes – a legacy from my grandpa's business trips to India. However, the pizza which she started to make in the 1960s after her trip to America was a delicious novelty in Tehran, which she introduced to our circle of friends and relatives. Except for the mozzarella which she bought from Iran-Super, the only western-style supermarket open at the time, she made the pizza from scratch: the dough with yeast, flour and water, the sauce with fresh fleshy tomatoes, and used home-dried and powdered *marzeh* instead of oregano.

Twice a year, for New Year and Easter, she made *nazook* in large quantities and summoned a porter to take them on a brass tray to the bakery around the corner. *Nazook* is a round thick pastry like a loaf of bread, made of butter, sugar and flour, glazed with saffron and egg yolk. When the porter brought the baked golden-colored pastry back to the house, we savored its vanilla and saffron aroma, and enjoyed it for months to come. Even now after all these years, we buy *nazook* from the Iranian-Armenian bakeries in Glendale, California. These bakeries have maintained the old tradition by baking it year round for the convenience of their customers.

Like her father, who had an orchard in New Julfa, my mother was a lover of nature. Since we lived in an apartment and didn't have a courtyard, she kept potted plants and showed me how to grow beans and seeds in springtime. She bought flowers at a kiosk around the corner from a one-legged young man who ran a profitable business, thanks to the sensible and generous customers of the neighborhood. As far as I can remember, the crystal vase on the table of our dining room was always full of seasonal cut flowers. In spring, it was fragrant daffodils and colorful tulips; in summer, gladioli and thick-stemmed rosebuds; in fall, gorgeous yellow and purple chrysanthemums; and in winter, multi-colored long-lasting carnations. Then in mid-January for a short period of time, we would indulge in the fragrance of the transparent yellow ice-flower that blossomed on its naked brown branches. Flowers made my mother happy. She said, "When I'm away from home and remember that I have flowers to return to, my heart swells with joy."

My love of flowers didn't directly come from my mother. It came from my little boy who told me once, "I love to go to grandma's home, because she has flowers in her vase." I wish she were alive and could see my backyard in California, with its year-round yellow and crimson roses, and white and purple azalea bushes, with coral red camellias that explode in color in December and January. I would especially like to show her my cream-colored orchids with purple hearts that last in a vase for as long as eight weeks.

My mother liked to improve her English and wanted to learn French, so she took private lessons with the best foreign language teachers in Tehran.

She was an avid reader and bought and read every new English book that the bookstore across the street could offer. During World War II and the occupation of Iran by Allied Forces, the pocket-books and army-editions of classical and contemporary novels were piled high in our house. After reading them, she would lend them to my uncles or her friends. When I grew up and began reading English books, I started pulling them out from cardboard boxes held in the storage and devoured them one by one. I remember *Tortilla Flat, Grapes of wrath,* and especially *Forever Amber,* about whose author, Kathleen Winsor, I read in the obituaries section of Los Angeles Times in May of 2003. For me, that book was an introduction and exposure to sex.

Uncle Johnny, who had a fiancée back in New Julfa, stayed in our house at that time. He too was an avid reader like mother. He was a warm person, gentle and patient, who filled the empty place left by our father. On Friday mornings (which is like Sunday here) when Emil and I woke up, we rushed to his room, sat on the edge of his bed, and asked him to tell us stories. He never disappointed us. He told us all kinds of stories. I am still amazed at the source of his knowledge. We were much fond of the stories he told us from the Greek mythology, especially the one about Cyclops, the one-eyed giant who stood at the opening of a cave like a prison guard, counting the sheep when they were filing past him, with the hero snuggled under the belly of one of them trying to sneak out to freedom. One story that has been etched in my memory and always makes me think about the bizarre situation of its protagonist is Washington Irving's story of Rip Van Winkle who had awoken after one hundred years of sleep to learn of the changes that had happened since he had fallen asleep. It has always made me wonder what would it be like if I died and woke up one hundred years later – would the world be hell or a paradise, or a little of both? Not unlike it is today.

Johnny also painted in his spare time. We had a few of his water color and oil paintings of landscapes and still life on the walls of our dining room. He showed us how to draw. He did an excellent job of drawing bicycles and automobiles which made Emil crazy about them. He had the habit of singing with every single line he put on paper, encouraging us to do the same.

*****

In the spring of 1937, a few months after my father's death, his sister, Mary, emigrated to Armenia in the Soviet Union. She was the middle one of the three sisters. She left Iran with her two sons, two daughters and her husband, a refugee from the Armenian Genocide, perpetrated by the

Ottoman Turks in 1915. He had fled from Turkey to Soviet Armenia and acquired Soviet citizenship. Then for some personal reasons, he had come to Iran, married my aunt and started a family. Mary didn't want to leave Iran and her bereaving family behind, but her husband was under the pressure of the government, either to acquire Iranian citizenship or leave the country. He decided to take his family to Armenia. The day the family left on a bus bound for the port of Pahlavi on the Caspian Sea, the atmosphere was somber. Deep down in our hearts, we knew they wouldn't come back. We were right. We didn't hear from them either on arrival, or during the six years of WWII which erupted in the fall of 1939.

*****

In late September 1937, when schools opened in Tehran, mother asked Uncle Johnny to walk me to the nearby elementary school, Tamaddon (meaning civilization). Ten months after my father's death she was still in mourning. It was the custom of the Armenian community for women to wear black until the first anniversary of the deceased person's death and not to appear in public places. I was five-and-a-half years old, nervous and frightened in my white-collared gray uniform that mother had sewed for me. I was going to a school where every subject was taught in Farsi, and I didn't know a word of the language. I was supposed to start in the preparatory class, but because of a shortage of rooms and the elimination of certain classes, I was taken to the first grade, where I started my education earlier than the regular age of seven.

The reason I was not going to an Armenian school was because they had been closed the year before. After a visit to Turkey the previous year, Reza Shah had ordered the Armenian schools to be closed. It was said that during a meeting with the Turkish leader, Ataturk, the leader had asked Reza Shah why there were no Turkish schools in Iran, whereas there were many other foreign language schools. In response, the Shah had decided to close all foreign language institutions instead of opening Turkish ones.

I started the first grade, with students of all ages who had arrived from other foreign language schools, some from higher grades, with little knowledge of Farsi. I had classmates who were four or even five years older than me. It was like the classes in the TV drama, *The Little House on the Prairie*, with the difference that all of us were educated at the same level. When we grew up and went to higher grades, the older girls started talking about the boys, parties and makeup, and scolded us younger ones who dared listen to them.

In order to raise its children with the knowledge of its language and culture, the Armenian community of Tehran started to run underground language classes and organized small parties, where they sang and danced to folk music, or performed in Armenian drama pieces. My mother enrolled me in a class but I never participated in any play. I only watched them. Emil and I were happy to mingle with other Armenian children of our age. Those classes and cultural events went on for several years until the foreign language schools were reopened after the fall of Reza Shah and the occupation of Iran by the Allied Forces at the beginning of WWII. It was then that a few Armenian cultural and professional organizations were established, of which I became a member when I grew up and attended college.

After I got used to my school, learned the language and found a Persian friend of my own age, with whom I could speak Farsi, I felt happy and satisfied. Every morning and afternoon (we had a two-hour lunch break for which we went home), Pari, a Baha'i by religion, who lived close-by, came to our door, and cupping her mouth with her hands yelled from under our balcony, "Elma...." Hearing her voice I, ready and waiting for her, would rush down the stairs or slide down the banister to the street and together, we would walk to school, chatting happily. Our school was located less than half-a-mile away, near a Jewish synagogue. I had another friend, a Jewish girl, Vajiheh, who lived next to the school and the synagogue. Sometimes after school she would invite the two of us to her courtyard

With my mother and brother, Emil, on our balcony.

and, depending on the season, we would pick either ripe persimmons or pomegranates from the trees and eat them on the spot smearing ourselves with their juice.

Every spring, mother would buy me a few silkworms which I would keep in a cardboard box and feed with mulberry leaves that Pari and I would pick from a tree on our way home from school. We would also pick a handful of the ripe, cream-colored, succulent mulberries and push them into our mouths as we carefully dodged the squashed fruit on the ground. For a few weeks, Pari and I patiently fed and cared for the silkworms until they wove a white or yellow cocoon around themselves. Then one day in our absence and without our knowledge, they turned into butterflies and flew away, leaving us with their pierced, hollow shells to wonder about.

During the month of Ramadan, as Pari and I walked home from school, we sometimes came across a man in tattered clothes who sold honey-soaked *zulubieh* and *bamieh,* delicious Ramadan treats, on a tray laid on a stool. As we stopped there hesitating, we would watch the man who, every now and then, would rearrange the yellow and brown sticky sweets around the tray, licking his fingers in between. My mother had strictly forbidden me from buying any food sold in the street. But Pari always had some coins in her pocket and would buy a few which the vendor would hand her in a piece of newspaper, and she would give me one or two. I knew that I was not allowed to eat them, but how could I refuse such a succulent offer staring me in the eye? Only God knew what that peasant had been doing with his fingers before touching those sticky sweets. I still am amazed at the power of our immune systems. How we didn't get diarrhea or any contagious disease is still a wonder to me.

Speaking of strictness, it seemed that the more I was forbidden from doing something wrong, the more it made me curious and eager to explore. Once I was invited to a play-date at a neighbor's house. The girl with whom I played had a pearl-colored purse with a golden chain-strap which we took turns in throwing on our shoulders and swinging to and fro as we walked around the room. I was so fascinated by that purse and tempted to own it that I sneaked it out on my way home (although I knew I shouldn't). The next morning, mother found it in the wardrobe and asked me about it. When I told her that it belonged to my friend, she got angry, slapped me on the cheek (that was common in those days), dragged me to their house, returned the purse, and made me apologize for my big mistake. I felt humiliated and furious, and didn't talk to her for a long time.

Chapter 4

My Grandparents' Home in New Julfa

In June, as soon as the schools closed in Tehran, mother packed my suitcase and sent me to New Julfa to stay with my grandparents until she and Emil could join me. On my departure, when she kissed and bid me farewell, I responded with coldness and reserve. I was still angry with her for humiliating me in front of my friend when she was returning the purse.

Our journey started in the early afternoon. There were five passengers in the big black Ford. My aunt, grandpa's brother and another man were sitting in the back. I was sitting in front, between the driver and a family friend, a huge man who rarely spoke, except for reluctantly answering my questions about the car and whatever I saw along the dirt road.

After passing the holy city of Qom, with distant views of the glittering golden and blue domes of its mosques, the driver made a short stop at a small teahouse on the side of the road to let the heated engine cool down and we thirsty passengers drink a glass of tea. Once we resumed the journey, we didn't stop until nightfall. The road was so straight and monotonous that I thought we would never see people again, but after a while, I noticed blinking lights in the distance and heard dogs barking. We were approaching a village where we would have dinner and would spend the night.

At a teahouse on the edge of the village, all they ordered was just a few tiny glasses of sweet tea with some freshly baked bread. Food prepared at the roadside teahouses was considered impure and unhygienic. Instead, my aunt had brought along two roasted salty chickens with some boiled potatoes which we all shared on the carpet-covered wooden beds that served as a table and a seat at the same time.

That night, I slept in the car with my aunt, while the rest stretched on those wooden beds with their own blankets trying to sleep for a few hours. At dawn, after we had a simple breakfast and the driver succeeded in bringing the car engine to life, we returned to the desolate road and headed toward our destination. The trip from Tehran to Isfahan, a distance of 405 kilometers (250 miles) took us twenty-four hours to accomplish.

*****

New Julfa, the Armenian quarter south of the historic city of Isfahan, is located on the southern bank of the Zayandeh Rood River. It was founded in the 17th century by the decree of Shah Abbas the Great for the Armenian population of the Caucasus that he had relocated to Persia.

Shah Abbas, who ruled Persia between 1587 and 1629, ended the country's anarchy that had been going on since the death of Shah Tahmasp I in 1576. He restored the Persian military forces and drove the Ottomans out of the province of Azerbaijan in the northwest, threatening to capture the entire Ottoman Empire. However, during one of his unsuccessful battles with them, he was defeated and forced to retreat from the west to the east of the extended empire, torching and sacking towns and villages along his way. When he reached the Armenian-populated villages and towns on the border of the Caucasus and Persia, and the most populous town, Julfa, he ordered its inhabitants, famous as artisans and for their craftsmanship, to leave their homes and join his forces returning to Persia. Since the Ottoman army was following and approaching them rapidly and there was no time to provide boats for the people to cross the border – the Aras River – he ordered them to swim its extensive width to the other side.

Out of 450,000 deported people only 150,000 survived. Of those who arrived in the province of Azerbaijan, some chose to stay in Tabriz, others dispersed to other cities, and the rest followed Shah Abbas and his military forces to the capital city of Isfahan in central Persia. They lived in Isfahan successfully for a few years and contributed to the cultural and economic welfare of the country. Later, they were given permission and the option of having their own quarter south of the city, where they built a town, complete with a cathedral and many churches, naming it New Julfa, being happy to be able to practice their religion, Christianity.

*****

I arrived in that small town the next evening and was greeted by my overjoyed grandparents. Tired from sitting for so long and covered in dust, grandma helped me wash and change as she opened my suitcase and hung my clothes in their wardrobe. Then she served us dinner while they took turns in asking me questions about my trip, my mother, uncle and brother. Later, she showed me to my bed, with the promise of going to the public baths the next morning.

I slept through the night like a lamb, only to wake up late in the morning to the smell of boiling milk that was wafting from the kitchen. It took me a few seconds to figure out my whereabouts before I jumped out of bed, dressed and rushed to the kitchen. Grandma was standing before a lit Primus stove, waiting to turn it off as soon as the milk rose. (Pasteurized milk still didn't exist.) Hearing my footsteps, she turned around, looked at me lovingly from behind her wire-rimmed glasses, smiled and gave me a big hug, pressing me tightly to her chest.

Grandma Mariam, a woman of medium height, with a head of brown hair and some strands of gray at the temples, was already considered old at the age of forty six. She had borne four children: my mother Lusik and three uncles: Hovik, Johnny and Hrand. None of them lived in New Julfa.

After a breakfast of hot chocolate, bread, butter and home-made apple jam (from their courtyard), she told me to get ready for the baths. Going to the baths was a whole day affair, a social event. So after grandpa left to run certain errands, and the Persian porter arrived, grandma showed him the necessary items to put on his round wooden tray which he carried on his head. The items consisted of an old blanket, a couple of small copper bowls, soap, towels and clothes in a bundle, and some food for lunch. With the man ahead of us, we walked to the nearby ancient bathhouse which was allocated to female customers in the mornings and to males in the evenings. In the ante-room, the porter unloaded the tray on a space on the platform, and spread the blanket on the warm slabs of stone that covered it.

Grandma and I undressed, wrapped ourselves in aqua-floral wraps, and walked in wooden sandals towards the crowded, noisy washroom, inhaling the sharp smells of wet clay, soap and henna that lingered in the steamy air. As we stepped inside, I saw women and children of all ages, even small boys, covered with colorful wraparounds, standing or seated on the wet slabs of stone next to the sunken hot-water basin, busy washing themselves. Suddenly, I noticed black cockroaches scurrying about in the corner. I screamed and shivered as I tried to summon all my courage just to dodge and walk past them. It was my first time at a public bath and everything I saw was new and scary to me. In Tehran we used a private shower stall in the public bathhouse with its own ante-room. However, my fear didn't last long and I felt at home when we found a space near the basin and grandma introduced me to a couple of girls my age. I soon joined them in filling our bowls with water, talking and laughing together. Once looking up at the glass domes on the high ceiling, I noticed the shadow of a man sneaking away, and I told grandma about it. But she shrugged and summoned a masseuse who approached and started scrubbing her body with a soapy *lufah*.

At lunch time we went back to the ante-room, sat cross-legged on the blanket and ate the food grandma had prepared: cold chicken breast, boiled potatoes, fresh and pickled cucumbers, with cherries and succulent cantaloupe for dessert which we shared with grandma's friends sitting next to us. The women knew each other there. They even made a date ahead of time to be there the same morning. They gossiped and discussed past and upcoming social events. As they became more intimate, they even revealed some personal secrets, after sipping some home-made wine that one of the women had poured into tiny glasses and passed around.

*****

I spent the entire summer at my grandparents' home, together with mother and Emil who joined me later. But for me, the first month was the best when I was alone with them and they tried to entertain and amuse me. Grandpa had bought a baby goat for me to play with. It was a mischievous pet that liked to run around the courtyard, with me trying to pursue and catch it. One day the goat jumped up and pulled down a bunch of hot red peppers which grandma had tied on a string and hung from a wall to dry. One little bite and the poor thing was howling and running around the courtyard. As soon as grandpa realized the situation, he reacted immediately. He brought milk from the house, caught the little thing in the middle of its run and poured it into its mouth and throat. He repeated it a few times before the baby goat calmed down. I have told this story to my two children and four grandchildren scores of times; even now that they are grown up, they still enjoy hearing it.

The big courtyard had an almond tree whose white flowers I hadn't had a chance to see in spring. One early morning, grandpa shook the loaded tree and when the green-coated almonds fell on the ground, grandma and I collected them in a basket, cracked and shelled them as we tasted one occasionally. There was also an apricot tree, its fruit called *shekar-pareh* (piece of sugar), as well as an apple tree called *golabi*, a hybrid of apple and pear, fragrant and juicy. On the other side of the courtyard stood a pepper tree with a cluster of bees buzzing and swarming in and out of it. When it rained or the wind blew, the tree let out a spicy, hot smell.

Twice or three times a week, grandpa, Haig, and I went to their orchard/ vineyard, where vines were elevated and spread on wooden arbors like a canopy, with bunches of grapes hanging from them. Grandpa opened the crude wooden gate with a heavy iron key, which he took from a hiding niche next to the gate, turning it in a large keyhole (through which I could see a part of the orchard). Once inside, he inspected the property for a few minutes then started cutting the grapes with his own hands, dropping them into a bucket. When it was full, he drew water from a well in the middle of the orchard and poured the cold water over the sun-warmed grapes. We ate some and took the rest back home.

In that orchard grandpa kept a couple of tortoises to kill the venomous snakes which sometimes appeared in the grass. Once I saw one of the tortoises grasping the head of a snake and holding it tight in its jaw. The ensnared creature tried desperately to free itself, by lashing its entire long body against the tortoise's hard back until it stopped struggling. A few moments later a raven snatched the snake's limp body from the grass and soared into the sky. As soon as grandpa noticed them, he yelled at me, "Be careful. Those snakes are poisonous!" He was afraid that something bad would happen to me. He always kept his eyes on me wherever we went. He seemed to have assumed full responsibility for protecting me. Sometimes he handled me like a china doll, afraid that if I fell I would break.

Grandpa liked to tend to his orchard personally, with occasional help from a laborer who came to trim the trees, till the soil, or to apply fertilizer. The orchard was irrigated by municipal water that flowed in twice a week. He took pleasure in introducing me to the mysteries of nature by showing and explaining about the fruit trees and varieties of birds and butterflies. Once he showed me how to graft a tree and form a new growth in order to improve the quality of the fruit. I remember him making a cut in an apple tree with his sharp pocket knife, inserting a new shoot, and then wrapping it tight with a thick thread. He showed me how to plant petunias in the flower bed and geranium cuttings by putting them in the soil of a flower pot, letting them grow into a new plant. I was very young when he taught me about gardening, but I have remembered enough to practice it in the backyards of my houses in Tehran and Los Angeles.

Grandpa didn't sell any of the fruit he grew in the orchard, because most neighboring families owned similar orchards. He didn't have a paying job. He had sold his store after his children had grown up and left home, but I guess he lived on the interest that the money earned for him. He kept himself busy with community commitments and for many years he had been a member of the diocesan council, and on the boards of the local schools and churches. He also took part in the activities of a theatrical group which produced and enacted original Armenian drama and comedy plays, or translations from English, French and Russian. In his better days, grandpa being a handsome and jovial young man was mostly given the part of the hero or the lover, which irritated grandma when she saw him rehearsing with another woman. In those days, theater was much in demand, being the sole entertainment for the population of that little town. People enjoyed seeing amateur actors and actresses performing on the stage, and encouraged or criticized them right on the spot, by shouting out their genuine thoughts and opinions.

Grandpa was a tall vigorous man. When I stood next to him, I had to hold my head back to see his face. He had brown hair and eyes and when he smiled he revealed his white regular teeth under his drooping moustache. I didn't know his age, but he was much older than grandma. He didn't like to talk about it. Years later, registering at a hotel in Qazvin on a trip to Hamadan for my Uncle Hrand's wedding, when the receptionist asked him, "How old are you?" He retorted, "Write down *one hundred*."

He was the third of his family's six children. His family had survived the Turkish massacres of the 1890s that preceded the horrendous Genocide of 1915 by fleeing from Erzurum, in eastern Turkey, to Tabriz in northern Iran, then to New Julfa, south of Isfahan. At an early age he had been sent to be an apprentice to a shoemaker, after which he had opened his own shoe store, making and selling shoes for men, women and children. That was before meeting grandma and falling in love. But when he asked for her hand and grandma's father refused to give his daughter to a shoemaker, he decided to change his profession and become a merchant. Apparently having a merchant as a son-in-law was much more desirable for that well-to-do Julfan family who had a pretty daughter like grandma and a wealthy son living in Calcutta.

So in the first decade of the 20th century, grandpa started following the footsteps of the New Julfa's community of merchants who had originated a trade network in the late 17th century, stretching as far as the Indian Ocean to Southeast Asia and beyond. He traveled with a caravan to India (a British colony) and brought home an assortment of goods which he sold in his old, renovated store. It took him a couple of years, however, to make his fortune and become eligible enough to marry the girl he loved.

On our way back home from the orchard, we walked down the narrow, unpaved dusty street which had houses and shops built on both sides. Other than Nazar Avenue in north of New Julfa, the rest of the streets were unpaved and dusty. So every day, in the early evening when the last rays of the sun lifted from the walls, a couple of laborers would arrive with their large water-sprinklers and douse the streets with water. I liked to watch the process. I loved the smell of the damp earth so much that every time I caught a whiff of it, I closed my eyes, inhaled the friendly odor, and was ready to lick the earth with my tongue.

Shops were not level with the street in New Julfa. To enter one, you either had to climb or descend a few steps to a higher or lower level. I have seen similar streets and shops in Old Quebec and in historic Old Tucson (before it burned down). It seems that, although remote geographically, their urban plans were products of the same era architecturally.

The streets were so narrow that the few cars that arrived from Isfahan only traveled on Nazar Avenue and came as far as the old *Vank*, the All Savior Cathedral, where they brought tourists or took passengers back to the city. The most popular vehicles were bicycles, motorcycles, horse-drawn carriages and donkeys, whose owners brought produce from the farms to sell.

Instead of having back yards, houses had front yards. To enter a house, one had to walk all the way across its spacious courtyard. The entrance doors were flanked by built-in stone benches where the owners sat in the summer evenings, met their neighbors and chatted, while the children played around them. The benches facing the street served the same purpose as the balconies did in Tehran. Behind the entrance door there was a covered porch which also had built-in benches, where neighbors usually gathered during the day for short visits. The thick-walled porch was warm in the winter and cool in the summer. Many years later, on a trip to Prague, I visited the old house of an Iranian friend, which had a similar kind of plan, with a porch and built-in benches around it.

I have seen something amazing in New Julfa that I haven't seen or heard about anywhere else. Since there was no sewage system, the waste from the toilets accumulated in shallow wells. The toilets were situated close to the streets with small trap doors conveniently opening outward. The farmers haggled with the owners and paid for the human waste, which they carried away in containers hanging on both sides of their donkeys like saddlebags. They used it as fertilizer. It was a profitable deal both for the owner and the farmer. The waste was so precious that sometimes the farmers stole it when the trap door was left open and nobody was around. This fertilizer was so effective in enhancing the quality of produce that we could see the result in the market square, the *meidan*, on Saturday mornings, when grandma and I would go grocery shopping. Every time we approached the crowded noisy market, I could smell the aroma of apples, apricots, cantaloupes and melons, even cucumbers, tomatoes, parsley and mint. It was a wonder what a stinking human waste could do to improve the quality, taste and smell of fruits and vegetables.

Grandma didn't buy cantaloupes, honeydew or water melons from the market. They were too heavy to be carried by hand. There was a farmer who brought them to her door on a donkey and she bought not one or two but the whole content of his saddle-bags, relieving his poor beast of its heavy load. She kept them in the cold cellar, which served as a natural refrigerator in those days, but she didn't keep meat or dairy products in it. She bought and consumed those on a daily basis. The milkman delivered milk, butter, cheese and eggs, and the butcher had freshly slaughtered lamb ready early in the morning for the customers to buy at his shop. The entrance to the cellar was a small, removable cover set in the floor of the veranda, above a flight of stairs. Each time grandma wanted something, she sent me down for it. There, I could see jars of melted animal fat, baskets of fruit, melons, and bottles of home-made wine, sitting on the shelves or on the floor. I didn't really like the place. It was dark and scary with its network of cobwebs. I always tried to finish the job as fast as I could and to climb up the stairs while she held the cover open for me.

Like many other vineyard owners, grandpa used to make wine with a special burgundy-colored grape that he cultivated separately in his vineyard. He made the wine by placing the grapes in a cloth sack inside a copper basin. He crushed them with his fists--sometimes asking me to wash my feet and tread on them as hard as I could. After the juice was extracted from the pulp, he went through the process of filtering, fermenting and bottling the wine, allowing it to age in the cellar for a year or two before consuming it at special events. Sometimes, at lunch, he poured some vintage wine in a glass, added some water, and gave it to me, saying, "Drink this and get strong. Drinking wine will keep you from getting sick."

On the other hand, grandma boiled the juice of the green grapes until it turned into syrup then poured it in shallow plates. She added pieces of walnut to the extract, leaving them exposed to the hot summer sun. After the excess fluid had evaporated, she cut the dried-up thick brownish substance into squares and treated us to it. It was something like the fruit roll my grandchildren like to eat here in America. It tasted sweet and sour, delicious, and very nutritious. After all, it was concentrated grape juice.

*****

At nights, my grandparents and I slept under the starry sky on a huge veranda in front of the brick building. The beds were covered and protected with mosquito nets, with their edges tucked under the mattresses. Grandma would tell me stories from the Bible, and grandpa those from *A Thousand and One Nights – Hezar Afsaneh, A Thousand Fairy Tales* – a story book in Persian and Armenian, with suspenseful tales of *Ali-Baba and the Forty Thieves, Alladin and the Lamp* and many others, with the disguised presence of Harun-al-Rashid, the wonderful, benevolent Kalif of Baghdad. The stories were told by Shaherezade, the young wife of King Shahryar, who had the habit of marrying a woman and beheading her the next night. In order to save her life, Shaherezade told him a story, stopping at a cliff-hanger point, with the promise of finishing it the next night. And thus, for a thousand and one nights, she kept the king so amused that at the end he abandoned his cruel intentions and spared her life and those of other women.

Shaherezade's captivating tales have not only remained in my mind and made me tell them to my children, they have also inspired generations of readers, writers, storytellers and artists. And what is more, her name has been immortalized by the 19th century Russian composer, Rimsky-Korsakov, who orchestrated a musical piece based on her succession of stories.

Grandpa also told me exciting stories about his travels to India where he went by a caravan every other fall to buy merchandise for his store, returning home in early spring. Every time the news of his upcoming trip to India spread in town, friends and relatives, even strangers came to his home or store, asking if he would take a package, a letter or cash for their children who studied in Calcutta. Then one week before his departure, envelopes of letters and cash would begin to pour into his house. Some would even take the liberty of sending packages of dried apricots, peaches or, the most popular one, a cluster of shriveled grapes preserved in sawdust and packaged in a small light weight wooden box.

The caravan would start from New Julfa for the port city of Mohammareh on the Persian Gulf (Khorramshahr today), with passengers consisting of merchants, a few women, and sometimes teenage boys. They were bound for India, Java, Sumatra, Singapore, Hong Kong, or elsewhere along the coast of the Indian Ocean, wherever an Armenian community with its churches and schools existed. The teenagers, however, were mostly bound for Calcutta to continue their education at the Armenian Philanthropic College, a high school founded in 1821 that had served generations of Armenian students in India and Persia. Some of those boys lived away from their families for so long that they forgot what their parents and siblings looked like. After graduating from college, they preferred to stay in Calcutta. They found a job, married an Armenian or a British girl and grew roots in their newly adopted city. So it was a really heart-breaking scene when these boys bid farewell to their mothers, who kissed and crushed their sons in an embrace, then beat their chests and plucked out their hair when they had gone, because they weren't sure they would ever see them again. Grandpa took Hovik, his eldest son, on one of his last trips. Hovik had been invited to study in India by grandma's wealthy brother, Peter, who had offered to pay for his nephew's education at a British college after graduating from the Armenian high school in Calcutta. Peter was married to a British woman and had no children.

When describing the trips, grandpa told me that on its passage to India, the caravan passed by many orchards, vineyards and vegetable fields, then crossed miles and miles of parched desert terrain before arriving at the foothills of the Bakhtiari Mountains. Climbing those rugged ranges and safely passing through the narrow gorges was an act of heroism, because not only was it technically difficult, but also because of the danger of being attacked by the bandits, who would either rob them of their cash on the way to the port, or of their precious merchandise on their way back home. However, once they safely put the mountains behind them, they felt relieved and stopped at numerous *caravansaras* along their way, where they ate and rested.

A *caravansara* or a house for caravans, was an inn, built around a huge courtyard on the edge of the thoroughfare. It accommodated travelers inside it, while taking care of their beasts of burden in the stables. The wonderful network of *caravansaras*, laid out by Shah Abbas the Great in the 17th century in Persia, served for hundreds of years as stopping places for the movement of Central-Asian commerce. Many years later when the roads were paved and caravans were replaced by cars, buses and trains, those *caravansaras* were also replaced by hotels, train and bus stations. As grandpa told his stories, I visualized him in the public room, eating a hot meal of rice and kebab, smoking a *chopokh* (a primitive Persian pipe), or sharing a water-pipe with his fellow-travelers as he listened to an entertainer playing a Persian tune on a *santour*. Then I imagined him sleeping under a soft warm quilt in his space among the others, only to wake up at dawn by the crow of roosters to resume his long journey.

Ordinarily, the journey to Mohammareh took them weeks or months, depending on the weather and road conditions. There, they had to wait for up to a week for the arrival of a British steamer. When it finally arrived and was ready to sail, they boarded it and headed for Karachi (then in India, now in Pakistan), where grandpa boarded a train to Calcutta, the city where grandma's sister and brother lived. It took him an additional week, as he stopped in a few other cities on the way to his destination.

Grandpa had many friends in Calcutta besides grandma's sister's and brother's families. He was sometimes invited to a wedding or a baptism at the Armenian church of Holy Nazareth, followed by a dinner party at a hotel or the host's house. Other than Calcutta, there were other large Armenian communities in Bombay (now Mumbai) and Madras (now Chennai), which he had visited with his brother-in-law, Peter.

Grandpa's brother-in-law, Peter Peters, the anglicized version of the Armenian Petros Petrosian, was a successful businessman who had married a beautiful British woman called Elizabeth. When grandpa was in Calcutta, Peter liked to entertain and honor him by throwing lavish parties in his elegant house where his Indian chef, Raj would serve his guests assortments of European, Armenian, and especially spicy Indian menus. The Indian recipes grandpa brought for grandma were so popular in the family that they were copied and used by his friends and relatives, and even handed down to the next generation.

One day while grandpa was trying to cross a crowded street, swarming with all kinds of people, rickshaws, wandering cows and vendors balancing overloaded baskets of vegetables, eggs, bananas, coconuts and mangos on their heads, a British police officer blew his whistle and signed to him to stop. Grandpa was first confused, then frightened. What had he done wrong? But before he could think, the police officer approached him, accompanied him to the sidewalk, and sizing up his tall, muscular figure, asked him, if he would be interested in becoming a policeman. Surprised, relieved, even pleased by the job offer, grandpa laughed and politely turned it down, indicating that he was just a visitor from Persia.

Grandpa stayed in Calcutta for the whole winter, spending time with his in-laws' families or selecting and purchasing merchandise for his store. The items he bought ranged from bolts of fabric, yarn, ready-made clothes, hats and shoes for men and women, fur, fake and fine jewelry, Christmas ornaments, toys, tea and spices to many gifts for his family and friends. He also bought a few jars of mango chutney, a favorite fruit of his which would perish if he carried it fresh. But he did carry a few coconuts, which would survive the trip. Then in spring, with all the merchandise in crates, he traveled back to Karachi and boarded a ship to Mohammareh.

One of the items grandpa once took home was a parrot with rare, silky, baby-pink plumage that could imitate and speak whatever he taught it. For many years my mother and uncles enjoyed the exotic bird, taking good care of it. How grandpa had managed to carry that caged bird from India to Persia is still a marvel to me.

On a spring afternoon during one of grandpa's return trips, the caravan he was in was ambushed by road bandits while passing through a gorge in the Bakhtiari Mountains. They appeared on top of the cliffs on horseback, then swooped down the steep rocks like birds of prey. There were about ten men, with guns, half their faces hidden behind black kerchiefs. The bandits cornered the passengers in the narrow place, attacked them, and after robbing them of their valuable possessions, climbed up the cliffs and vanished.

The travelers were grateful that they were still alive. They continued their journey to the nearest village, where they reported the robbery to the gendarmerie which was sometimes able to catch the roadside thieves, salvage the valuables, and hang the robbers on the gallows in the town square. They were also lucky that the bandits had spared them their mules, because without the mules, they would have been stranded and separated from the nearest village by miles of treacherous mountain terrain. Every time grandpa started that long dangerous journey, he was well aware of the fact that he might never come back. Still, he was courageous enough to take the risk for the welfare of his family. Years later, when Reza Shah took the throne in 1925, he cleared the roads of bandits and made them safe for travelers.

I liked to hear the exciting story of the bandits, maybe because he told the story in a flamboyant manner or because I already knew that he had survived the attack. But when I told that story to my eight-year-old granddaughter, she refused to listen, retorting, "I don't like bandits."

In India, Grandpa had learned from a yogi how to tell someone's fortune by reading the lines on a person's forehead, but had given up the skill after predicting my father's death. I wish he had taught it at least to one of his children. He also could heal certain minor physical discomforts by teaching some easy yoga postures or by means of a certain diet. I don't remember any of them, but forty years later in America when I was afflicted with severe allergies, and after having futile long-term medical treatment, I remembered grandpa's yoga postures, and signed up in a Hatha Yoga class where I exercised twice a week for two semesters. It helped me get rid of those allergies.

On one of his visits to Calcutta, grandpa found Peter afflicted with an infection of the gallbladder. The doctors wanted to operate on him, but Peter didn't trust the local surgeons, and decided to get it done in Switzerland. Grandpa tried to discourage him from making the trip, but Peter didn't listen. He made arrangements, and traveled to Geneva with Elizabeth. A few days after the designated date of surgery, grandpa and the rest of the family received a telegram that Peter had died. Later they found out that the surgeon had left some cotton wool in his abdomen that had caused a fatal infection. They brought Peter's body back to Calcutta and buried him in the Armenian cemetery. Peter's cook, Raj, who had the same medical problem had surgery in a local hospital, survived and lived a long life.

When my broken-hearted grandpa returned to New Julfa and tried to keep in touch with Elizabeth through a letter and didn't get any response, he sent a telegram to grandma's sister, who informed him that Peter's wife had returned to England suddenly, taking along most of the wealth that her husband had accumulated throughout his lifetime.

On one of his trips, grandpa took along his mother-in-law to see her younger daughter in Calcutta. She contracted cholera by eating or drinking contaminated food or water, either on the road, while staying at a *carvansara*, or an inn in Mohammareh, waiting for the arrival of a ship. After boarding the ship, she suffered for a week and died. Her body was thrown into the sea after a special funeral ceremony conducted by the captain of the ship according to the naval regulations. Later, they gave my devastated grandpa a death certificate. He had to bear the horrible news to his wife back home, and to his sister-in-law in Calcutta who was impatiently waiting for her mother's arrival.

Grandpa was a tough man. After having witnessed and survived the Turkish massacres of the Armenians in the 1890s, he was capable of handling any crisis in life. However, he never told us about the brutalities and atrocities the Turks had inflicted on the Armenian people in Turkey. It seemed that he was keeping that part of his memory hidden in a dark recess of his mind, as if it was Pandora's Box which, if opened, would spill out all the evils in it and afflict mankind with them. Instead, he fired my imagination by telling children's stories from Armenian writers like Hovhaness Toumanian and Ghazaros Aghayian. One night I was very sleepy when he started the mythical story of *Hazaran Blbool (The miraculous nightingale)*. I only heard the first part then fell asleep. In the morning when I asked him if he had told the story, he said, "Don't you remember? I told it to the very end."

*****

My grandparents took turns in spoiling me. While grandpa took me out to the orchard or the club for ice cream and raisin cake, grandma amused me at home, by inviting one or two girls of my age, children or grandchildren of her friends. When I played with those girls, I always felt good about myself. Unlike my classmates who always reminded me of my father's death, here my new friends not only didn't mention it, they idolized and pampered me just because I had arrived from Tehran, and most importantly, because I had been *born* in Tehran.

I listened to an old-fashioned His Master's Voice horned phonograph with those new friends, playing dozens of popular records grandpa had brought from Tehran. They stayed all day, had lunch with us and took a nap afterwards. Sometimes my grandparents packed a picnic basket and took us to the nearby woods where, for drinks, we used natural spring water which jetted out from under a rock. A few days later, I would go to their homes and play with their dolls and toys. It was somewhat like the play-dates my grandchildren have here in America. One of the favorite meals grandma cooked for us was rice with fried eggs on top. Many years later on a trip to Patzcuaro, Mexico, I ate the same meal at a restaurant. It was considered to be a novelty by my fellow-travelers.

One early Saturday morning when I was still asleep, a Persian woman came over to bake the flat *lavash* bread with pure white flour. Grandma said that the woman had a heavy schedule during the summer, so she had set that date two months ahead of time. The baker-woman, with sweat running down her pink face, kneaded the dough in a copper basin in a corner of the spacious kitchen, then took a chunk and flattened it with a rolling pin on a flour-smeared table. Then she spread and formed it on a round, firm cushion and stuck it to the red-hot walls of the cylindrical oven built into the floor. As soon as she pulled out the crusty flat bread, she tossed it to grandma, who put it on a table to cool and dry. The woman did the job with such speed and skill that in no time the table was covered with thin sheets of steaming *lavash*, the aroma filling the house.

After she was done with baking bread, she took a small batch of the rest of the dough, rolled it out with a smaller rolling pin and filled it with powdered sugar, crushed walnuts, nutmeg, cardamom and cinnamon. Then she rolled the dough into a long thin roll, cut it into sections and baked it on a heated metallic device. The thin, crisp pastry was called *yokha*. That day I ate so many of them that I got sick in the stomach and grandma gave me the homemade remedy of *dagh-nabat* – a solution of caramelized sugar and boiling water – to ease my pain. The next morning, before going to church, she stored those dried sheets of bread on the shelves of a wooden bin to be used in winter by sprinkling some cold water to soften them.

*****

New Julfa is famous for its twelve churches and especially the *Vank* (monastery), the All Savior Cathedral, which is located within walking distance of my grandparents' house. Although its unimpressive exterior cannot be compared with the colorful intricate Islamic domes and facades of Isfahan's mosques, its breathtaking, richly-decorated interior equally attracts tourists from all over the world. I saw a sample of that interest on a TV program in Prague when I visited the city in 1999. The program was about those twelve churches, with an in-depth story of the *Vank,* its library and museum, the *Matenadaran,* a citadel of chronicles, religious and precious works of art that have been gathered there during the nearly four centuries of New Julfa's history. What is more, the *Vank* can boast that the first Armenian language Bible has been printed in its printing house in 1634 or 1638, about two centuries after Gutenberg completed printing the first Bible in 1455. It was printed on a printing machine which arrived in New Julfa with all its wooden and metallic type (raised characters on small blocks) as well as the printing paper and the ink. The printing house of the *Vank* is still active at the beginning of the twenty-first century, printing newsletters, announcements, flyers, and books. It works with modern tools, with the original ones preserved and displayed in its museum.

On Sundays and religious holidays, grandma dressed me up and took me to the *Vank*. She was a religious woman and a regular churchgoer. In a small town with twelve churches and the frequent, inviting chimes of their bells echoing in the neighborhood, how would someone dare not to be religious? She was a believer in the power of prayer. She prayed regularly at home and in the church. When she was confronted with some kind of problem she couldn't solve, she sought help through prayers. When I got sick and ran a high fever for several days and the medication didn't work, she prayed for me. It was not the kind of prayers we say at bedtime. It was kind of ceremonial. I remember her inserting an open safety pin in my pillow and murmuring a long prayer as I slowly fell asleep. Miraculously, the next morning the fever had disappeared and I went on with the routine of the day. I wish I had asked her how she did it. Even my mother didn't know about the nature of that prayer.

In the church, after uttering a brief prayer which she also had taught me, she would follow the liturgy, as I would relax on the pew watching the women in head-scarves lighting white candles on a bordered table filled with sand. Looking at the oil paintings that represented God's revelation through the Old and New Testaments and the frescos that covered the rest of the walls, I wondered which of them interested me most. Was it the picture of Heaven with its saints and martyrs in the glorious company of angels and cherubs, or the picture of Hell, with the horrified faces of the people struggling with the horned beasts and Satan who eternally poked them with a red hot pitchfork?

What I liked most about going to the church was listening to the music. The deep sound of the organ and the heavenly voices of the choir elated my childish spirit and made me indulge in its relaxing harmony. I have traveled the world extensively and visited many churches of different sects throughout my life, but to this day I haven't heard much sweeter and more inspiring ecclesiastical music and songs than those used in the Armenian Church, which observed all the religious festivities throughout the year. The two feasts celebrated in summer were called *Vartavar*, the name-day of *Vart* (rose), and the Feast of Grape Blessing, Mary's name-day.

Vartavar is a popular feast that has originated in pagan Armenia and later has been associated with Christianity. On *Vartavar* morning grandma took me to the crowded *Vank*, where a special service was taking place, with a full-sized choir and a soloist singing to the music of the organ. After the service when the congregation dispersed and we walked into the street, I saw the rest of the *Vartavar* ritual. Children and youngsters were running up and down the street, shouting and sprinkling water on one another and passers-by.

The tradition of dousing or sprinkling people with water on *Vartavar* is as old as biblical times. Noah, the patriarch was chosen by God to build an ark to save the lives of his family and specimens of animals from the flood. When the water subsided and the ark descended from the peak of Mount Ararat, Noah ordered his children to sprinkle themselves with water in order to keep the memory of the Flood alive in their hearts.

*****

A month after my arrival in New Julfa, when mother and Emil arrived, I still was a little angry with her. But when she opened her suitcase and gave me a present, I relaxed, wondering what it was. In those days we didn't get any presents except on New Year's Day and birthdays. My hands began to shake as I carefully untied the white ribbon. I didn't tear the paper at one attempt, just made one tiny tear at a time. It seemed that I was enjoying the suspense, dragging the time. When I finally opened it, I saw something that I readily fell in love with. She had brought me a purse just like the one I had sneaked out of our neighbor's house. It was even prettier. When I looked at it and held it at arm's length, I suddenly burst into tears, I'm not sure why. Was it the one-month-old tension that had broken between the two of us? Was it the happiness that had overwhelmed me for possessing my favorite item, or was it a bit of both?

After mother's arrival, our daily program changed entirely. Her cousins and friends arranged picnics in the woods or on the banks of Zayandeh Rood River, where we swam, played on its banks, and chased gray crabs staggering about on the pebbles, sometimes carrying two baby crabs by their tiny arms. In the meantime a couple of men in the group caught fish with their nets, and the women fried them over an open fire. The men also shot tiny birds called "yellow bellies," and barbecued them on skewers on the same fire. We all enjoyed a delicious lunch after hours of swimming and getting hungry.

Once we packed and went to a nearby village for a week. My grandparents stayed at home, together with little Emil. Grandma was not much of a traveler anyway. She always said, "If I don't go to a better place than my home town, then it is not worth the trouble." She left her home town only once, to move to Tehran near her four children. She never showed any interest in accompanying grandpa on any of his trips to India. Maybe she did, but he had refused to take her along. Come to think of it, grandma had every right not to go with us. The distance between the town and the village was not far, but the road was so bad that it took us a whole day to accomplish a two-hour trip. It was not a road for a sedan. Maybe SUVs or the army Hummers of today would have fared better. Still, our hired driver of the old Studebaker did his best by twisting and dodging, splashing through numerous streams or abruptly stopping for flocks of sheep or cows to pass.

Eventually, we got there before nightfall. We stayed in the village school with our own bundle of bedding brought from home. I made friends with the children of mother's friends. For breakfast, we drank fresh milk, and ate fresh cream, butter, cheese and honey, with home-baked thick loaves of bread that a villager delivered to us. For lunch we had rice-pilaf with the tender meat of a deer that the men had gunned down, skinned and barbecued on an open fire. In the mornings, we hiked the nearby hills and explored the vegetable fields and orchards, and sneaked a slender cucumber here or a ripe sweet pear there. We rode donkeys and had the time of our lives. In the afternoons we wove baskets with wheat straws which we had soaked overnight in water. In the evenings we gathered inside the school hall and listened to a storyteller.

I loved every moment of living in that village, except for something that touched and bothered me when I came in contact with it – the presence of many trachoma-afflicted children, even blind ones, with pus-covered, half-closed eyelids whom we were instructed to stay away from. Although I sympathized with them, there was nothing I or my elders could do about it. Trachoma was an infectious eye disease that was widespread in many villages in Iran, long before the early 1950s and the arrival of the mobile health-units of the U.S. Point IV Organization (an off-shoot of the Marshal Plan) which treated them on a regular basis, gradually eliminating the disease.

Back in New Julfa, one Sunday in August, on the feast of Grape Blessing and the name day of St. Mary, my grandparents, mother and I went to the *Vank*. After the religious ceremony, I saw huge copper trays of grapes arriving and being placed on the edge of the altar. They were filled with varieties of seedless, luscious red and amber grapes, all freshly picked that same morning from the vineyards, which the priest blessed by holding the cross over them. Then the congregation passed along the altar in a file, each taking a bunch, placing it on a napkin or a kerchief to take home and share with the rest of the family.

Since it was grandma's name-day, guests arrived in the afternoon and she treated them with tea and homemade cake, *yokha;* and specialties of the city of Isfahan: sweet *gaz* and almond brittles. On the dining table with the sweets, there was a large basket of fresh fruits: apples, pears and peaches, with two bowls of cut melon and watermelon, and of course varieties of grapes. Although the day was called the feast of Grape Blessing, I thought the other fruits equally deserved to be blessed. I learned later that the reason they rated the grapes higher than other fruits was because they made wine from them which was used in the church for services, communions and marriages.

Our family's pleasure didn't last for long. At the end of the summer, my brother, Emil, contracted diarrhea. When the doctors of the British Hospital couldn't cure him, mother decided to take him back to Tehran to our family physician. Those were the days when children died of diarrhea left and right. Emil was so weak he could hardly move. The only thing he said was, "Water." But he was not allowed to drink any liquid.

Grandpa rented a car with a driver he knew who drove us to Tehran and straight to the doctor's office, with a few short stops along the way. The Russian-educated Armenian physician said to my mother, "If you want to see this child alive by tomorrow morning, you'll have to follow my instructions step by step."

With mother's given directions, the driver stopped at a dairy and a bakery on our way, then drove us home, helped us with the luggage upstairs, and after getting paid, wished mother good-luck and left. As soon as we got into the apartment and put Emil to bed, mother sent me to the neighbor's to borrow a jug of drinking water, then to the balcony to look for a passing water carriage. Fortunately, it didn't take me long to catch the attention of a vendor, who stopped his horse-drawn carriage in front of our building, filled two buckets of water from its tank, and balancing them with his hands, rushed up to our apartment, filled the earthenware containers and left. In those days the pipes of the houses didn't carry filtered or chemically-treated water; we bought it from the vendors who filled their tanks from the *ghanats* – underground passages that brought fresh water from the mountains to the plains and to certain man-made covered spots. For the kitchen and bathroom, we hired the garbage-man to pump water from the underground reservoir to the tank in the attic. Water in the reservoir came from the open streams in the street, which flowed once a month for a few hours. The dirt in the water subsided in the reservoir and was disinfected by means of throwing in pieces of charcoal.

While I was busy buying water, mother was beating the whites of two eggs in a glass bowl until they foamed. She added washed pieces of ice that she had bought at the dairy, but before assuming her nursing duty, she sent me to bed after feeding me milk, bread and butter.

That night my mother didn't sleep a wink. Every ten minutes throughout the night, as the doctor had instructed, she awakened Emil from his constant sleep and put a teaspoon of the mixture of egg-whites and melted ice on his tongue. He sucked it slowly and went back to sleep. In the morning, with the first light of dawn, he opened his eyes wide and smiled. That was his first smile in two weeks.

The doctor's knowledge and resourcefulness, and my mother's efforts and persistence saved my brother's life. He is a successful architect, over seventy years old, living in Los Angeles now. Many years later when my eight-month-old daughter's diarrhea didn't go away after a week, I was terrified. But our children's pediatrician who was also a family friend said to me, "Listen, Elma, don't be scared. She'll pull through eventually. Gone are the days when the doctors forbade liquid for a diarrhea-inflicted child. Those children mostly died of dehydration."

Now in her forties, that little girl is an emergency-room physician who has treated hundreds of adults and children with diseases which are much more serious than diarrhea.

Chapter 5

Two Weddings

In the spring of 1939, Uncle Johnny gave me my first job when I was seven years old. For the wedding procession of the Crown Prince Mohammad Reza to the Egyptian Princess Fawzieh, the sister of King Farouk, the government had sent large cardboard sheets to organizations and business owners. The sheets were imprinted with the national emblem of the Lion-&-Sun that had to be cut out individually. Those cut-out emblems were going to be distributed among the people who would wave them along the streets where the floats, parade, and especially the motorcade of Reza Shah and the married couple were going to pass.

Uncle Johnny promised to pay me one *Shahi* for each cut-out. With one *Shahi* I could buy a red lollipop shaped in the form of a rooster. The job looked easy in the beginning, but after I had cut a few, my fingers began to hurt. I took a pair of smaller scissors, at mother's suggestion, which helped in cutting the corners more smoothly. I remember the yellow and brown image with the profile of a standing lion, a sword in paw, and the rising sun behind it, which I would see later on the white section of the tri-colored (green, white, and red) flag of Iran.

Triumphal arches – temporary monuments – were erected in most of the squares of the city. They were dedicated to the royal couple by various Iranian communities and religious minorities with their own motifs. Close to our house, near the Armenian club, the Armenian community's arch stood with statues of ancient gods, flanking and guarding its passageway.

On the day of the parade some of our relatives and friends came over to watch the procession from our balcony. I remember the royal bride, Princess Fawzieh – whose marriage to the Crown Prince didn't last for long – was so beautiful with her green eyes and dark hair that even years later, people found her the prettiest of the Shah's three wives. Unfortunately, no one had a camera among us to capture those precious moments of history in pictures, but I, a little girl, did capture those colorful images in my memory, and recalled and told my children of them about a quarter of a century later. I also remember the formidable gray eyes of Reza Shah the Great who looked at our balcony and frowned, then stared ahead as his open motorcade passed us by. Was he afraid that the balcony would collapse under the weight of that crowd and ruin his son's spectacular wedding parade, or perhaps he knew that it belonged to the man who had down-sized his car's rear window and painted it with a unique royal purple.

*****

In the summer of 1939, my mother, brother and I traveled to New Julfa together. To my mother, New Julfa was *home*, just like Tara was to Scarlet O'Hara in *Gone With The Wind*. She looked forward to the trip all year long. In her parents' home she would forget her daily worries and frustrations, and would relax and enjoy the company of relatives and old friends. That year, we all had something else to look forward to: Uncle Johnny's wedding to his fiancée, for whom I was going to be a bridesmaid.

Something strange happened on the way to Isfahan. We were traveling on a bus. Not only was the bus full to capacity, its isle was also loaded with the passengers' cargoes. We were sitting on a bench-like seat, on the driver's side and were the only Armenians going to New Julfa. The rest were Persians going to Isfahan. Next to our seat, sitting on his bundle of belongings, was a handsome young man holding a small pillow on his lap. Every now and then, he looked at us and smiled. He started a conversation with mother and introduced himself as Ahmad, asking about my brother's and my ages, our destination, and so on. Then looking at me with concern, he said to my mother, "Lady, why don't you take this pillow and let your daughter sit on it? She's too skinny and the hard bench will hurt her bones. It will also lift her up and she can see better through the window." And he extended the pillow, which I grabbed and prepared to put on my seat, but I immediately gave it back as I noticed mother glaring at me. But Ahmad didn't leave us alone. He kept asking and repeating his offer to the point that mother got angry and raised her voice. The driver, who apparently was following the conversation through his rear view mirror, looked back at Ahmad and yelled, "Stop bothering the lady! One more word and I'll throw you out of this bus!" Ahmad fell silent and held the pillow firmly against his chest.

A few miles further on, we were stopped at the edge of a village, and a gendarme, the highway patrol, entered the bus and began checking the permits – which were needed then for traveling from city to city – and the belongings of the passengers. He made his way through the congested isle, asking the owners to pull their luggage aside. When he approached our row of seats, he ordered Ahmad, who was sitting on the pillow, to stand up. "What is this?" he asked, taking the pillow and weighing it in his hands.

"It's a pillow, don't you see?"

"Rip it open!" the gendarme yelled.

Ahmad hesitated for a second but having no other choice ripped out the thread of the pillow-case, then the cover of the pillow. Inside the pillow, instead of cotton-wool or feathers, we saw a brownish yellow substance:

illegal opium. "A pillow, huh?" the gendarme grunted, kicking him out of the bus together with his bundle of belongings.

When they were gone and the driver started the bus, the passengers breathed a sigh of relief, thanked my mother for her cleverness and applauded her. If mother had accepted the pillow, she would have been arrested. No need to say that the owner of the opium wouldn't have come forward to claim his belongings. She had narrowly escaped a dangerous drug dealing set-up. Even now I dread to think of what might have happened if mother hadn't been cautious enough to refuse that opium-filled pillow.

Opium trafficking and addiction, a legacy of the weak governments of the previous dynasty were still going on surreptitiously despite Reza Shah's rigid regulations to eradicate them.

*****

When we arrived at my grandparents' home in New Julfa, they had already made the major preparations for Uncle Johnny's wedding, with the final touches to be added in the last days before the event which was a month away, so we had plenty of time to enjoy our vacation and go wherever we pleased.

We went to Isfahan several times in a horse-drawn cab and visited its numerous ancient mosques, among them, Masjed-e-Shah or the royal mosque, with its brilliant enameled tiles, situated on the southern end of Meydan-e-Shah (a huge square), with Masjed-e-Sheykh Lotfollah on the eastern side, which had been Shah Abbas' private mosque. On the western side of the square stood Ali Qapu with its walls, inlaid with precious gemstones, mirrored panels, and an immense balcony from where the Shah and his guests would watch polo games or other events. The two-story building led into gardens, pavilions and courts, one of which was called, Chehel Sotun (forty pillars), with twenty columns on its veranda, and twenty more when their reflection showed in the clear waters of a huge pool in front.

Every time we visited the city, mother and her cousins liked to buy local handicrafts, as well as Persian candies, *gaz* and *sohan* (almond brittles). The shops were on Chahar-Bagh, a four-way, tree-lined avenue which ran from the center of the city southward to the Zayandeh-Rood River, ending at the edge of the Sio-Se-Pol Bridge. We walked along the avenue and at lunchtime stopped at a restaurant that served the best chelo-kebab in town. I remember the crowded place and its waiter, who carried a skewer of scalding kebabs in his hand, walking among the tables, looking for empty plates to unload the kebab onto. In that restaurant, as long as you had rice in your plate, they would serve you hot kebab. I liked that place so much and looked forward to a delicious meal and drink of chilly *dough* (diluted yogurt with water, laced with powdered mint) that I didn't mind to be dragged along in the museums, mosques and shops.

Once mother and I visited one of her friends, the wife of Dr. Karo Minassian, in whose library we found an enormous collection of rare books. Many years later in Los Angeles I learned that the UCLA's Charles E. Young Research library had acquired many of those manuscripts in Armenian, Persian, Arabic, Turkish and Urdu, which dated from the 14th to 19th centuries, with subjects ranging from philosophy, literature, history, law, astronomy to science.

One day grandpa took me to *Matenadaran*, the *Vank*'s museum and library. There, with the help of a friendly attendant, he gave me explanations about all those rare manuscripts with tempera and gold-leaf on parchment, masterpieces of 14th-century Armenian illumination. I saw well-kept silk attire of men and women with intricate gilded needlework on mannequins in glass cabinets (one of them belonged to my grandma's aunt, Vartuhi). Then years later, at an exhibition at the Getty Center (where I volunteer), I saw similar masterpieces of 14th-century miniatures which illustrated the life of Christ in commemoration of the 1700th anniversary of the establishment of the Armenian Church. Although I was too young then to appreciate all those historic landmarks and rich collections, they made me curious enough to revisit them in my college years when I had more background in history.

Nowadays the *Vank* is a mecca for students who come from everywhere to do research at its library and museum for their Ph.Ds in Middle Eastern studies. Many years later in America, I met an Iranian scholar, the head of the Middle Eastern Studies Department at the University of Arizona in Tucson, where I was invited to talk about my historical novel, *Under the Blue Dome,* set in Iran, who told me that he had lived in New Julfa for a number of years, in a house just opposite the *Vank* where he had done some of his research for his Ph.D. and where his son had been born. I thought to myself: what a small global village!

In the late 17th century New Julfa became a cultural and intellectual hub for the Armenians of the Diaspora. However, since nothing is permanent in the course of history, the Afghans invaded Iran from a few miles east of Isfahan in 1772, surrounded and sacked the city, defeating the powerful Persian army. The Armenian population of New Julfa was a small percentage among millions of Persians who perished of famine or were ruthlessly raped and massacred. Of those Julfans who had survived, some fled to the Caucasian countries in the north, and some to the south-eastern countries of India, Thailand, Hong Kong, Singapore, Burma, Java and Sumatra (Indonesia), leaving only three hundred families behind.

These wonderful, courageous survivors of the Afghan massacre and plunder continued living in New Julfa for about a century. They took excellent care of the town, its churches and its people's cherished and invaluable treasures, before a great part of the refugees returned to their home town. These expatriates shared their novel foreign experiences with the community, helping it flourish once more. They established the boy and girl-scout organizations, a playhouse and an orchestra in which they only used percussion and brass instruments.

On September 1, 1939, when the news of the outbreak of WWII exploded in that tiny town, it was my uncle's wedding day. Everybody talked about Adolph Hitler, blaming him for invading Poland, starting a full-scale war in Europe, and most importantly about the impact that the war could have on their uneventful lives, here in New Julfa. But as far as I remember, nothing extraordinary happened. Everything went on as usual.

At my grandparents' home, the bride and the groom – who were called the "king and queen of the day" – with their two bridesmaids and all the guests were treated to tea, pastries, sweets and fruit. Then they all walked toward the *Vank*, with two musicians walking ahead of them, playing a drum and a *duduk* – an ancient Armenian woodwind musical instrument- with the bells of the cathedral chiming and echoing in the narrow streets, with people lining the sides to watch and clap their hands. After a long religious ceremony in the cathedral, the bride and groom drank the wine that the priest offered them, accepted the guests' congratulations, went into the street, and walked in front of the procession to the nearby local club. In the spacious courtyard of the club the guests were treated to a lavish dinner with a three-tiered, white-frosted wedding cake (prepared by the club's chef), and were entertained by the local band. They didn't call the bride and groom "king and the queen of the day" in vain. They treated them as if they were.

Uncle Johnny's wedding was one of the happiest days of my life. My bridesmaid's dress made of pink organza with ruffles around the neckline and the bottom of the long skirt which was made by mother at home. It was a beautiful dress for the occasion, but I didn't like it because of its coarse fabric which made me feel restricted and uncomfortable. I didn't like it because in the days to come, grandma would make me wear it on every trivial occasion: to go to the local club for an ice cream or to visit a friend. I remember running around the courtyard while she followed me with the dress in her hand. But to my frustration, she usually succeeded in her intention. To this day, I haven't liked dresses that make me conspicuous or cooped up. I'm a person who prefers to keep a low profile in order to feel self confident.

Although I was sent home to bed at an early hour, the guests danced until dawn to popular waltzes, tangos, foxtrots and the newly arrived Lambeth-Walk, a 1937 song composed by the British song writer, Douglas Furber, and choreographed into a cheerful, brisk ballroom dance.

I'm still amazed at the spirit of the people of that small town, who were capable of enjoying life even at such a critical historic time with the approaching war on the horizon. But then, I try to remember that these people were the descendents of the same courageous generation of Julfans who had survived the atrocities of the Afghan invasion and had refused to die. Instead, they had treasured and maintained their own traditions while following the latest trends of fashion coming in from the outside world.

Part II

The WWII Years

1939-1945

Chapter 6

Iran Is Occupied

In 1941, two years after the beginning of WWII, the Allied forces invaded Iran, turning the country into a strategic stronghold and a safe supply-line for American armaments going to the Soviet front. The Iranian road system and the newly founded trans-Iranian 1000-mile railroad (1938) that ran from the Caspian Sea in the north to the Persian Gulf in the south was just right for the purpose. By taking over Iran, the Allies were also trying to forestall a German invasion whose armies were advancing toward the Caucasus. In his *Grand Alliance*, Winston Churchill explains: "Our only interests in Persia are, first, as a barrier against German penetration eastward, and, secondly, as a through route for supplies to the Caspian basin."

"On August 23, 1941, both countries invaded Iran without warning," documents Mohammad Reza Shah in his *Answer to History*. "To the north, strong, motorized Soviet forces crossed the frontier at Azerbaijan and Khorasan and along the whole frontier. Five British divisions came up from the southeast, the south and the west. The Royal Air Force bombed military targets such as Ahvaz, Bandar Shahpour and Khorramshahr, avoiding the petroleum plants. The Soviet air force bombed Tabriz, Ghazvin, Bandar Pahlavi and Rasht."

When the Soviet air force began bombing the port city of Pahlavi and was approaching Ghazvin, ninety miles west of Tehran, people panicked and not knowing what to do, just hoarded food items, such as rice, beans, flour, sugar, animal fat, as well as kerosene and basic emergency medicines. Nevertheless, we were in a vulnerable situation, and had no idea how we should protect ourselves when the bombs fell. There were no underground shelters and no basements in our or other apartment buildings. There were no government instructions or plans for the security of citizens. News about the invasion and progress of the enemy came from the radio and newspapers. Most of the times we heard them from the newspaper boys who called out the headlines while selling "Extras" in the street.

Fortunately the air attacks stopped in the north and the south, when on August 28, Reza Shah ordered a cease fire after he was notified that on September 17, the Allied forces would enter Tehran. So on September 16, one day before their arrival he abdicated in parliament, paving the way for his successor, his twenty-two-year-old son, Mohammad Reza. It was after the ceasefire that Tehran, which had been holding its breath for five days, exhaled again and resumed its ordinary life. I remember my mother who had left aside the dress she was sewing for me, taking it up and using the sewing machine, with all the mess scattered around it.

With the swift collapse of Persian resistance, Iran was completely occupied by the British and Soviet forces that met in Tehran after the Shah's abdication. Reza Shah, who was considered too pro-German by the heads of the Allied countries, was sent to exile in South Africa with the rest of his family. Iran, a peaceful country, with a homogenous, multi-faith, multi-cultural population, suddenly found itself trapped and isolated from the rest of the world, with food shortages and the fear of infectious diseases.

Churchill's interest in creating "a through route for supplies to the Caspian basin," was soon realized by sending steamers with cargoes of American weapons, trucks, food, clothing, medical supplies and military equipment to the southern port of Khorramshahr. The Iranian drivers drove the trucks and the cargoes in convoys across the country to the north, to Old Julfa in the Soviet Union on the border of Iran. Over a period of four and a half years, five million tons of supplies traveled across Iran, either by road or railroad.

In the fall of 1941 my grandparents relocated to Tehran and rented a three-bedroom apartment, sharing it with Uncle Johnny and his wife who moved from a two-story house they had been living in since their marriage. They had brought us sweet *gaz, yokha,* and lots of *rish-baba,* large golden grapes, laid in layers of sawdust, preserved and sealed in air tight tin containers. Back then I thought there were two categories of grapes: the bunches of fresh juicy ones which hung from the vines, and those which were preserved in sawdust, shriveled half-way between grapes and raisins. I liked both of them.

At that time, mother had sub-let Uncle Johnny's room to a middle-aged Armenian couple from Bulgaria, refugees from the Armenian Genocide of 1915, who had fled from Istanbul to Sofia. They had sought opportunity and security in Iran, long before the start of WWII. The woman whose name was Surpik was a little chubby with thin grayish hair. She was a good-natured woman whose contagious laughter helped raise the general mood in our house. Laughter was missing in our lives, and Surpik brought it back to us. Gales of their laughter bounced between the ceiling and the tiled floor of our kitchen where mother and Surpik worked together. She had kindled the embers of mother's happy nature, which in turn had a great impact on me and my brother's moods. As they say, "When momma ain't happy, ain't nobody happy." Surpik was a great cook whose new western-Armenian recipes entered my mother's ordinary menus. Unlike my mother and aunts who used butter or animal fat, she used pure olive oil, and the delicious smell of the potatoes she fried in it wafted through our apartment.

The couple had many friends from Istanbul who had also escaped the persecutions of the 1915 Genocide, and who often visited the couple, and got acquainted with mother. They were distinguished families with university degrees in medicine, law, or other professions who spoke about Constantinople (Istanbul) with pride and nostalgia, calling it, *our Polis.*

We called Surpik's husband, Mr. Artin. Like his wife, he too was a good-natured, resourcefu person who repaired and fixed anything that went wrong around the house. I don't know what he did for a living, but I remember him working with his tools on our second balcony. Emil loved to squat next to him, watch and ask questions. Those sessions taught my little brother how to do similar repairs in our house and, much later, in his own house. He became a curious person, someone who was eager to learn.

*****

Shortly after my grandparents moved to Tehran, I contracted scarlet fever, a contagious and dangerous disease that they said, was wrecking havoc among children in Europe. I was isolated and on a strict liquid diet. I had a patchy rash in my skin, inflammation in my mouth, throat, and on my tongue which the doctor jokingly likened to a strawberry. It was a time when antibiotics, even sulfanilamides still had not been discovered. My mother was very anxious to follow the doctor's orders and give me the best care she could afford. In the mean time, she sent Emil to our grandparent's home as a precaution. With the bitter experience of my father's untimely death still fresh in her mind, she had every right to be scared.

Then one late afternoon, as I was lying in my bed feeling a little better reading a children's magazine, much to our surprise, my best friend, Pari, rang the bell of our front door and wanted to see me, but mother wouldn't let her in, warning her of the dangerous consequences of her visit. Pari was a stubborn girl and insisted on seeing her sick friend, to which mother relented and led her to the bedroom on one condition that she sat near the door, far from my bed. A few minutes later when she brought Pari a cup of tea and cookies, with a glass of milk for me, Pari had pulled her chair next to my bed and was blabbering excitedly about our classmates and teachers.

From that day on, every afternoon on her way home from school, Pari would stop by our house to give me my homework, update me with the news about our school and friends, or a funny incident she had seen in the street. We would laugh from the bottom of our hearts, then she would leave.

Pari never caught the disease. After six weeks when my rash turned into scales and peeled off my whole body, Emil returned home with the doctor's permission, but not before mother fumigated and disinfected the entire apartment.

A few months after I had resumed school and regained some of my strength, grandma, who had made a vow to "light a candle" for my recovery, came over on the eve of February fourteenth to take me to the church, two blocks away, from where we could hear the bells chiming. Nobody could blame her for making a vow for a ten-year-old girl who had survived a dangerous disease that was killing children left and right. Grandma could have lighted the candle by herself at any Sunday service, but apparently she wanted to kill two birds with one stone by also attending the ceremony of *Tiaruntarach*, a festival that occurred forty days after January sixth, the Armenian Christmas. It is a combination of a Christian and Zoroastrian ritual dating back to the time when the latter was the religious faith in Armenia. It is a ritual that the Persians have also preserved and carry it out on the last Wednesday of the year, before *Now-Ruz*, the first day of spring. However, I didn't know that grandma had made another vow for that night, but I soon found out when the time came.

In the center of the churchyard, we saw laborers piling up armfuls of chopped wood, dry tree barks and shrubs to build a bonfire for people to jump over after the service.

Inside the crowded church, the scent of burning incense mixed with the deep sound of the organ and the soft voices of the choir had created a heavenly atmosphere. Grandma looked for a seat, and noticing one on the middle of a pew, pulled my sleeve as she made her way toward it. The space was so narrow that we barely fitted in, but she didn't care, and as soon as she found her breath, she concentrated on the words of the priest and forgot everything else. As for me, I indulged myself in my favorite ecclesiastical music and began to daydream.

After the service, grandma bought three white candles that were sold in the doorway. We approached the image of the Virgin Mary, under which stood a rectangular metallic table with raised edges and covered with sand where scores of candles were burning and melting. I stood next to her and watched her every movement with fascination as she slanted one of her candles toward the light of the nearest one, caught its sizzling flame and pressed it into the soft sand of the table. Then she crossed herself and uttered a prayer that seemed to have come right from the depths of her heart. She looked younger, prettier and happy, with a pink glow on her cheeks. I wondered where that change came from – was it from the heat and reflection of those flickering tiny lights, or from something within, like her strong faith, gratitude, or a general sense of spiritual satisfaction?

The simple process of "candle lighting" is a long-standing tradition which has been handed down from our ancestors. It symbolizes the light of God's presence and also a way of expressing one's gratitude to Him for a wish He had helped fulfill. Years later in the Latin Church in Mexico, I noticed a somewhat similar concept with a different form of expression. At the entrance of the church, the grateful person went down on both knees and walked on them all the way to the altar to thank God for the blessing He had bestowed him or her.

In the courtyard that night, the bonfire that had been lighted with the flame of a candle from the church was already crackling, blazing and shooting its red and orange tongues into the dark night, with heat, smoke and the smell of burning wood filling the cold atmosphere. A dense crowd was standing back on both sides of the bonfire, allowing for the passage of a single file of youngsters who were inching their way toward the fire, getting ready to jump over it. Grandma encouraged me to join the line, but I refused. I was scared. What if the edge of my coat caught fire? What if I fell into the fire? But there was no time to think twice or hesitate, because grandma pushed me into the line, where I stood still, astonished and terrified. There was no turning back, especially when I noticed in the line a few older girls from our school staring at me. To them I didn't look younger. I was leggy and tall for my age. I had no other choice but to summon all my courage and concentrate on what I was going to do next. I looked ahead. There was quite a long distance between the beginning of the line and the bonfire, enough space to run, gather some momentum and jump. I thought to myself: there's nothing to be afraid of. It's like jumping over a hurdle in the physical educationi class. But I panicked when the girl ahead of me fell down on the other side of the fire. Worried, I glanced at grandma in the front of the crowd who in turn looked nervous, but still nodded with encouragement. It was then that I pulled myself together, toned up my muscles, ran, and finally jumped over the flames. The next thing I knew, I was standing on the other side of the fire, relieved and energized, even surprised at my own courage and achievement.

The idea behind jumping over the fire was that one would purify one's tarnished soul by casting one's worries, sickness, and darkness of spirit into the fire, thus acquiring its glowing warmth and bright colors. On the night of *Chahar-shanbeh-Souri*, the Persian version of the ritual, girls and boys jumped over the fire as they sang: "Let my pallor be yours, and your red hue mine."

In the end after everyone in the line had jumped and the fire had started to die down, grandma and I, like the other worshipers, lit our two remaining candles from its embers and, cupping the flames with our hands, walked silently home. The trick was not to allow the breeze or some wicked passer-by blow it out. For us who lived close-by, carrying it home safely was not so hard, but for those who lived further away, it was a challenge. Once we got home, we both felt satisfied: grandma for her accomplished missions, and I for overcoming my fear of fire, and also for safely taking home my candle still lit, whose sweet odor of burning wax would nestle forever in my heart. Then we blew them out and placed them in a box to light again when a disaster would strike or someone in the family would get seriously ill. (In the past when there was no electricity, they lighted kerosene lamps with the candle's flames.) Grandma believed in that candle's constructive and healing power, especially when it was accompanied by her special prayers.

That night my mother treated us to hot tea, hard-to-find white fresh bread, butter and home-made apple jam and, to my great satisfaction, grandma stayed overnight in response to my constant pleas.

When I think about it now, I can't believe what motivated grandma to shove me into that line. She was a gentle, considerate woman who wouldn't force anyone into doing something one didn't want to. But then, having been born a Pisces, she was at her best at times of crisis. To achieve her goal and not to miss that once-a-year opportunity because of my stubbornness, she had acted fast and on impulse, without any hesitation or show of weakness. I'm sure she, like mother, was scared to death when I was in bed with scarlet fever, and had prayed every night until I had pulled through. She had then made a second vow to make me jump over the bonfire.

Now when I look back at that night and the similar ones that followed year after year, I can still, with awe, visualize that glorious spectacle – hundreds of people of all ages, emerging from the church holding lighted candles, fanning out and filling the broad half-dark Naderi Avenue towards the east and west, illuminating it for miles. I can see myself as a little girl, wrapped in a winter coat, carrying a flickering yellow-flamed candle cupped in my hands, trying hard to watch my steps and concentrate on keeping the flame alive, as if it were the flame of my life. It was a dramatic scene that made a group of passing American soldiers stop in their tracks, eagerly watching us with wistful eyes. It was a scene that might have brought to their minds Valentine's Day (it was February 14th). It was a scene my favorite painter, Edvard Munch, with his themes of love, sickness, death, and a feeling for community might have liked to paint.

In the beginning of summer of 1942, like every summer in the past, my mother tried to talk me into getting my head shaved. I had thin hair and it had thinned even more after having the disease. She was convinced that a better quality of hair would grow by shaving it off, but I fiercely fought against the idea and never let her get my hair cut more than its standard shoulder length. I had seen girls with gray shaven heads who were the target of ridicule at school. It took them more than six months to grow a few inches of hair and even then it didn't make much difference in its quality. After I started high school, she stopped trying, but sometimes teased me by saying, "Why don't we shave your head this summer?" After puberty, the quality of my hair improved. It was still thin, but had grown dense and I had learned to take better care of it by washing it with raw egg yolk.

*****

With the occupation of Iran by the Allied forces and the removal of Reza Shah the Great from the Peacock Throne, the foreign schools of Iran, including the Armenian ones, were reopened. I was in the fifth grade at the time and stayed in my school, as did most of my Armenian friends in the class. The Persian language school with its established curriculum would prepare us much better for the stringent sixth-grade national exams than the newly-opened bi-lingual Armenian school. Mother did, however, register Emil at the new Armenian school and hired a tutor to continue teaching me our language that I had started in the underground classes.

In the millde of the year, the number of the students in our class suddenly doubled. A nearby elementary school had closed and the majority of its students were transferred to ours. Among them there was a pretty girl named Flora. She was a neat, studious girl whose grades surpassed those of the rest of us. Within a short period of time, much to our envy, she won the heart of our teacher and became her pet, who lovingly ordered her around, "Flora, do this, Flora, do that. Flora, I'm going to the principal's office. Write down the names of those who talk. You are an angel, Flora."

One morning when the teacher came to the class, she looked more serious than usual, perhaps with a touch of resentment. She called our names on the roster and we raised our hands to indicate our presence. When it came Flora's turn, the teacher read her name, told her to stand up then asked, "Flora, why didn't you tell me you are a Jew?" Flora blushed then went white as she stared at the teacher like a deer caught in the headlights. She stood there silently, then opened her mouth to say something, but closed it and hung her head – defeated, unable to defend herself.

The teacher's attitude toward Flora changed drastically after that day. She completely ignored or treated her with contempt, as our feelings toward Flora shifted from envy to sympathy. It was odd. In our school and class there were a variety of religious minorities, all treated equally. It was a mixture of different religions and cultures, like Christian Armenians with their own Indo-European language; Assyrians who spoke Aramaic, an extinct Semitic language; Azeri Moslem Turks from the northwestern province of Azerbaijan who spoke Azeri, a Turkish dialect; Baha'is, an Islamic sect; Jews and Zoroastrians who spoke Farsi. They all had their representatives in the parliament too. Those were the times when the Jews had long been accepted in the mainstream of Iranian life after Reza Shah had abolished the Jewish ghettos in Iran. It was also the times when in other parts of the world the Jews were mistreated and executed.

After all those years, I still can't get over that incident and don't understand the teacher's motive. Was the school management behind it? I doubt it. Or was it a personal matter. Maybe the teacher had felt betrayed or cheated for not knowing in advance that Flora was Jewish and she had pampered her beyond limit. This seems more likely. The misunderstanding was neither one's fault. Most of the Jews' last names were Persian and Farsi was their spoken language. In that community, one couldn't tell a Jew from a Moslem Persian.

From that day on, Flora, an eleven-year-old girl who was considered one of the best students in our class, suddenly withdrew into her shell. She was so quiet, we sometimes thought she was absent from the class. Her grades dropped, she fell from the top of the list to the bottom, and she kept her distance from the rest of us. She failed the finals, and we didn't see her in sixth grade.

Ordinarily, it was not common for parents to challenge the teachers or question their judgment. They always sided with the authority and found their children guilty of some wrong doing. In this case, however, Flora's parents kept silent but changed her school.

Chapter 7

Nourbakhsh High School

When I passed the much dreaded sixth-grade national exams and graduated from elementary school, I thought I already knew enough about the basics of arithmetic, science, history, geography, and Farsi –with its Arabic roots and difficult dictation– that I didn't need any more education.

The elementary and high schools in Iran followed the French method of education with all subjects mandatory throughout the academic year. Most of the subjects were taught for five-and-a-half days a week, Saturday through Thursday noon, with Fridays off. The day mother bought me a desk for my graduation after postponing it for years, I thought it was already too late and a waste of money because I wasn't going to use it. During my school years, I had wished for a desk but mother either didn't or couldn't buy it for me (I did my homework on the dining table). Every time I asked for one she told me the story of Abraham Lincoln who did his homework on a log. When the desk entered our apartment, I asked her why she kept telling me the same story over and over again. She said, "Ah, that's the point. I wanted you to learn about that great man and liberator in history" – and she was right. I did learn much about Abraham Lincoln by reading his biography, which helped me get a high mark in history in the twelfth grade national exams.

In an in-depth essay I had written about Abraham Lincoln, the 16th president of the United States of America, a self-educated lawyer, who brought about the emancipation of slaves and preserved the Union (23 Northern states) during the American Civil War against the Confederates (11 Southern states). He was assassinated shortly after his victory, becoming a martyr and a hero for the generations to come.

And yes, I did use that desk throughout my higher education.

On the same occasion, Uncle Johnny gave me the largest metallic globe that the nearby stationary store could offer. The moment I received it, I fell in love with it. Having studied geography intensely for the previous three years, I had learned so much about the subject that even with my eyes closed, I could show the location of every single country, its capital, seas, mountains and rivers on the maps of the five continents. That globe, which I treasured for many years, became my source of interest about the world, my comfort zone – just like reading and writing – and had a major role in turning me into an itinerant, setting a life-long trend of travel and exploration of worthwhile places both at home and abroad.

At Nourbakhsh High School, with a group of
the folkloric choir (1947).

In those days, unlike our children and grandchildren who begin celebrating a string of graduations, starting with kindergarten, we didn't have any ceremony or party. All we had was a gathering in a classroom at the elementary school where our teachers talked and talked but never cut the creamy cake they had bought with the money gathered from us.

In the fall of 1943, I was registered at Nourbakhsh High School, previously an all-American girls' high school. In the 1940s, Nourbakhsh was considered one of the best educational institutions for girls in Iran. It had high academic standards and a modern campus. The school was also renowned for its athletic education and a sports club, with basketball and volleyball fields, tennis courts, a running track, swimming pool, and facilities for gymnastics, all of which were also used for competitions with teams from other schools. The club also housed a few ping-pong tables, bicycles and roller skates that the students could use during their free time or in the physical education classes. Skating was just becoming fashionable, with skating rinks opening in Tehran.

Every year on the fourth of Aban (October 26th), the Shah's birthday, we participated in the sports festival that took place in Amjadieh sports stadium with students of other high schools, in red tops and white shorts. We paraded and performed synchronized exercises which we had practiced in the school courtyard for a few months ahead of the event – one hour every morning before the start of the classes. I also participated in the school's choir where we sang Iranian folk songs and prepared for the annual variety show of Char-Shanbeh-Souri, the last Wednesday of the Iranian year. A month before the concert we helped our teachers make us costumes with colorful crepe papers which we wore only once.

We went on several field trips by bus in spring. Once we visited the Institute of Producing Serum in the town of Hesarak, and another time the sugar factory and the faculty of agriculture in Karaj, with its farms and ranches, which ended with a picnic on the premises. During those trips shooting photos was the highlight of my day. I had an Eastman Kodak box camera that mother had given me for one of my birthdays. It had six photo rolls and took pictures only in sunlight. Still, the pictures I shot with it were good enough to excite my friends. It was not that there wasn't a more advanced camera in the market, but she thought it was enough for a beginner to make mistakes with and learn in the process.

At Nourbakhsh, we had the best teachers, mostly with higher degrees obtained from universities in France, Belgium, Germany, England or the United States. I remember some of our female teachers attending the University of Tehran full time while teaching some courses at our school. One of them, our science teacher, Mrs. Parsa, was a young married woman who was studying at the Medical School. After graduating, she was appointed to the post of principal. Many years later she was assigned to the prestigious post of Minister of Education in the Cabinet of Prime Minister Amir-Abbas Hoveida. I don't know if she ever practiced medicine. I was in Los Angeles in 1979, the year of the Iranian Islamic Revolution, when I heard with dread about her execution in Tehran by the Islamic government's firing squad. What was her crime? She had worked with the previous regime. She was a grandmother then.

*****

During the second year of high school, mother enrolled me at Madame Cornelli's ballet school. She thought that exercise and dancing would shape and strengthen my thin, growing body, while music would train my ear and cultivate my sense of rhythm and style. Madame Cornelli, who was married to an Italian, was a middle-aged Russian émigré, a graduate of the world famous Leningrad Ballet School, who ran her six classes three times a week. On Thursdays and Saturdays my class began at 6:00 p.m. and on Fridays (the weekend), at 10:00 a.m. for one hour each session. The first half hour of the class consisted of exercises and a workout, followed by thirty minutes of dancing. The classical dances were pieces from *Copelia, Swan Lake* and *La Sylphide*. We also learned ethnic dances, such as the Hungarian *Chardash*, Italian *Tarentella*, Polish *Mazurka* and Russian *Kazachok*. The music was produced live by an elderly woman who accompanied us on the piano.

The ballet school was located a long way from our house. It was still within walking distance, but closer to my grandparents' residence. I didn't mind walking on Naderi and Ferdowsi Avenues in daylight, but I didn't like to cross them at night when they were full of American soldiers hanging around the bars or flirting and haggling with the much-in-demand prostitutes. I was not even bothered by any of the local pests that sometimes lurked in a dark corner and made amorous or abusive comments to a girl or a woman walking alone. Normally, the streets were considered safe. If not, mother wouldn't let me go alone. Still, I detested that lonely walk and I usually went to my grandparents' on Thursday nights and stayed overnight to attend the class on Friday mornings.

Once when I entered their apartment, I found them shocked and distraught. Their old grandfather clock, which used to chime on the hour and half hour, was lying on the floor broken. "It happened just before you came," my grandma lamented.

"It just exploded by itself and spread all over the room," grandpa added. "But you know, I'm going to fix it with some help from you."

After dinner, I gathered in a bowl, the nuts and bolts and every single tiny piece of metal and wood my sharp eyes could see on the carpet. Grandpa put the half-empty clock on the table and carefully studied his next move in the complicated project. Then he awkwardly started to put pieces together and add the nuts, bolts and screws to a small part which had remained intact inside the clock. In the meantime, he told me to separate and put together similar parts, and to give him the required piece when he asked for it. He worked like a surgeon, with me as his assistant. He said he hadn't done such a job before but, much to our delight, he did succeed in fixing the clock, using all the parts, except for a single extra screw.

The next fall an Armenian girl who lived in our neighborhood joined our ballet class and we walked there together. Her name was Emma. Her family had immigrated to Iran a few years before from the Soviet Union, and shortly after had applied for the American quota, a permanent visa for a family to immigrate to the United States. Since there was a long waiting list of applicants, families had to wait for many years before they received an acceptance letter from the American Embassy.

Emma's parents didn't send her to an Iranian school because she didn't know enough Farsi to be accepted at a high school. Instead they hired a tutor to work with her at home, something that seemed strange to some of my classmates who didn't approve of her academic situation. Emma was a charming, ambitious girl with a strong personality and a self-confident posture. She liked to talk about her dreams which she hoped to fulfill in America. Sometimes she invited me over to her family parties where the two of us would dance to the music provided by a gramophone. I enjoyed her company so much that I sometimes didn't go to my grandparents' home on Thursday nights, but walked and talked with her along the way home. When I was with her, I felt happy and more secure.

The ballet school organized a concert at the hall of the Palace movie theater every other year which was sold out as soon as the tickets were issued. The concert was consisted of solo and group classical ballet pieces, Russian and Eastern European ethnic dances with the appropriate decor, and a live performance by the best band in Tehran. One time while practicing for a concert, Emma fell down and twisted her right ankle. Despite the doctors' best efforts, the ankle didn't heal in time for her to dance at the concert. Madame Cornelli gave me her role, which made me embarrassed, but fortunately, two weeks later, when the concert was repeated due to popular demand, she was able to perform her part. That was the last time Emma danced in the concert. That year, they received their quota and emigrated to America. We kept up our correspondence with each other, until I met her in America many years later. As for our quota, we lost it because when we received the invitation letter, mother didn't follow it through. She saw no reason in leaving Iran. She was happy there, surrounded by her parents, brothers, in-laws and many friends.

During my high-school years I also danced on the stage of our school's assembly hall at a few festivities. I danced Johann Strauss's *Blue Danube* with another student, I in the role of the male, and she in the role of the female (because I was taller than her). On another occasion, I danced solo the *Hungarian Dance No. Five* by Johannes Brahms, accompanied at the piano by one of my classmates. Ordinarily, my mother attended those performances, but if for some reason she couldn't make it, Uncle Johnny was always there to replace her.

Chapter 8

The WWII Years

Part of my life during the WWII years was spent at the elementary school and a part at high school.

Because of the war, the import of certain food items had come to a halt and the local products had become scarce or of poor quality. Bread, the staple of Iranian people, made of impure flour, was so bad that made headlines in papers and periodicals. I recall a caricature of a sliced brown bread embedded with screw driver, knife and blade. For that kind of bread, Emil and I had to wait in line for hours. Even then, we sometimes went home empty-handed because the store had run out of stock. Once we didn't have bread for a whole week, then one day someone knocked at our door and gave us a large package. When we opened it we found, to our extreme delight, twenty large sheets of *lavash* bread. My youngest uncle, Hrand, who worked at a branch of UKCC, a British firm in the city of Hamadan, had heard about the shortage of bread in Tehran and had sent it to us through a truck driver who routinely drove between the two cities.

In those days, one of my father's cousins, Simon, who was working at the National Iranian Oil Company company in the Caspian city of Rasht had also heard about the food shortages in Tehran and did our family a favor by sending us a live goose. We kept the bird on our second balcony, feeding it for a week and coping with its frequent squawks, until my mother decided to cook it. But when nobody volunteered to slaughter it, she took it to the nearby cold-cut meat factory-store, run by an Armenian family, whose employees could also pluck its feathers and empty its internal organs for a fee. We enjoyed the meal mother had cooked with some dried prunes, and forgot about all the trouble it had given us. Then a week later, we received a piglet, which we also kept on our balcony for a few days, then took it to the meat factory again. This time they didn't cut the throat of the piglet. Its neck was too thick to be cut by a knife, so, instead, they stabbed it in the heart, did the preliminary cleaning and gave it back to us. This time, mother got it roasted at the bakery's oven, which we shared and enjoyed with our sub-tenants, Mrs. Surpik and Mr. Artin.

However, the third time when Simon sent us a turkey, my mother became angry and yelled at the bearer, "Not Again! Go tell Mr. Simon not to send us any more *live* gifts!" And poor Simon stopped in his tracks. But, when Mr. Artin heard about it, he volunteered to take care of the bird; first by fattening, then killing and making it ready for cooking. Every morning, he fed the bird a whole walnut, the size of a ping-pong ball, as Emil and I gaped at the bizarre procedure. He opened the noisy bird's beak with his fingers, put the walnut into its mouth then forced it down the bird's throat. We saw how the walnut bulged inside the long, narrow throat, then slowly slid down and disappeared, as the fowl winced and swallowed hard. I don't really know if the walnut had any role in making the meat so tasty, but I do know that when it came home from the baker's oven on Christmas Eve, it was a rare feast in those lean years of WWII.

Somehow, certain canned foods, like spam, corned beef, salmon, dried powdered eggs and custard came out of the American military canteen and were sold in the Iranian markets. My mother had experimented and learned to make delicious meals with those canned foods, combining them with vegetables, rice or pasta. The meal she made with vermicelli (angel hair pasta) and spam was my paternal grandfather's favorite, who came over for lunch every Wednesday. Grandpa Grikor had lived alone since my grandmother's death. He was retired and had worked for the German firm, Ziegler, as an English-Farsi translator. I remember him throwing some English phrases into his Armenian statements, like "One thing at a time," which I learned to use later.

Shoes were rare items in those war years. For summer, the shoemakers made sandals. Because of the leather shortage, however, we seldom had new winter shoes. Our same old shoes were repaired over and over again by a wonderful shoe repairman on Naderi Avenue, who did an excellent job of nailing new soles and heels to our shoes and polishing them like new.

In high school, noticing that some of my classmates were wearing high-heeled strapped shoes, I insisted on having a pair myself. In spite of the shortage, mother found a full-heeled pair of sandals which made a lot of noise when I walked on the bare floor. I wanted to look older. Besides, there was an Armenian boy from the nearby boys' high school who stood on the side of the street waiting for me to pass, casting admiring glances at me. I don't know why he showed interest in me, because I still hadn't quite matured. I was skinny and tall, something that was not much appreciated in that community, where men preferred a layer of flesh over a woman's bones. However, those encounters didn't go any further than waiting and a few complimentary comments thrown at me. Nonetheless, I felt good about myself. Those high-heeled shoes had boosted my self-confidence making me walk more erect with my head in the clouds.

In the war years, the shortage of fabric, yarn and household items which used to be imported from European countries forced the women to recycle old ones and make magical creations with them. For instance, my mother unpicked our old sweaters and knitted new ones in a different style, or if there wasn't enough yarn, she coordinated it with a matching color. Sometimes, she reversed a coat and skirt to give it a new look. Once she reversed an overcoat and removed its lining, which I wore under my school uniform. Although it was thick and heavy, it kept me warm in the dead of winter. As the old saying goes, "Necessity is the mother of invention." Parallel to the women's frugality and creativity, a few local factories started to come to life. One successful factory belonging to an Armenian family – whose one daughter-in-law, a beautiful lady, happened to be my cousin – supplied the Iranian nation with assortments of woolen fabrics, yarns and blankets. They were coarse and scratchy in the beginning, but became softer and better as their quality improved over the years.

Knitting, an old family tradition that had made a comeback, took women's minds off war problems as they focused on the colorful yarn and the movements of the needles in their hands. Knitting became so popular and in demand that many housewives not only knitted for the members of family, but knitted shawls, scarves and sweaters for charity events. Grandma was busy all year round knitting for her eleven grand children for Christmas and birthdays. In those days, we appreciated whatever was given to us as a present. I remember one Christmas how getting three pairs of pink, yellow and blue hand-woven socks had exhilarated me as I wore and showed them off to my friends.

I see the same interest flourishing today in Los Angeles among women of all ages at knitting classes held by local libraries, women's book clubs, among Hollywood celebrities, and simply in women's homes. It has become a way of relaxing by focusing their minds on the work. It is also good exercise for their wrists and fingers while watching TV, baby sitting, and to fight boredom. And what's more, to save money.

In those days, everything seemed so precious. God forbid, if I lost, ruined or broke a valuable item in the house, life became miserable for me. Here is one example.

One summer in New Julfa, we were going to a picnic on the banks of the Zayandeh-Rood River and mother had borrowed a swimsuit for me from my father's cousin, Manoush, in whose house we were staying. A swimsuit was not a regular item one could buy from a store. It was a rare luxury item which cost an arm and a leg, and could hardly be found in Tehran, much less in Isfahan, and especially not in New Julfa. However, Manoush, who was a petit woman, lent me her old swimsuit, which was a couple of sizes too large for me. But I didn't mind as long as I could go into the water in it.

We all had a great time on that gorgeous warm day. We swam, chased one another on the river bank, climbed the extended staircase to the bridge above, ate the most delicious food in the world until the sun sank behind the horizon and we collected our belongings and left. Once back at home, when mother and Manoush were taking out the wet swimsuits and the towels to hang on the rope, mother asked me, "Where is the swimsuit you were wearing?"

I said I didn't know and panicked.

She said, "Try to remember. Did you rinse it and put it back into the bag?"

I shook my head. Apparently, I had removed and put it on a rock, gotten busy drying myself and putting my clothes on that I had forgotten about it. It shouldn't have happened, but it had. Mother apologized to Manoush for losing the swimsuit, and promised to buy a new one in Tehran and send it to her, to which Manoush protested and said it didn't matter and it was an old one anyway. As for me, not only was I punished for my carelessness, I was not allowed to go to the club for ice cream and cake and she refused to take me along to the next swimming picnic (I didn't have a swimsuit anyway).

In Tehran mother bought and sent Manoush an imported red-and-cream colored one-piece swimsuit for ninety *tomans*, one-third of the rent of our apartment. Actually, it was not over-priced, considering the fact that during the war the import of merchandise, especially such a luxury item, was limited to a trickle. Nonetheless, I cringed every time she repeated the same story to a friend, blaming me for all the trouble I had caused.

That bitter incident taught me two things in life; first, to be responsible for my own belongings, especially during trips; and second, when I had children myself, to teach them to take care of their personal possessions, but more importantly *not* to blame them if for any reason they would fail to do so. I would let them enjoy themselves and not hurt their feelings for the sake of a replaceable material item.

Now when I look back and think about it, I find mother guilty of the mishap. She was the one responsible for the borrowed item. After all, I was a little girl, carried away by childhood fantasies, involved with friends and games, whose only care in the world was to have fun during those precious hours.

*****

When we were growing up in the war years, we often went on a picnic in spring time, as soon as the weather turned mild and the poplars on the sides of the street began to bloom. Since we lived in an apartment and didn't see any vegetation around us, we yearned for the outdoors, the fresh greenery of nature, the shade of a tree or the gurgle of a brook. So mother would pack some food and a couple of blankets, and with a few of our relatives we would rent a city bus and travel to the foothills of the Alborz Mountains, near a spring or a small waterfall. There we would run on the green meadows, yell at the top of our voices, and play with other children whose families were picnicking like us. Some of those children were blond and blue-eyed. They were refugees of war from Poland who lived in Iran at the time. Life was so good for us children. We enjoyed freedom and good food, and took home bouquets of wild poppies and violets we picked in the fields. One of those picturesque fields that we often visited was called Evin. Years later, during the reign of Mohammad Reza Shah, a piece of that land was transformed into a modern prison to be shown off to the representatives of the Human Rights Organization whenever they visited Tehran. However, Evin prison gained notoriety after the Islamic Revolution, when hundreds of prisoners were held and executed on its premises.

In addition to those picnics, there was an annual picnic/garden-party we looked forward to. That was *Hambartzoum,* the feast of Christ's Resurrection (Ascension), forty days after Easter. On that day, after a religious ceremony at the church, we would go to a picnic in the garden on the outskirts of town, held by the Women's Charity Organization, of which my mother was a member. There, we would see many booths and stands erected under the shade of weeping willows. At one of them, women sold lottery tickets which always won a prize. Those prizes were hand-made items, such as knitted sets of caps and scarves, children's outfits, crocheted tablecloths, doilies and runners, or fake jewelry and perfume, mostly donated by the organization's members or certain shop owners. They also sold home-made pickles, fruit jams in small jars, cookies and cakes in cardboard boxes.

At lunchtime, mother would take Emil and me to a food stand where they offered home-made *dolma* – vine leaves stuffed with ground beef, rice, and chopped fresh herbs – *piroshky* (a kind of meat pie), and rice pilaf with lima-beans. Then with our full plates in our hands, we would walk a few feet away toward a man who was pulling chunks of lamb through iron skewers and putting them on a brazier, as another man rotated them and fanned the glowing wood coals with a straw fan. Waiting for our order, we inhaled the appetizing smoke that rose from the embers: sizzling with meat juice and fat. When it was ready, the man pulled pieces of the scalding shish kebab from the skewer and, wrapping them in a loaf of flat *lavash* bread, urged us to eat while it was still hot.

As we sat at a table, we saw in the distance, grown up girls gathered around an older woman with long braided hair, her head and face covered with a short transparent veil. She was dressed in an old-fashioned Armenian costume, with long sleeves and long-skirt. She had a blue, glazed earthenware jar in her hand, which she held in front of each girl to draw a lot, singing the traditional song of *Jan Gulum,* (a song special to the feast), while the girls nervously opened their lots to find out about their futures. It was such a delightful scene that if the American William Eggleston and John Humble had been there, they would have liked to shoot pictures and add them to their collections of award-winning photographs.

The Feast of Christ's ascension is both a religious and social event in the Armenian community. *Anoush* opera, a tragic love story by Hovhaness Toumanian, the 19th century Armenian national poet and children's story teller, with scores by Armen Dikranian, a Soviet Armenian composer, is based on this event, especially on the fortune-telling lottery. When Anoush, a pretty girl in love with Saro opens her lot and reads, "Death and unfortunate future," she is terrified. The prediction comes true when her brother, Mossi, commits a crime of passion by killing Saro and driving her mad. *Anoush* is a popular opera, a magnificent production of which we saw at the State Opera House of Yerevan when my husband and I visited Soviet Armenia in 1985, during the presidency of Mikhail Gorbachev.

The annual religious celebrations that we looked forward to included the eves of Armenian Christmas, on January fifth, and Easter. From the time my grandparents moved to Tehran they invited my mother and three uncles with their families to dinner at their small apartment. As it was not common to eat red meat on those holy nights, the menu was always the traditional dishes of rice-pilaf, *kookoo* – omelet with fresh herbs – and smoked, salted white fish. Grandma would also roast a whole goose with prunes, and make salads of pinto beans, yogurt with spinach, and sometimes *baba ganouj* – mashed roasted eggplants mixed with *tahini* paste – dotted with pomegranate seeds. It was a healthy and delicious menu, part of which was also used during the forty days of Lent. We all looked forward to those evenings *and* the next day left-over lunch, which we would have after returning from the easter ceremony in the church. These family gatherings went on for many years as long as grandma was alive. My mother kept the tradition alive after grandma's death. When we came to the United States, I continued the tradition by inviting my brothers to dinner on those festive evenings. Then after my children got married and had their own families, we also invited their in-laws.

For us children, Easter was an exciting event to which we looked forward throughout the year. When in high school, one Easter morning, clad in a new two-piece suit, I went to church with my classmate, Vera, carrying a couple of Easter eggs that I had helped mother color on Good Friday. The church was full to bursting point. Even its courtyard was filled with people, mostly youngsters in colorful outfits, busy playing the Easter egg-game. The idea behind playing the game was to break the other person's egg, with the intention of winning it. However, some people were so obsessed by winning that they cheated on the game by using a hard wooden egg or an eggshell filled with melted wax.

Vera and I decided to stay in the courtyard and maybe play the egg game. As we were standing there aimlessly, a good-looking boy approached me and asked if I would like to play. I looked at my friend for approval then nodded at the boy. Covering most of his shining red egg, he graciously offered to "sit" (holding his egg ready to be hit by mine). Delighted, I held my yellow egg with the tip of my fingers and landed a powerful blow to the little-exposed part of his egg. To my disappointment, the top of my egg cracked. Grinning, he told me that it was my turn to "sit." I turned my egg, with the bottom portion now pointed upward. He broke it again. Then he asked if I would like to play with the other. I nodded, and when that too broke on both ends, I reluctantly gave him the broken eggs. He asked my friend if she would like to play, but she shook her head, and pulling my sleeve, dragged me along. Later I learned that before starting the game I should have tried the other party's egg by knocking it against my front teeth to make sure that it was real.

When I grew up and went to a party at Easter, my experience with the egg game became more enjoyable. The girls and boys played the game over something like a book, going to a movie, or a visit to a confectioner's for an ice cream or cream-puff. That was a good excuse for a girl and a boy who secretly admired each other to spend a few hours together.

*****

In those days going to the movies was the highlight of our lives. We went with our parents or friends, depending on the subject of the film. Among the children's movies I had seen were *The Wizard of Oz, The Blue Bird,* Walt Disney's *Bambi, Snow White and the Seven Dwarfs, Fantasia* and many others. During my teenage years, I remember the movie stars Greer Garson, Walter Pigeon, Judy Garland and Mickey Rooney. One of my favorite movies was *First Love* featuring Deanna Durbin and Robert Stack, whose TV series, *Unsolved Mysteries* I would watch much later when we lived in Los Angeles. Collecting photos of the movie-stars was another pastime which we cherished. We either bought them at stationary stores, or exchanged duplicates with those of our friends, and then arranged them in photo albums like those of a family.

Unfortunately, we couldn't enjoy even that small pleasure for some time because of an epidemic of typhus that had spread among the soldiers of the Allied Forces stationed in Tehran. We were forbidden from going to public places until the opening of *Kaj Nazar, (Courageous Nazar)*, a comedy written by Hovhaness Toumanian and filmed in Soviet Armenia. It was the hilarious story of a peasant who, contrary to his name, was a coward, but through pure luck and a series of misunderstandings became a respected hero. It was a popular story, which we had heard scores of times and were excited and looked forward to see the movie. Then after some debate and deliberation among the mothers of other children in the family, they came up with a bright idea. They sewed two little pouches for each of us and filled them with naphthalene which we placed in our pockets. The sharp-smelling solvent would repel the typhus-infected lice that could find its way toward our skins, bite us and transmit the disease. So we went in a group, enjoyed the movie, and didn't catch typhus.

When I think back to that mediocre movie, I can't believe how we endangered our lives and put our parents through all that anxiety. We certainly didn't have any notion of danger or death. As long as we were surrounded by family and friends, we could enjoy anything, a bad movie or a piece of impure brown bread. For us, life was good in those prime years, no matter what was going on around us. At the movie theater, my friends and I shared those wonderful images that were projected on the screen, about which we talked and fantasized later. As film director Martin Scorsese says in "The 100 Best Movies" in an extra issue of Newsweek in the year 2000, "Movies can transport you to another place and time. And that's magic. They take you away to another world. It's like a dream state." I couldn't agree more. Those movies, even the mediocre ones, could take us to a more beautiful world and amuse us for a few hours.

I was so fascinated by cinema that later in life, in Los Angeles, I took two film courses in college. The first one was called Cinema 5, "Film and Society – the 1950s," where I saw films like, *Rebel Without a Cause, The Defiant Ones, Paths of Glory, From Here to Eternity, Shane, Asphalt Jungle, The Man With a Golden Arm, The Day the Earth Stood Still, Some Like it Hot, Viva Zapata, Born Yesterday, Psycho,* and many more, most of which are among

"The 100 Best Movies," of the year 2000. The second course was "Many Faces of Love," where I saw *Camille, Wuthering Heights, Rebecca, Casablanca, Red Shoes, Now Voyager, Romeo and Juliet, Son of the Sheik,* and *Vertigo,* stories that carried an air of sadness and melancholy about them. In that course, I saw director Rouben Mamoulian's *Love Me Tonight,* a 1932 musical film, with Jeanette MacDonald and Maurice Chevalier, in which for the first time in the history of cinema, he had used a sound system, applying rhythm, sound and music to the scenes, even in people's dreams. A few years later I saw an Italian movie named *Cinema Paradiso.* It was so nostalgic. It took me back to Tehran, reminding me of the Italian films we had seen in the fifties and sixties, and our fascination with them.

Throughout my years in the United States, my love affair with movies has helped me get closer to my American acquaintances, with the subject of stars and movies being a common thread of conversation. To me, they are like a bridge, a foundation for mutual understanding.

Part III

The Post-WWII Years

1945-1976

Chapter 9

The End of WWII

In 1945, a series of surprising things happened that dramatically changed the course of our family's life.

Mr. Artin contracted pneumonia, just like my father, and passed away within a week. After his death, his devastated wife, Surpik, not having a source of income and unable to make a living just by crocheting and knitting items for customers, decided to go back to Bulgaria where she still had a few relatives. So after the ceasefire of Europe and the disastrous atomic bombardment of Japan, she sold her household items, some of which my mother bought, and vacated our room. She took a bus to the port city of Pahlavi on the Caspian Sea, where she boarded a steamer bound for Baku in Azerbaijan, then a train to Sofia in Bulgaria. Although she promised to write us a letter, she never did. We later heard from one of her close friends that she had arrived safely in her home town and was doing fine.

After Surpik left, my mother decided not to sub-let her room, but to turn it into a living room. So she got it painted, bought fabric and sewed new curtains. She decorated the room with one of Uncle Johnny's oil paintings, a winter landscape; and one of her own, a water color of red poppies. She also bought a couch, a few armchairs and a coffee table. In furnishing the room, Emil and I helped her as much as we could, but most of the credit went to our housekeeper, a young girl named Margo, a cute girl with curly hair, whom we had brought to Tehran from a village near New Julfa a few years before. When Surpik was still there, Margo helped her in sweeping her room and washing dishes. She also helped our Jewish neighbor on Saturday mornings by striking a match to light their kerosene stove in return for a few *rials*. In Tehran, the majority of families (not necessarily the rich ones) had a housekeeper, who either worked daily or stayed overnight, depending on whether she had a family in town. Over the years, we had a variety of maids, ranging from an inexperienced teenager girl to a woman housekeeper/cook, who were either Persian or Armenian.

Margo sent her wages to her parents in her village. My mother taught her to read and write in Armenian, and I taught her the same subjects in Farsi. When she was nineteen, Margo fell in love with the owner of a nearby convenience store, an Armenian from a village near Tehran. We notified her parents, and she married the young man with their consent. Mother gave her a modest trousseau, and held a tea party on her wedding day. Margo left us at the end of that summer, but she regularly visited us even after having two children. She was lucky to get married before the age of twenty, because in her social class, they believed that "A girl whose age has passed twenty, you should weep for her adversity!"

*****

In February of 1946, after the end of WWII and nine years after my father's death, mother remarried the son of my father's elder sister, who had been trying to talk her into marriage for many years. Vartges, whom I will call father from now on, was a few years younger than my mother. He had graduated from Tehran University Medical School, specializing in pathology, and worked at its Pathology Department, becoming its chairman and a tenured professor in the years to come. Their wedding ceremony was very simple. One afternoon they went to the church, got married and came home with their best man, a collegue friend of Vartges. There was no celebration and no honeymoon.

Our bedroom was renovated, curtains changed and mother's bed replaced with a new double bed. Every night, Emil and I would bring our bedding from the bedroom to the dining room and sleep there; in the morning we would fold and take them to the bedroom, piling them in a corner against the wall. Our dining room became a dining/sitting-room during the day and a bedroom during the night.

Our small storage room began to function as a kitchen, as our old kitchen was remodeled and converted into a laboratory, with the equipment that Vartges bought from a retail medical supply store. He ordered a fluorescent-lit glass sign that read "Alborz Laboratory," in Farsi and English, named after the Alborz mountain range in the north. By running the laboratory part time, he wanted to have his own business on the side, although it took him a couple of years before the business started to pick up. Meanwhile, my father's car-painting factory, under Uncle Johnny's management, helped support Emil and me through our high school and university years.

After mother's marriage, our newly decorated living room suddenly sprang to life. It started receiving a variety of visitors, ranging from Vartges' Armenian and Persian colleagues and their wives to frequent dinner parties that mother enjoyed to throw with the help of a housekeeper/cook she had hired after Margo had left. During the afternoons, the room served as a waiting room for laboratory patients, and on certain evenings as a meeting-place for the board members of a few Armenian community councils, in which Vartges was actively involved.

Ordinarily, children don't like it when their mothers or fathers remarry, but Emil and I felt ecstatic about mother's marriage. We would not be fatherless anymore, and we could boast in school that we had a physician father in the house. We were already close to Vartges, whom we had admired and loved since our early childhood. He came to our house frequently and joined in our family gatherings, picnics, and helped Emil and me with our homework, and sometimes took us to a movie. Before attending medical school, Vartges had graduated from the American College of Tehran when Dr. Samuel Jordan was its principal. Dr. Jordan, who called Iran his second homeland, was an accomplished educator who during his forty-two years of tenure, had taught and shaped many of Iran's future leaders. Vartges had an excellent command of English, and helped me in writing compositions in English.

Vartges was always there when one of us was sick. When my tonsils were removed at the age of eleven, something went wrong in the night following the surgery. I felt the constant taste of blood in my mouth. The surgeon was notified and came immediately to our home. After a bit of struggle, he was able to stop the bleeding. Prior to leaving, he warned mother and Vartges – who had been present during the entire procedure – not to let me cough and cause recurrent bleeding. All night long, I was tormented by trying to stifle a cough which continuously irritated my throat. Both of them were on the alert, watching my every move, sometimes giving me drops of water, propping pillows behind my head, or helping change my position in bed. They stayed awake throughout the night, sometimes taking turns, with me dozing on and off. Vartges had also helped mother when I had scarlet fever two years before. He stayed with me when mother had to leave the house for shopping or running errands. Among her duties there was an occasional visit to a sick lonely friend with heart disease, whose family had abandoned her because of a marriage they hadn't approved.

Vartges was one of the founding members of the Armenian Society of University Students and its branch, *Bujaran*, a free medical clinic for needy Armenians. *Bujaran* was especially founded for those thousands of homeless villagers who after WWII had traveled to Tehran from various villages in Iran to emigrate to Soviet Armenia by permission of its government. Armenia having lost hundreds of thousands of its citizens to war and famine had planned to fill in their places by admitting Armenians from Iran who were looking forward to live in their homeland.

Some registered families had already emigrated within a year, but most were still waiting and hoping for admission while living under unfavorable conditions. To make matters worse, the Iranian government, displeased by their intention of mass exodus, not only didn't help them to settle in Tehran, but urged them to go back to their villages, where they didn't own any homes or land, having sold them for minimum prices. However, with the mediation of the Armenian diocesan council, those displaced families were permitted to erect tents on a vacant lot in north of Tehran – which were gradually replaced by sun-baked brick houses. Their children were accepted at Armenian schools for free, and the Women's Charity Organization, in which my mother was actively involved, served the students of one school nutritious lunches and clothed them in winter. I remember how one month before the New Year, women of the organization came to our house, working at our dining table with fabrics, measuring tape, scissors and patterns spread all over it. They worked frantically, with mother at the sewing machine, trying to make those garments ready before the end of the year.

In those days many rumors and stories circulated around the emigrated families, some of them so exaggerated that they could pass as an anecdote. I recall one story that went like this: There were two families of a brother and a sister, one of which was allowed to emigrate, and the other was still waiting for its turn. On departure, the brother told his sister that on arrival he would write her a letter. But since he was not allowed to explicitly describe his condition in Soviet Armenia, he would set a secret code between the two of them. He would enclose a photo of himself. If he was in a standing position, it would mean that every thing was fine, and she should follow in his footsteps. If he was seated, the conditions were not so favorable, and she should better think twice before leaving Iran. Two months later the sister received the long-awaited envelope. She read the letter, in which her brother had extolled the virtues of the life and privileges they had in a village near Yerevan, about the abundance of food and clothing (which everybody knew Armenia was badly short of). At the end, he encouraged her to emigrate. But when she peered at the blurred photo, she winced and shuddered at what she saw. Her brother was neither standing nor sitting. He was lying down on a bare floor.

With the help and sacrifices of the Armenian community, fifteen years later those hardworking displaced families had done so well that they gradually moved to other parts of Tehran. The sun-baked houses were demolished and the vacant lot turned into an open market. Most of the children of those families finished their schools, some were accepted at the university and some learned manual skills and established successful businesses.

One of those boys, who had been regularly fed at the school luncheons, and now owned a profitable welding workshop, had bought a three-story apartment building on Ferdowsi Avenue. He lived in one of the apartments and rented out the other two. One of the tenants was my eldest aunt who had just become a widow. The young man who had recognized her from those school luncheons had rented her the apartment for a minimum amount. Some times life has strange ironies. My aunt, who had volunteered to help those impoverished children in her middle age, was reaping the harvest in her old age. There's a Persian proverb that says, "Do a good deed and throw it in the Tigris, so that God will give it back to you in a desert."

That same year, 1946, when the baby boom began in America, our brother Armen, was born in Najmieh hospital at the end of December. I was fourteen years old. Although I liked babies and was happy to help mother take care of him, I sometimes was frustrated by his frequent cries which interfered with my homework and sleep. We were still living in our three-roomed apartment, with a crib added in the bedroom. Once I asked myself in frustration: when will this baby grow up and let me have a normal life? That baby is over sixty years old now, a Stanford University graduate and successful computer engineer, with a wife, children and grandchildren. Now I wonder: where and how did all those years go by?

During the next spring, my paternal grandfather, Grikor, died of old age. He had been living with my eldest aunt during the final years of his life.

*****

In July 1949, shortly after my high school graduation, with no proms, ceremony or celebration, I was invited by an Armenian classmate to her birthday party. It was my first co-ed party and I was looking forward to it. I washed and set my short hair, wore a sleeveless yellow cotton dress – one of a few mother had sewn for me – and was about to leave with the gift in my hand, when she said to me, "Remember to be back by midnight." I nodded and left. Of course I would be back by then. It was 7:00 p.m. and still light, my friend's house was within walking distance, and there were five hours to spend.

The party was going full blast when I arrived and was welcomed by my friend. There were about fifteen Armenian boys and girls, most of whom I knew; talking, laughing, dancing, and munching on chips and dips and cold cuts from the table. It didn't take me long to blend in and find myself completely at home. More than that, I was having the time of my life, oblivious of the passing time. But suddenly remembering my curfew hour, I checked my watch. It was 11:50 p.m. I panicked and cut short the dance, apologized to my partner, went to the host and told her that I had to leave. She was appalled, "This early? The party is just warming up!" I told her about my time limit and the promise to my mother. She nodded but didn't let me leave alone. She asked two of the boys to walk me home. When we got home, mother was awake waiting for me. I was about to say goodbye to the boys when, to my surprise, one of them asked her to let me stay to the end of the party which wouldn't exceed beyond one or two o'clock. My mother, caught in an impasse, relented and allowed me to stay. So we returned, talking and laughing all the way back to the party.

When I returned at 1:30 a.m., mother was asleep, but next morning, she warned me, "Don't you ever bring someone along to stand up for you! Remember too, that from now on whenever you go to a party, you have to be home by midnight. Understood?"

Yes. I understood that from that moment on I had to obey my mother's rules as long as I lived in that household. And more importantly, my male friends in the group also learned to walk me home before midnight every time we went to a party.

Chapter 10

College Years: 1950-53

In early October 1949, I took the Tehran University *concours* – entrance exams – at the Department of Literature, Faculty of English Language/ Literature. Hundreds of applicants had to write an essay in English on the subject "Necessity Is the Mother of Invention." A week later when the names of the accepted students were posted on the college bulletin board, I was delighted to find my name on top of the list. In general, I was good at writing, regardless of the language – Armenian, Farsi or English – for which I usually had gotten high grades in high school. My younger brother and two male cousins – who later attended Stanford and Berkley Universities in the United States – usually borrowed my essays, copied them, and much to my frustration, got even higher grades than I did.

After twelve years of segregated, all-female classes, it was strange for us girls to share them in college with male students who seemed to be in the same situation as us. They didn't know how to handle the girls who were maybe 20% of the class. They usually looked down on us girls, scarcely talked, but sometimes teased us. Our curriculum, in addition to subjects related to English literature and reading assignments of books by British and American authors, playwrights and poets, also included Persian literature and French language. Our professors consisted of a few Britons and Americans, the majority being Iranians with Ph.Ds obtained in England or the United States.

In Iran and Middle-Eastern countries, knowing foreign languages, especially English and French, was a valuable asset for those who intended to continue their higher education abroad. It was also instrumental in finding employment in American or European firms, embassies and consulates, or wherever English and French were required.

The final year of high school was divided into three branches: math, science, or literature. I was among the majority of the students in the class who had chosen literature in high school. Those who were graduates of math and science and were less acquainted with literature had difficulty in keeping up with the pace of the class and sometimes made stupid mistakes. One of those blunders happened during my class speech.

In order to improve our language skills, one of our professors asked if anyone among us would like to make a speech on a subject, such as "Invention of the Wheel." Being a shy person, I thought it would be a good idea to volunteer and speak in front of all those male students. First, I wanted to prove to myself that I could do it, and, second, to prove to those boys that we girls had good heads on our shoulders and were not lesser than them. So I raised my hand and volunteered. But as soon as I accepted the assignment, I regretted it. How was I going to find material about a subject I knew nothing about? How was I going to speak in front of all those young men who were waiting for an excuse to tease or criticize a girl? But it was too late and I couldn't do anything but comply. When I told my parents, they encouraged me to start the project and work on it. Then with some help from Vartges and material from college reference books, I was able to write something about the "wheel": one of man's most important and useful inventions, how it was first cut in one piece from a solid log to move heavy stones, then came the separate axle and wheel, sliced from a log in a circular shape, eventually to be replaced by metal. I wrote about its usage through time: for pulling water from wells, for millstones to grind grain, for potter's wheels to spin clay, for chariots in ancient Rome, carriages, bicycles, cars and a variety of machinery. I developed and expanded the writing, read it several times, memorized it, and underlined its important parts.

On the designated date, I made the speech in front of a full class. I was scared and nervous in the beginning, but relaxed and found my composure when I saw signs of interest on the faces of the audience. At the end I answered all questions, except for one. A young man who had mistaken the word "wheel" with "will" started asking irrelevant questions about "will," making me confused, and causing the whole class to roar with laughter. On the whole I thought the speech was good, but there must have been something more to it when at the end the professor and a few girls congratulated me. Then later on campus, students from other faculties approached and asked me, if I was the person who had made the excellent speech. From that day on, the boys stopped teasing the girls, and showed them more respect.

In late June 1950, when I had passed my exams and didn't know what to do with my long summer vacation, I welcomed my youngest uncle Hrand's invitation to join him on a trip to Hamadan. Hrand who used to live and work in Hamadan during the war years, but now lived in Tehran with his family, had sent his pregnant wife and little son back to Hamadan where she would give birth and enjoy the support of her parents. I had once been to Hamadan for Hrand's wedding, but I was looking forward to spending my summer vacation there and indulging in a change of pace.

Hrand was a handsome jovial man with reddish blond hair who had lived with our family for a year when he was attending a technical school in

Tehran. My brothers and I called him by name, unlike the two others, whom we called "Uncle." During most of the trip, he made me laugh by telling jokes or singing the popular songs of the day with his sweet voice.

Located in the west of Iran, with long cold winters and cool pleasant summers, Hamadan is a historic town, the birthplace of Abu-Ali-Sina (Avecina) the ancient Persian scientist and physician, whose tomb and shrine, together with the shrine of the famous poet, Baba Taher Oryan are popular tourist destinations. Its Mount Alvand still holds carvings of King Darius, and the shrine of the Jewish Queen, Esther, the wife of King Xerxes and that of her cousin Mordechai.

When we arrived in Hamadan late that night, the city seemed to have sprung to life. When I expressed my amazement, Hrand reminded me that the month of Ramadan had started the previous day. Those who had fasted and had slept all day long had emerged from their shell of lethargy and were catching up with lost time. Ramadan had turned their ordinary lives upside down.

Hrand drove straight to his in-laws' residence, where his wife had just come home from the American Hospital. We were glad to see them all, but sensed that the atmosphere of the house was somber. We were told that the condition of the new-born baby-boy who had developed severe diarrhea seemed hopeless.

The next day, the family's physician, a huge man, with spectacles, came to check on the baby and to inject him with some medicine. When he boiled a syringe and inserted the long needle into the baby's emaciated thigh, I shivered with fear and sympathy. The baby was so weak that he couldn't even whimper.

A couple of days later, Hrand had to make a short business trip to a nearby town. In his absence, the baby's condition worsened. The doctor said that any hope for the baby's recovery was slim and he might die any moment, so we better send for a priest to baptize him. While the priest was praying and applying holy water to the dying baby's forehead and cheeks, his mother was crying softly in the next room. When the priest called and asked her for a name with which to baptize the baby, she couldn't come up with one. Maybe she had one in her mind but in her intense grief she couldn't think and concentrate. "What's the use?" She sobbed. "He's not going to live anyway." Then noticing me in the room, she added, "Why don't *you* choose a name for him? After all, you are Hrand's only relative here." Caught by surprise, I started thinking of names that I knew, and came up with the name Shahen. Although it was considered an Armenian name, it was originally the Persian word *shaheen*, which meant a "hawk." So that skinny sick baby was baptized Shahen.

After the baptism ceremony, the priest left. The next morning, the doctor who had visited the house daily, didn't show up. But the baby *didn't die*. On the contrary, his condition improved gradually. He sucked his mother's milk and gained weight. It was then that I asked myself: is the force of nature challenging the inadequacy of science? Or did I have a spiritual ability and didn't know about it? Whatever the answer, I felt proud and happy that the name I had chosen for my cousin had been a lucky one and had saved his life. That skinny baby is a nearly sixty-year-old, handsome man who now lives with his wife in Los Angeles and works for a major airline.

In September, I resumed my studies at college. The years that followed coincided with the turbulent era of the Prime Minister Dr. Mohammad Mosaddegh, his power struggle with the Shah, the nationalization of oil, and constant student protests and demonstrations. These usually took place on campus, with police beating the students with batons, or using fire arms when the clashes turned ugly. Our professors, especially the British and American ones were surprised and angry at the frequency of the student strikes that happened without prior notice. The rest of us, who didn't participate in the protests, didn't mind missing classes. We either went to the library to read or to the cafeteria with a couple of classmates to chat over a cup of tea or a glass of lemonade about politics, our professors, books, films or boys.

I was going to graduate from the university in 1953. My thesis was a translation of the 19th century British novelist Thomas Hardy's novella, *The Romantic Adventures of a Milkmaid* from English into Farsi. I received the assignment in early January and had to turn it in before the final exams in June. Doing an acceptable, high quality translation from one language to another and within such a short period of time was not an easy task for me. However, I worked on it along with my daily homework and during my free hours, both at home and at the university library.

During one of those library visits, something happened that made me realize there was more to the dark side of politics that met the eye. One morning, after the Now-Ruz holidays, I was on my way to the library to work on the translation and do some research about a paper I was writing, when I saw a large group of students chanting slogans against the Shah. Those activities around campus had become so common that we no longer paid serious attention to them. However, a little later, I had just taken a couple of reference books and was about to settle behind a table in the library when I heard a cacophony of quick foot steps, muffled thumps and screams. Instinctively, I grabbed my handbag, rushed to the end of the hall, pulled myself behind a half open door that led down to an alley, closed it as much as I could, leaving only a narrow opening to see what was going on inside. I was scared, but too curious to leave.

What I saw in that hall terrified and irritated me. I saw how the huge entrance door was thrown open and a crowd of panic-stricken students poured in, chased by a group of policemen who rushed to the open windows, shut them and attacked the defenseless students with their batons and rifle butts. I saw a boy desperately fighting with a policeman, his face awash with blood, and how the butt of a rifle landed on the head of a skinny girl, with a subsequent gush of blood. I saw one of my classmates jumping on the shoulders of a policeman, trying to grab his rifle. During the struggle another policeman rushed at them, held his rifle with two hands and struck the boy on his head and the back of his neck. Blood streamed down the boy's nose and ears as he collapsed on the floor. I was numb with fear, unable to move, but somehow managed to sneak out through the narrow opening, descend a flight of stairs and find myself in the alley, walking toward the bus stop in the main street. How I had escaped the fate of those unfortunate victims is still a marvel to me.

Seated in the bus on my way home, I felt shocked with disbelief, unable to understand the situation. We had always been told that the university campus was considered a safe place, a sanctuary, immune to police and army attacks. Then what had gone wrong? Why had the police broken the rule and invaded it? Had it gone overboard in taking action, or was it one of the dirty tricks and intrigues of politics? Whatever the reason, as the Persian saying goes: "The fire of conflict equally burns the dry and the wet, the innocent and the guilty".

After that bloody confrontation the campus was closed for a week. When classes eventually resumed, we found out that the police had dragged and crammed the injured students into a truck, then driven them to the police station for interrogation. The library incident was only the tip of the iceberg. Many other incidents happened that led to the events of the summer of 1953 and the CIA-backed uprising of 28th of Mordad.

For me, 1953 was the year of living dangerously. It was a year full of police and student clashes, strikes, class cancellations, occasional university closures, and the constant dread of police attacks looming over our heads. However, I was able to finish the translation of the novella on time, get Vartges' approval (which was important for me), type it on a Farsi typewriter, and give it to a book-binder to make it ready for presentation.

Although I passed my final exams successfully, I didn't get the result of the translation that I had personally given to our professor. When I tried to inquire about it at the university administration, I found it closed after the recent student-police clashes. Still, I was glad that at least I had done my share of the work without being affected by the circumstances, and if worse came to the worst, and for some reason the thesis got lost in the system, I had another copy at home. In the words of TV anchorman, Walter Cronkite: "That's the way it is." And I couldn't do anything about it.

*****

Summer came early with its choking dry heat hanging over the city, blistering the asphalt, and rusting and burning the leaves on the trees. People like us who lived in apartments with no courtyard or nearby park had to seek refuge in a cooler location or a summer resort. So in late July, we welcomed my father's elder brother, George's invitation, and traveled to Ahmad-Abad, a village in the foothills of Damavand, the peak of the Alborz Mountains, to spend a few weeks at his summer home. Having lost his wife a decade before, Uncle George liked to have company while vacationing there. The road from Tehran to Damavand was narrow and treacherous, winding up the dirt surface of the rocky mountain. A quick look through the window of the bus down the ravine – where dozens of cars and buses had fallen over the years – was enough to make us dizzy and scared.

We finally arrived in the small town of Damavand, and completed the last few miles of the journey to Ahmad-Abad, using a different mode of transportation: local mules. Each of us rode a mule, except for my mother and little brother who shared one. Two extra ones carried our luggage. Our joy began the moment we saw my uncle's red brick house that peeped through the lush green weeping willows and apricot trees, with their branches hanging over the roof. We were welcomed by my uncle at the gate, who showed us to a table in the shade. He introduced us to another family from Tehran that was vacationing in the neighboring house. During lunch, Emil and I soon made friends with their two sons, making plans to hike and explore the nearby woods and hills the next day.

Uncle George lived in that house for the entire summer with his male house-keeper/cook, entertaining friends and relatives whenever they visited him. In his late fifties, he was a vigorous, healthy man with an athlete's body, who used to swim in the cold pool early in the mornings while we still were asleep. He knew how to enjoy and make the most of his life. He had good taste in food, and showed his appreciation for any meal that was set before him at the table. He had a small vegetable garden in the backyard, from where Emil and I happily picked fresh squash, eggplant, carrot, string beans and tomatoes when the cook asked us for them. Uncle George was retired then, but before that he had been tailoring uniforms for the ministers of the Iranian Cabinet. I remember seeing samples of elegant double-breast dark-blue suits with golden buttons displayed in a glass case in his shop on Saadi Avenue.

He had two married daughters and a son. His elder daughter and her family lived in Tehran, while his younger daughter and her family had emigrated to the United States after WWII and lived in New York. His son, who had been studying at the Armenian Muradian School in Paris – affiliated to the prestigious Mkhitarian Catholic Institution based in Vienna, with a branch on the Island of St. Lazarus in Venice – was brought back home shortly before the invasion and occupation of France by the Nazis. Although he wasn't able to complete his education, he later became a successful businessman/contractor who worked in the oil-fields of Kuwait, with one of Paul Getty's sons.

Throughout the two weeks that we stayed there, we swam in the swimming pool, went hiking in the woods and while passing by the fields, sneaked slender cucumbers and firm red tomatoes, and ate them along the way to the Superior Springs up north.

The village of Ahmad-Abad was situated at the foot of the mountain and had many springs from which the villagers got their daily supply of drinking water, as did my uncle's household. Superior Springs was a huge natural fountain of water which was formed by hundreds of rivulets that streamed down from the snow-covered mountains, getting filtered by passing through sand and gravel. The ice-cold water that collected in a small pool was protected by a man-made wall, with an opening for people to help themselves to it. The surface of the water was so clear that you could see your face shimmering on it, and when you drank from it, you never had enough of its natural cool and light taste. The place was a hang-out for the villagers and visitors from town who came to picnic under the cool shade of the old walnut trees and to carry water away. Damavand also had some hot springs in another village, around which cabins were erected for people suffering from rheumatism, arthritis, or other diseases, who benefited from its heat and mineral qualities.

We all enjoyed every minute of our stay in that quiet village, playing cards and monopoly in the evenings, as we listened to the old and new popular songs on the phonograph, oblivious of the world outside. In Ahmad-Abad, we were cut off from the news and happenings in Tehran. There were no telephone lines in that remote village.

The day we left Damavand, I felt well-rested and relaxed, ready to face a new life and new challenges. We took an earthenware container of golden honey with us, which was famous for its high quality because of the village's apricot orchards. We didn't have a chance to eat the fruit, which ripened much earlier in the season, but we did carry along plenty of naturally-dried ones.

In Tehran, we were appalled to learn that the Shah and his second wife, Soraya, had left Iran to "seek medical help" in Europe. In our absence there had been some bloody clashes between the followers of the Shah, including the police and the army, and the opposition forces, including the followers of Prime Minister Mohammad Mosaddegh, and the Communist Tudeh Party. The next morning, we heard a mixture of screams and motors coming from the street, and went to the balcony to see what was happening. A huge procession of men was passing through Naderi Avenue, followed by buses and trucks full of people. They waved their fists and shouted in a rhythmic, harmonious, almost rehearsed tone of voice, "*Zendeh-bad* Shah – long live the King! *Mordeh-bad* Mosaddegh – death to Mosaddegh!" Frightened by the intensity of the crowd that had filled the length and width of the avenue, we went inside and closed the French window. Vartges ran down the stairs to shut and shore up our main heavy gate with the planks that we kept there for such occasions.

We were all home except mother who had gone to the market and still hadn't returned. Although the demonstration was peaceful, there was a chance that the supporters of the rival parties could emerge from the opposite direction. In that case, a bloody clash under our balcony would be almost inevitable. Fortunately, it didn't happen there, but it did happen elsewhere because we saw injured people being transported to the Russian Hospital across the street from our window. We were amazed to see, however, that the gates of the hospital, which was always open to the public, were closed and remained shut despite the angry screams and an avalanche of human fists that landed on their metallic surfaces.

After the procession had passed, we heard a loud knock on our gate. When we looked down from the balcony, we saw mother standing with the grocery bag in her hand. She told us that she had found refuge at a neighbor's house near the store and waited until the street had cleared. She said that the frightened shop-keeper, who had been standing in front of the door, hesitating to raise its shutters, had sold her whatever she needed.

Throughout the day, none of us dared leave our home. We were glued to the radio, uselessly trying to find out what was going on. Then in late afternoon, the voice of the speaker who was talking about something irrelevant was suddenly drowned in an uproar, as an exhilarated voice boomed in the speaker, "General Fazlollah Zahedi is prime minister! Long live the Shah!" Then the General himself read the Shah's decree, which confirmed his appointment to the position. On that 19th day of August, 1953, the 28th of the Iranian month of Mordad, the "people's revolt," supported by the American CIA had triumphed, Mosaddegh was arrested, and the Tudeh party defeated. When the Shah returned to Tehran, the newspapers announced in bold letters: **"The King of Kings is back on his throne again!"** In a short period of time the King of Kings who had regained the reign of the country with new, reinforced authority, strengthened his position by adding to his title, *Arya-Mehr* – the Light of Aryans. The 28th of Mordad became a national holiday which was celebrated every year in Iran until the Shah's downfall in February 1979.

*****

In October 1953, after the country had calmed down and I had received the result of my thesis and a bachelor's degree, I applied for a job at *Asle-chahar*, the American Point IV Organization--an offshoot of Harry Truman's Marshal Plan – which was spreading its network all over Iran, hiring employees by the hundreds. With my degree in English literature and knowledge of typing and shorthand, I was hired as an executive secretary/ translator with a high salary in the Engineering Department of the organization.

The year I had started college I had become a member of the Armenian Society of University Students. Its center was located in a large rented apartment within walking distance of our home. There, we had monthly educational lectures, meetings and briefings, field trips, picnics and parties on various occasions, such as New Year, Easter, and Now-Ruz. For participating at those parties thrown in the center's hall, the members paid a fee for a dinner of cold cuts and desserts then danced to the music and songs of American, French, Spanish and Italian singers, played on a stereo. Then after the party began to pick up, we held one another's hands and danced Armenian folk dances in a circle. Those parties gave the boys and girls a chance to get to know each other and choose their life partners.

In that community, the boy-girl relationship didn't venture beyond eye contact, holding hands, kissing, or tightly hugging during a tango. The tango we danced was not like today's ballroom figure-dancing seen on the TV screen, with jumps, somersaults, cartwheels, and other acrobatic movements. It was an intimate dance, sometimes cheek-to-cheek to a romantic music and the song of a popular singer, which helped stir and

My birthday party in our house (1954).

blend the emotions of the dancing couple. Our parents were strict. Out-of-wedlock sex was out of the question. There was no pressure, harassment or anger on the part of the males. A couple would wait patiently until matrimony, which sometimes lasted for years before they were ready to start a family.

Among those students, there was a smaller group of boys and girls with whom I had been friends since the start of my college years, and Seboo was one of them. Together we went to birthday parties, picnics or movies. Throughout those years, my relationship with Seboo was purely platonic. I didn't pay him any more attention than the other boys in the group. Then one day at a picnic, my feelings changed toward him. It is strange how things happen with the heart and without any prior warning.

That day at the picnic, in the outskirts of Tehran, with other girls and boys seated under the shade of a walnut tree, with a brook gurgling nearby, I saw him in quite a different light: the way he laughed, told jokes and stories about his long-distance bicycle rides, or talked and argued about a political issue. As I looked at his tall muscular body, I compared him with the other boys I knew, present or absent, in terms of sex appeal, attitude and personality, and surprisingly, found myself attracted to him. I also noticed that he wasn't indifferent toward me either. We talked about the new movies we had seen, the new books we had read, and more importantly, a common-ground subject – our jobs at Point IV. At that time he was the co-chief of the Public Health Cooperative Organization, Tehran Team, Engineering Department, with frequent travels to various Iranian towns and villages to inspect certain engineering projects, including the Malaria Control Project.

For years, malaria had been a widespread disease in Iran. So when PHCO started its work with the Ministry of Health, it launched a massive assault against the disease by spraying DDT in rural areas, especially in the humid northern Caspian towns. The organization also controlled other contagious diseases by starting a large-scale vaccination program through its mobile health units. "The Malaria Control Project was the biggest single Point IV project," says William E. Warne in his *Mission for Peace*. "Its success justified its priority. Every time the spray-men entered the village with their tanks on their backs, they sprayed every spot as they moved from alley to alley, cottage to cottage, stables and even empty lots, painting the Point IV emblem on their mud-walls. They dug wells for drinking water, drained malaria-infested swamps, built bath-houses *(hammam)*, dug toilets *(mostarah)*, finished paving roads and trained rural teachers and farmers."

After that picnic, whenever Seboo came to our office for a meeting, we would go to the cafeteria for lunch, where we would meet colleagues and other acquaintances. Among the people we saw, I recognized my high school English teacher's daughter, having lunch with a girl friend. Many years later, I found out that the girl friend's name was Farah Diba, the future third wife of the Shah: Shahbanou Farah.

*****

In the spring of 1955, Point IV offered a one-year grant to graduates of Tehran University to study education, public administration, sociology and other subjects at the American University of Beirut. I applied for sociology, as did two of my college girl friends. After passing an English language test, I applied for a student passport. Having business at a governmental office was not the highlight of anybody's life, and I was not an exception. I would rather have root canal treatment at the dentist than go in quest of a passport. At our office we were off for two days a week, Friday and Sunday, the Iranian and American weekends. So I went to the passport office one Sunday morning when the government offices were open. It was my first experience at the establishment and I felt nervous. I turned in all the required documents to the officer in the crowded office, and was told to return two weeks later. Two weeks later my passport was not ready. They requested more documents. Then after a few unsuccessful attempts, one day, complaining about the time-consuming Iranian red tape to a co-worker, he gave me his visiting card and told me to take it to a friend of his who had a responsible position in the passport office. That visiting card did the trick and I finally got my passport within a week.

I learned from that experience that you could easily get lost in Iran's complicated bureaucratic system unless you knew somebody in it. They would treat you like a speck of dust as long as you were nobody. But the moment they realized you had connections, they would help you, willing to serve or even bend the law in your favor. Of course this was with an expectation of compensation from the person who had introduced you. That meant I had to do my part which was to buy a gift for my co-worker in appreciation of his help.

The next day at lunch break, I went straight to the Education Department to ask for some details about our trip to Beirut. When I spelled out my name, the man in charge looked at the list and shook his head. My name was not there. Nor were the names of my two friends. He said that the course of sociology had been eliminated from the list because of few applicants. The bottom line was we were *not* going to Beirut, and they hadn't even bothered to notify us.

Thinking quickly, I tried to switch to the course of education or public administration. It was not important which one of those subjects I chose. They would all expand my knowledge of the English language which I needed to become a writer. Besides, I couldn't get a degree in one year in a subject in which I didn't have any background. But to my distress, the man told me that all those courses had been filled already.

I was devastated and angry. It was not fair to disillusion three young girls because of the carelessness of a bunch of administrators. They apologized later for the inconvenience with a formal letter, but that didn't restore my shattered dreams or heal my wounded feelings. After going through the trouble of passing a difficult exam and getting a passport, I had achieved nothing, except that I was standing in the same spot I had been in a few months before.

I got over the frustration gradually as some good things happened to me. My boss, who was no less angry at the situation than me, increased my salary. My relationship with Seboo became stronger, and my parents who were going on a one-year sabbatical to London with a WHO grant encouraged me to join them there and continue my education. After some thinking and calculating, I decided to go to England and get a certificate from Pitman's Secretarial College, while taking courses in creative writing. I knew that a certificate from a prestigious British business school would do wonders in Iran in terms of position and salary. So when my parents and

Armen left in late April, I stayed in Tehran with Emil – who had just been accepted at the Architecture Department of Tehran University – until November to save more money for my trip to England. After all, I wanted to use my hard-gained student passport which would expire within a year.

I went to work during the day and spent the evenings with Seboo and my friends, having dinner at the Armenian club, going to the movies or on Friday afternoons to a *thé-dansant* – a tea-dance at the ballrooms of Ritz Hotel or Mehrabad Airport. There, by paying an entrance fee, couples were served with tea and pastry, and danced to the music of a live band. One memorable event that I attended with Seboo was a sold-out Harlem Globetrotters basketball game, which took place at the Military Sports Stadium. The world famous U.S. basketball team, established in 1927, consisted of tall and agile black players who entertained and exhilarated the Iranian fans by giving a spectacular show of ball handling and humorous gestures.

One Friday morning, while cleaning the refrigerator at home, the door bell rang. When I opened the door, I was surprised to see a sophisticated young lady, wearing a wide-brimmed straw hat with artificial flowers, and a suitcase in her hand. She smiled nervously and asked in English, "Excuse me, do you know where these people are?" She pointed to our neighbor's door. "I rang their bell but nobody answered."

I knew that the Hashemis were expecting a guest from Tel Aviv, their new daughter-in-law's sister. One of their sons had married in Israel and brought his wife over to live with the family. I also knew that for the last few days, the family had been busy preparing the house, cooking and cleaning, and bragging about their guest, whom they had gone to meet at Mehrabad Airport.

When I told her about them, she laughed and said, "*I am* their guest. My name is Rachel. The plane arrived earlier than scheduled. I couldn't find them, so I took a taxi and came straight to this address." We both laughed and I invited her in to wait for the family to return and claim their guest.

Rachel stayed in Tehran for a couple of months. She was a charming girl, a little younger than me. She had completed her military service in Israel and liked to boast about it. We became friends. We went to the movies and shopping, or just sat on our balcony and talked. I liked the company of friends. I had many friends and took pleasure in keeping them. And I partly owed the secret to mother for teaching me how to maintain good ties with my friends: not to hurt their feelings, and to respect and treasure their trust and sincerity whenever extended to me.

One evening, seated in our balcony with Seboo, talking about our jobs and friends, he suddenly changed the subject and began making jokes about a relative's up-coming wedding. I laughed and asked, "When are *you* going to marry?" Suddenly, he got serious and looking into my eyes, said with a hoarse voice, "Whenever *you* are ready."

I stopped laughing and felt embarrassed. I hadn't meant to ask him a question that was so delicate and yet so important to both of us. But there was no return. I was caught in a trap. He waited for an answer that I didn't have, even wasn't prepared for an impromptu question like that. Actually, it wasn't a question but a strategic maneuver around a question I had asked him on impulse. For a moment I fell silent. All I knew was that I wasn't ready for marriage, at least not in the near future. I was only twenty-three years old and wanted to go abroad, continue my education, return to Tehran and work, and then consider such a serious commitment, and told him so.

That was his proposal; not pre-meditated nor pre-planned, much less cultivated, just a-spur-of-the-moment thought – and yet, a decisive one. He didn't propose again. He took it for granted that he had already fulfilled a difficult duty, and I had made it easier for him by innocently initiating a question. Once again, our balcony became a witness to a crucial turning point – this time in my own personal life.

In those days in the Armenian community of Tehran, a marriage proposal was not announced until it was put on a formal basis with the knowledge and approval of the parents of the two parties. It was nothing like a proposal in America these days, which becomes public knowledge as soon as the girl says, "Yes." Even the places and moments men choose for a proposal are unusual. For example, my daughter was proposed to by her boyfriend on a kayaking excursion. My daughter's friend was proposed to in Magic Mountain on a frightening roller-coaster ride: "Honey would you marry me?" Another one was proposed to in Disneyland, in the Haunted Mansion, with the sudden appearance of a ghost between them while standing in front of a mirror looking at their exaggerated images. Sometimes to make matters worse, the couple would choose an odd hour to give you their good news. For instance, at 5:00 a.m. one morning I was awakened by the ringing of the phone. Terrified that it was bad news (I always assume that when it is at the wrong time), I picked up the receiver. It was my brother, Armen, calling from Athens, Greece, where he was vacationing with his family. "I have good news for you," he chirped. "Arby has proposed to Alina, and she has accepted!" (Arby is Armen's son, and Alina Arby's girlfriend.)

Before having a relationship with Seboo, I had a boyfriend, whom I'll call my Old Flame. I used to see him on my way to ballet class. He attended an all-boys school, not far from our home. Later I met him at a girlfriend's birthday party and was formally introduced to him. We were together only for a few times at parties, picnics, and group visits to the movies before he went to England to continue his higher education. Our relationship didn't last beyond a year and a half of regular correspondence and exchange of our photos. It ended when he wrote to me that he was planning to go to Canada after the completion of his studies. I wasn't really hurt, but I was so furious about his unilateral decision on such an important matter that I didn't even bother to write back. That was the end of it. I knew from the beginning that the relationship wouldn't last long. First, we both were very young; I was eighteen and he was twenty one. Second, with a distance of thousands of miles between us, how could a romance flourish and survive for years to come? I began to believe in the old saying: "Out of sight, out of mind."

As for our correspondence, suspecting that my mother would be surprised, even angry, I had told my boyfriend that instead of sending his letters to my address, to send them through his close friend, who faithfully fulfilled his duty for as long as we wrote to each other. Then, many years later in Los Angeles, I met an acquaintance from Tehran, who told me that during the same period of time, she too had a boyfriend in Italy who was sending his letters through the same person who was receiving and giving me mine. Her story made me feel relieved and happy. After all, my mother was not the only parent who was strict with her daughter. Now when I think about those restrictions imposed on us young girls, I wonder how those mothers expected us to find a mate in life. But it seems that they knew what they were doing, because it worked and we *did* find a mate at the right time.

Chapter 11

London: 1955-56

The day I arrived at the Heathrow Airport after an almost twenty-four hour flight, with lengthy stops in Baghdad, Beirut, Frankfurt and Amsterdam, I was welcomed by my parents in a depressingly foggy and rainy London. We caught a taxi to the suburb of Wimbledon Park, near the world-famous tennis courts, where they had rented two rooms in the semi-detached, two-story house of an Armenian friend. The room on the first floor served as a dining-sitting room, where I would sleep on a hide-a-bed sofa, and the other, a bedroom on the second floor, which belonged to my parents and Armen. We didn't even have a radio, much less a TV which was a novelty in those days. But the landlady, who lived in the house and had just bought a set, sometimes invited us to her living room to watch interesting programs, such as a musical or a ballet performance, or hilarious stand-up comedians, like Peter Ustinov or Victor Borge.

To get to Pitman's College, I had to catch the District Line underground train at Wimbledon Park, change to the Piccadilly Line at Acton, and get off at Russell Square (one of the deepest underground stations in London). I remember when the elevator was filled, the conductor – always the same hefty woman – would yell, "O.K. Harry," after which the door would hiss close and the elevator would rise to the street level. I never found out who was Harry and where was he hidden. I spent the whole day in various classes of the noisy, crowded Pitman's College, and made friends with some of my classmates, most of them from other countries. We had to walk to the nearest coffee shop for lunch and wait in a long line for a sandwich and tea. (I don't know why I didn't take a sandwich from home.) Then in the late afternoon, I took the same route back to Wimbledon Park. As I walked the quiet suburban street of Vineyard Hill Road, I saw big black carriages in the front yards of some houses with babies peacefully sleeping in them. This friendly residential area became like a comfort zone to me. It gave me a sense of security and tranquillity after having spent the day in the hectic, crowded city of London.

Sometimes, when my classes ended early at Pitman's, I walked to the close-by British Museum to browse through its various sections. One late afternoon, a few days before the Christmas holidays, dusk had already fallen at 4:00 p.m. when I visited the section of Egyptian mummies. I was so busy walking around and studying them that I didn't realize I was alone with those ancient corpses. Suddenly I panicked and looked frantically for the exit, but couldn't find any signs in that huge hall. All I saw were rows and rows of mummies in coffins. Then I noticed at the end of the hall a woman with her teenage son taking notes, perhaps for his homework or a project. I was so relieved to see other living people that I waved to them and they waved back to me. At home when I told my parents about the experience, Vartges laughed and said, "Never be afraid of dead people who are unable to harm you. Better beware of the people who are alive!"

On New Year's Eve of 1955, my mother and I, our landlady and her daughter bought tickets for the Albert Hall where they were celebrating the event in the form of a fancy-dress ball. We did not participate in the ball. We were among the spectators who watched the event from the balcony. We were in our casual outfits; there was no dress code for the spectators. For the event, the whole sitting area of Albert Hall, down below – which was usually used for concerts – had been converted into a sprawling ballroom, with three different bands playing in turn. Guests of all ages in a variety of costumes were dancing

Before boarding the airplane to London, at Mehrabad Airport, with my grandparents, aunts, Uncle Johnny, and his son (November, 1955).

on the polished floor. They represented animals, such as a grizzly bear and a cuddly rabbit; a historical character, like Queen Victoria or Mary Antoinette; or a particular occupation, like an amateur physician, in white scrub, with a large "L" (for learner) appliquéd on his back. When the band played the last tune and people started to leave, we hurried to the street to catch the first early morning underground train to Wimbledon Park.

The celebration of that New Year's Eve was so different from the way we celebrated it in Tehran. In the Armenian club, women dressed in evening gowns with men in formal attire. They were served dinner at tables and danced until dawn, wearing funny paper hats. But what was even more interesting for us was what we saw on our way to the station. My mother and our landlady were appalled to see teenage boys and girls, the cuddly rabbit and the grizzly bear among them, checking into a nearby hotel in pairs. It was the first day of 1956, *not* 1965. It was long before the advent of the sexual revolution and the arrival of the hippies who would shock the older generation by breaking the British moral code of conduct by exploring a new lifestyle, based on peace and love.

*****

My parents and brother went to Manchester in mid-January for a period of two months so that Vartges would complete what was left of his research project and sabbatical. As for me, since my course of studies at Pitman's College was not complete and I still had exams to take, I stayed in London in a boarding house, sharing a room with a family friend from Tehran. The house, into which I moved on a Sunday afternoon, was located in Hammersmith, much closer to my school and much more centrally located. Other than me and the other Armenian girl, there were three other girls: the daughter of a Belgian diplomat, an Italian, and a British girl from Liverpool. They all attended a nearby prestigious private school (called "public" in England).

The owner of the boarding house, Mrs. Hayman, whose husband had been killed in WWII, had a daughter who attended the same school and befriended the girls. Music being mandatory in their curriculum, all of them played an instrument in the school's orchestra. On Sunday evenings, after having our "high tea" (tea with milk, ham-and-cheese sandwich, scones, sometimes kidney-pie or fish-cakes), we went to the study where the fire was burning in the fireplace, and listened to the girls who played pieces from Bach, Mozart, or Beethoven on the violin, cello and flute. Sometimes Mrs. Hayman's boyfriend, a family physician and a widower, joined us in listening to the chamber music. Although the girls were much younger than me, they trusted and included me in their gossip about the two old love birds.

I went out on weekends with Armenian friends, who had come to London to study medicine, engineering, nursing, or music. Together, we would see places that I hadn't visited before, such as St. Paul's Cathedral, Fleet Street, the center of newspaper and magazine publishing houses, the world-famous Madame Tussauds Wax Museum, the National Gallery, with its 13th to 19th century paintings, and the Tate Gallery with its modern and contemporary art, and a special exhibit of the Mexican artist, Diego Rivera.

Finally, after long walks in the overcast, chilly climate of London, we would stop at one of those quaint "coffee-bars" that had sprouted in the crowded areas of town, and order some sandwiches, a cup of trendy Italian espresso or cappuccino, with glistening brown sugar, and a slice of cheesecake. Being tired and cold, it would hit the spot and boost our mood

With my parents, Armen, and our Cypriot neighbor in
front of our residence in Manchester (February, 1956).

and energy. Then we would go to one of the newly-opened "music bars" on
Oxford Street, called, His Master's Voice, that carried a huge poster of its
trademark: a dog sitting next to an old-fashioned horned-phonograph (like
the one my grandparents owned back in New Julfa). There, for a couple of
hours, we would listen through headphones to the latest recorded classical
music, or the popular tunes from "Top of the Pops".

Later, we would go to a cafeteria in Marble Arch, called "A Guinea, A
Piggy" where an all-you-can-eat-feast could be had for a pound and a
shilling from its sumptuous salad bar. Also on Sundays, after attending the
service at the Armenian Church near High Street Kensington, we would
have lunch either at a Greek *taverna*, a Chinese eatery, an Indian curry
house, or an Iranian kebab-house. We enjoyed the food, admired the exotic
scenes on their trendy, newly-installed wallpaper, and relaxed under the dim
lights as we shared our recent experiences.

Those coffee shops, record stores and boutiques were full of young
people who met one another there and wasted their hard-earned cash on
things they didn't really need. It seemed that the war and the post-war era of
food and money shortages that our friends had gone through on their arrival
in England was over. Now the financial independence among the youth had
created a new world for them – youth culture – in whose pleasures and
consumerism they had started to bask.

One of our male friends in the group was my Old Flame. He was still
studying in London. One night, he invited me to see the ballet *Les Sylphides*
at Covent Garden Opera House. Having been a ballet student myself, I
enjoyed the graceful performance of Margot Fonteyn, the prima-donna of
the Royal Ballet Company. After the show, he asked me to have a cup of

cappuccino at a nearby café, which I accepted after some hesitation. I was afraid that Mrs. Hayman would reproach me for getting home late. As they say, old habits die hard. I had been brought up in a strict household that had taught me to be at home on time.

There, in the noisy café, he tried to renew our old relationship, but I laughed and told him that it was too late and I had another boyfriend back in Tehran. By confessing that to him, I suddenly realized that I had overcome my doubts about Seboo's proposal, and felt good about it. I don't think I broke my ex-boyfriend's heart, but I did make him understand that he was paying for his past tactlessness.

He didn't go to Canada after all. He returned to Tehran a few years later and married a nice girl he had met in London. That night when I got home, contrary to my expectations, I found Mrs. Hayman and everybody else asleep, my bedside lamp on, and a hot-water bottle under the blankets, with my nightgown wrapped around it.

*****

After completing my studies at Pitman's College, one rainy morning, I boarded a train at Victoria Station and travelled to Manchester. At lunch time I didn't go to the train's restaurant, the prices of which, in Mrs. Hayman's words were "outrageous," but enjoyed the ham-and-cheese sandwich and a juicy apple with a small bottle of soda that she had packed for me. When I arrived in Manchester in the late afternoon, it was overcast, but not raining. I took a taxi to my parents' address, and rang the bell of one of a series of terraced houses. After a while when I didn't get any answer, I knocked at the next door. A chubby woman with an apron around her waist opened the door and when she found out that I was her neighbor's daughter, invited me in to wait. I thanked her and asked if I could just leave my suitcase. She laughed and nodded. Then I asked for directions to the nearest movie theater and headed there. I had to kill the time in some way.

I saw a film called *River of No Return*. I believe Marilyn Monroe was the actress. It was a good movie and I later read a positive review about it. But I couldn't enjoy it much because I was tired and a little worried about not finding my parents at home. They knew I was coming that day but apparently didn't know when as I hadn't given them a definite time of arrival in my last letter. In those days, the cost of long distance telephone calls was enormous and I didn't dare place a call to Manchester from Mrs. Hayman's house. Then after two or more hours (most of the movie theaters showed double-feature films, one of them a documentary), I walked to the house and rang the bell. My mother opened the door. She was delighted to see me, but surprised that I didn't have a suitcase. But at that moment, the neighbor opened her door and gave it to me. The reason they had missed me was because they had gone grocery shopping.

The furnished house my parents had rented had two bedrooms and a living room with a dining area, a kitchen and a bathroom. The gas fireplace in the living room also heated the water-tank which contained rainwater. The fire roared all day long because of the on-going humid cold weather. I remember mother and I having a good heads of hair while living in Manchester. I think it was because we washed them with rainwater.

During the day, Vartges went to his research center at the University of Manchester and Armen walked to the elementary school in the neighborhood. Mother and I, depending on the weather, either stayed at home and cooked, wrote letters to our relatives and friends in Tehran or went out shopping. We didn't have a television set, but sometimes would go up and watch a good program at the invitation of our second-floor neighbor, a young Armenian from Cyprus, on his TV. In return, mother would invite him for lunch on Sundays. We would talk about our families, current affairs in England, the world, Iran, Cyprus, and Soviet Armenia.

While in Manchester, in addition to many newly-released British and American movies, we saw the musical *South Sea Bubbles* with Vivian Leigh and Rex Harrison; a visiting circus under a huge tent, and some variety shows at the town's hippodrome.

The six months that I spent in England (contrary to my first impressions of its bad weather) was one of the best periods of my life. Not only did I complete my studies, I was also exposed to the rich British culture. The number of classical concerts, musical shows, ballets and operas that I saw in London were more than I had experienced in my entire life. Among the musical shows, I remember *The King & I, Kismet* and special Christmas shows. In addition to the performance of Spanish flamenco dancers, I saw the opera *Carmen* at Covent Garden, the ballets *Coppelia, Giselle* and *Sleeping Beauty,* with virtuoso dancers like Dame Margot Fonteyn, Alicia Markova, Ludmilla Cherina, Nadia Nerina (whose obituary I saw in the L. A. Times in 2008). I saw plays ranging from Shakespeare's *Hamlet, Macbeth,* and *The Merchant of Venice;* Henrik Ibsen's *Hedda Gabler* and *The Wild Duck,* to a couple of "straight" plays (as the British call the plays based on people's ordinary lives), and also a "kitchen-sink drama" (a new kind of play), like John Osborne's *Look Back In Anger.*

I listened to Manouk Parikian, the premier violinist of the London Philharmonic Orchestra, the pianists Arthur Rubinstein and Clara Haskil, and the legendary conductor, Herbert Von Karajan, performing at the Royal

Festival Hall, and got their autographs on my programs. I also saw the newly-released American movies: *Love is a Many Splendored Thing*, with William Holden and Jennifer Jones, *The Picnic*, with William Holden and Kim Novak, *The Long Hot Summer*, with Paul Newman and Joanne Woodward, and many others. I saw *The Dambusters* three times; not that I was crazy about it, but because my kid brother, Armen, had fallen in love with it. It was an early representation of Britain during WWII, with heroism glorified. I also enjoyed fashion, flower and home-design shows among other things. Because of its year-round, affordable programs, London had become the most vital and active city for classical music as well as avant-garde art and theater. It was full of tourists who constantly visited it from the European countries, the Middle East, the Far East, and the United States.

On our way back to Tehran, we stopped in Paris for one week, took city tours, visited its landmarks during the day and went to grandly-staged operas and night-club shows in the evenings. At the end of the week, we all yearned for our home back in Tehran.

Later when I thought about my frustration about the AUB fiasco, I realized that my trip to England, if not more educational and enlightening, was surely not lesser than going to Beirut. I remembered a Persian proverb that says: "If God wisely closes one door, He blissfully opens another."

Chapter 12

Back Home to Tehran

Our flight from Paris to Tehran made a short stop in Beirut. In the airplane my parents and brother were sitting in one row while I was in front of them, sitting next to a white-haired man with a white goatee. The old man who had overheard the conversation with my parents, turned to me and said in Western Armenian, "I can see that you are talking Armenian. Where are you from and where are you going to?"

I told him about my parents' year-long trip to England, the visit to Paris and our return to Tehran, our home town. Then it was my turn to ask him the same questions. He said, "They call me Malkhas. I'm a writer. I live in Boston and I'm going to Beirut as I've been invited by the Lebanese-Armenian community to give a series of lectures about my books. Later, I'm going to Tehran for a similar series of lectures." At the mention of his famous name, my mouth fell open. I couldn't believe my eyes and ears. It seemed like a dream come true, sitting next to Malkhas (his pen name), a favorite and revered writer of my generation, whose five volumes of historical novel, *Zartonk, (The Awakening),* and its two follow-up volumes I had read in my high school years.

When I introduced him to my parents, they started an animated conversation with him, about his books and Boston's Armenian community. He said that in addition to his lectures in Beirut, he wanted to oversee the second printing of his novel which had first been published in Boston in 1933. Then he talked about his family, blaming himself for his frequent absences from home and for leaving his wife alone, who during one of his trips had fallen ill and died, causing him deep sorrow. The conversation throughout the flight was so fascinating that when we arrived at the Beirut Airport, we were surprised at how quickly the time had passed.

When he left with the promise of calling us in Tehran, I began to think about his novel, *Zartonk,* trying to recall its plot and characters. The story was about the Armenian national revolutionary movement that had originated in 1850-60 in Czarist Russian-dominated Eastern Armenia. The goal of the revolutionaries was to protect and secure the rights and safety of those oppressed Armenian people who lived in Ottoman-dominated Western Armenia subject to unbearable taxation, confiscation of land and property, with endless atrocities inflicted on them, just because they were non-Moslem "infidels." The story was set in the Caucasus, Eastern Turkey and Persia. The characters consisted of courageous young men who either successfully carried out the dangerous assignments entrusted to them, or heroically fell in the line of duty, ignoring death and danger with courage, even contempt. *Zartonk* is a captivating historical novel that has fired the imagination of young generations of the Armenian Diaspora, past and present.

When Malkhas came to Tehran, he stayed with the family of an old friend. Mother invited them to dinner a few times. He gave several public lectures, autographed his books, and after a month of staying and attending dinner parties thrown in his honor, left Tehran for the United States. Like some characters of his books, he was an interesting character who told us funny stories about his literary and personal life, always blaming himself for not having been an attentive husband.

After my return from England, Seboo and I got engaged to be married in January of the next year. It was a simple engagement. One evening, he visited us with his father and stepmother, bringing us a basket of red roses, a bottle of brandy, and a box of chocolates, as was the custom. He fitted a gold Swiss watch around my wrist, and mother served us dinner.

A few days later, he introduced me to the American consulting engineering firm of Litchfield, Whiting, Panero, Severoud and Associates, where he was working as a civil engineer. I was immediately hired with an excellent salary as an executive secretary at the accounting department. I was amazed at the difference between the salaries I had been receiving at Point IV and the one they were offering me at Litchfield. It seemed that the saying: "A degree from England or the United States does wonders in this country," held true for me. In reality, nothing much had been added to my knowledge of office work. I already knew most of the subjects they had taught me at Pitman's College, but maybe they had polished and cultivated them in the process. Whatever the truth, I was happy with the outcome.

When I was in England, Seboo had resigned from Point IV and was hired at almost double his previous salary by Morrison & Knudson Company, an engineering firm that was building a dam and a water-reservoir across the Karaj River to supply the city of Tehran with sufficient water. To work there, he also had to live in its dormitories to be able to get up at dawn to start his work. He resigned after a few months, and found employment at Litchfield, Whiting Co. When I started work, every morning on his way to the office, he picked me up and drove me in his used Plymouth he had bought in my absence. The secretary to the chief officer, with whom I soon became friends, was an Iranian lady by the name of Amanpour, whose husband was an anesthetist who, much to our distress, was later executed in the early days

Seboo and I at our wedding, with members of our two families (1957).

of the Islamic Revolution. Now when I watch Christianne Amanpour on CNN, I wonder if she is related to her.

Our office was located in the northern part of Tehran. It was a rented, two-story, multiple-roomed residential property. The management consisted of American engineers, architects and administrators, mostly from New York where the main office was located. The rest of the staff was Iranian, with a few European women who were married to Iranians. They worked as engineers, architects, draftsmen, or in the personnel and accounting departments. In summer the employees worked from 7:00 a.m. to 2:00 p.m., after which some of them had lunch at the cafeteria then used the office swimming pool where they swam, talked about work and relaxed. I usually stayed and tried to improve my swimming skills. But Seboo did not, because he had to work in his own office in a fledgling corporation named Zohal that he had established with three other partners. They were trying to get construction contracts from the private sector, other companies and government offices.

The next winter, shortly before our wedding, we were able to find a two-bedroom apartment within walking distance of the office, where we sometimes went after work and tried to furnish, one room at a time. To pay for my trousseau and pricey custom-made bedroom furniture (a cream-colored double-bed, a three-door wardrobe, a mirrored dressing table and its chair), for which the bride was traditionally responsible, I used a portion of the proceeds that I had received from the sale of my father's factory a couple of months earlier. The factory that had supported two families throughout its twenty years of existence wasn't needed any more. Uncle Johnny, who had been looking for a change of pace, finally opened a paint shop and went into his favorite movie business, making documentary films on the side.

For our wedding, our parents decided to throw a small dinner party in the house of Seboo's parents, choosing Friday, January 25, 1957 for the event. Two weeks before the designated date, something unexpected happened that frustrated all of us. The landlady of the house, who lived on the second floor of the duplex, became seriously ill and the doctors said she had only a few days to live. The problem was that if she died before January 25th, it would be impossible for us to have a reception in the house or anywhere else because of the respect we had for the old lady. My mother-in-law who was a religious woman decided to pray for her. For two weeks, every single night, she knelt by her bed and prayed to God to spare the old lady's life until after the wedding day. Believe it or not, her prayers worked, the woman pulled through and lived on for many years.

Since we hadn't had a religious engagement ceremony before, my parents decided to throw a cocktail party at the spacious home of a friend prior to the wedding ceremony. The guests consisted of the members of our two families, our friends, co-workers, and our parents' friends.

In the stylishly decorated living room of my mother's friend, dressed up in the latest fashion of the day, the guests watched as the priest blessed us, touching our heads with a cross. He also blessed the fluffy lace wedding gown and the veil, which the bridegroom's family had brought in a box. The hand-made box that was covered with white silk fabric and delicately decorated with flowers of the same material was designed and prepared by Seboo's father. After the ceremony, the box was raised over his head by a young man, as others joined him in a circle and danced an Armenian folk dance, played on an accordion. In another room, with the help of a few female friends, I changed from my crimson chiffon engagement dress into the wedding gown and the veil, and returned to the living room. I was cheered and led to the middle of the dance circle where I started dancing myself. Later, the guests were treated to drinks, sandwiches and the engagement cake, and were given wedding favors at the end.

When leaving the house, grandpa sang the traditional, moving song of "They're taking away our daughter…," after which, we were driven to the Armenian Church, where Seboo and I got married and received congratulations from the guests, who passed us by in a single file.

From the church, the guests went to Seboo's parents' home and waited for my parents' arrival. There was a tradition that the parents of the bride shouldn't go to the wedding party by themselves. They should be taken there by a relative of the bridegroom. In the meantime, the guests were not supposed to sit, but had to wait on their feet to welcome the bride's parents. But my parents didn't arrive and the guests, many of them elderly people, had to remain standing for more than an hour. Finally, they came with Seboo's eldest uncle, and apologized for the delay. They had a flat tire and had to get it fixed.

After dinner, some of our friends created a happy atmosphere by singing and dancing the Armenian folk dance *Hoy Nazan,* encouraging the guests to join in by holding hands and dancing in a circle: two steps to the right, one step back, two steps to the right, one step back. Later, we continued dancing to the music of a stereo until a little past the midnight, after which Seboo and I, accompanied by our close friends, were driven to the Darband Hotel in the foothills of the Alborz Mountains. I still don't know why we had chosen that cold spot in the middle of winter for our honeymoon.

Something happened late that night in the hotel that snapped me out of my girlish dreams and put me right in the middle of reality. I met a college classmate with her husband and friends in the lobby. When she showed surprise to see me with a man, I quickly introduced Seboo, "This is my husband. We are here on our honeymoon." The moment I uttered the word "husband" it echoed three fold in my brain and my ear lobes began to burn. The woman just smiled and wished me happiness. However, the word "husband" tortured me for a while until I got used to it in the course of time.

Although it had snowed in Darband, we felt hot, nervous and hungry (we hadn't been able to eat properly at the party). When we called the room service at 2:00 a.m. and asked for some snacks, someone yelled from the other end of the line, "Do you realize what time it is?" So we went to bed hungry.

We had planned to stay in that hotel for a week, to enjoy each other's company, to relax and make plans for our future. But no such luck. On the first morning after breakfast, when I pulled the curtains aside and looked through the large window which opened to a magnificent snow-covered landscape, I suddenly noticed Seboo's stepbrother, Shahen, the son of his stepmother, getting out of his Volkswagen Beatle down below and heading toward the hotel entrance. For a second I panicked. What was wrong? Was he the bearer of bad news? Had something bad happened to one of our family members? If not, what was he doing there on the first day of our honeymoon? It turned out that he was the bearer of some cash for us.

Apparently, before the wedding, Seboo had given him his wallet to hold until after the wedding, but both had forgotten about it. We were so grateful to him for taking the trouble of driving the icy road between Tehran and Darband and bringing us the money, because Seboo didn't have any cash with him.

We were preparing to go to a nearby village the next morning when someone from the Ararat Cultural Society came with a problem. Since Seboo was a member of its board of directors, he had to leave me in the room and take care of the problem in the lobby. Then the next night we had to drive to the church in town to be present at a close friend's wedding ceremony. So after three days of "honeymooning" we decided to go back to our newly furnished apartment, a place that we would call *home* for the first five years of our married lives.

We liked our home and the neighborhood, especially the nearby convenience store which was owned by an old Zoroastrian. It was a mini-department store with merchandise ranging from aspirin to potatoes and onions, bicycle and china sets as well as clothing. What was more, it had a public telephone from where we could make our calls for as little as two *rials*. We had applied for a telephone line for our house and would be on the waiting list for two years at least.

Once organized, we told our friends and relatives that we had a *jour fixe*, open house, on every Wednesday evening. Since we were the first couple to marry in our group, every single boy and girl was thrilled to come to our new apartment, to admire it, to tell jokes, to look at our fledgling family, and to learn in the process how and when to start their own. The warm, friendly atmosphere of our home encouraged some of the boys to expedite their marriage proposals to the girls they loved. During those long evenings, we served them tea, pastries, sandwiches and fruit. We talked, laughed and listened to music, sometimes dancing till late, only to wake up at 6:00 a.m. to rush to work.

*****

One evening in late May after work, four months after our marriage, we showered and dressed to go to my elder uncle's house to a dinner party they had thrown in honor of my in-laws and our extended family. On our way we had to pick up my father-in-law and his wife. As we arrived, we noticed the wife standing by their front door waving to us. She was not dressed and there was an expression of anxiety on her face; we knew something was terribly wrong. When we hurried toward her, she said that her husband had had a stroke and she had called their family physician. While she was talking frantically to us, a taxi pulled up and the doctor climbed out. He examined my father-in-law and sent Seboo to get some leeches from a pharmacy, which he did with incredible speed. When he returned with the leeches in a box, the doctor applied them to the patient's neck and temples, one at a time. The small suckers bit at a vein, making y-shaped incisions with their sharp teeth, sucking out the patient's blood, and bulging like a miniature balloons. I had seen them applied to my grandma, who suffered from high blood pressure and felt much better afterwards.

During the procedure, the patient doesn't feel any pain, because the leech's saliva anesthetizes the area, dilates the blood vessel, and most importantly, prevents the blood from clotting. However, in case of my father-in-law the treatment didn't work, and he died shortly after. This might sound like a primitive way of treating hypertension, but for centuries leeches have been used for medical purposes in Iran and elsewhere in the world. Even here in America, medicinal leeches are used in hospitals. As a volunteer in the purchasing department of a hospital many years later, Seboo regularly put in purchase orders to a leech vendor.

*****

The death of my fifty-four-year-old father-in-law was ironic. He died much earlier than his landlady, for whom his wife had prayed every night until the day of our wedding. I had known Mr. Mushegh only for a year or so. In 1950, he had lost his forty-two-year-old wife to congestive heart failure. Two years later, he had married a widow who had two grown-up sons, Bobby, the same age as Seboo, and Shahen, (the one who had brought us Seboo's wallet on our honeymoon). After marriage, Mushegh had moved into his wife's large first-story duplex with his own sons, Seboo and Rubik.

In his youth, Mushegh had taught math at the Armenian school in Tabriz, and had served as the principal of another school in the Caspian port city of Pahlavi. After the closure of Armenian schools in 1936, he had worked as an accountant in several construction companies in Tehran. He was a social activist and in his spare time liked to organize plays with other theater-lovers. He staged them at the Ararat Cultural Center, with the income from ticket sales going to Armenian charities. He was a jovial person who liked to tell anecdotes and funny stories about his experiences on the stage. I hadn't seen any of his productions, but those who had seen his plays said that he was an excellent actor and director. He was even compared to well-known foreign actors and directors.

On one of my trips to London, my old high-school friend, Vivian and I had gone to see the comedy of *Charlie's Aunt*. When it ended and we were walking towards the underground station, she said to me, "You know Elma, your father-in-law in the role of Charlie's Aunt, wearing a woman's wig, a fur jacket and good make-up, acted so much better than that famous actor, Tom Courtney. I can't imagine how a small Armenian community in Tehran could accomplish such a difficult task with a few theater-lovers and minimum of funds."

I haven't had the chance to see my father-in-law on stage, but we have a picture of him in our living room which I see every day. The picture has been professionally shot by a photographer on one film and in a unique technique that shows the actor, cast in eight different roles, surrounding his regular picture in the middle. It is a masterpiece of photography, done in Tabriz, in the year 1930.

*****

In the winter of 1958 my boss, a disciplined German-American, developed a pinched nerve in his vertebra and was in great pain. In the beginning, he would come to the office later in the day, and after going over the mail and giving us necessary instructions, would leave early to rest at home. He had his own private office, whereas the three accountants and I worked in a large room at our desks. While working, we talked, drank tea, or made phone calls. But all those stopped when he appeared on the threshold. He was a strict boss and didn't want to see us idle for a second. He said to us, "Even if you don't have work to do, *pretend* that you are busy." However, there was an instantaneous change in his personality when his blond wife came to the office. He stood up like a soldier and sweetly asked her about her day, then spent hours talking to her.

There came a day when his pain intensified and he was ordered by his physician to take a one-month leave of absence and lie flat on his back. That morning before leaving, he put me in charge of office administration, with our Dutch-American accountant in charge of the accounts. The other two, a father and daughter, were Turkish-speaking Iranians, originally from Baku in Soviet Azerbaijan.

In addition to my new office commitment, I had to report to my boss personally on a daily basis by taking the mail to his residence in Gholhak in the suburb of Shemran. So every afternoon, the company driver would drive me in the office van on the congested Old Shemran Road, up the hill, past many old mansions and the Tehran radio station. The five-kilometer ride would usually take us about an hour to accomplish.

Although Seboo and I had been at my boss' house for a couple of parties, I was nervous on my first business visit, not knowing what to expect. When we arrived there, the driver, who was familiar with the place, pushed the gate open and we were suddenly welcomed by a pack of bulldogs. I was terrified, but the driver held them back and told me to ring the bell. The door to the house was ajar, so I pushed it open, entered quickly, and closed it behind me. There was nobody in the hallway. I called their last name, but got no answer. At that moment the driver came in and led me into the bedroom. My boss was lying on his back all alone in the house. He told me that his wife had gone to town to play bridge with some of her American friends. Their maid had gone grocery shopping and had left the door unlocked for us to enter. I gave him the mail and sat on a chair.

As I was waiting for him to go over the letters, I saw with dread the door being pushed open, and the four bulldogs coming straight toward me. My heart skipped a beat and my mouth dried up. "Don't mind them," my boss said without taking his eyes off the papers. "They're harmless." But how could I not mind them? They had already approached and surrounded me, placing their muddy paws and large square jaws on my knees and skirt and were staring and growling in my face. I was terrified and told him so. "You see," he said with affection, "they *do* like you, but if you don't like them, just ignore them." Then he called the driver to lead them out. Maybe he was right and they did like me, but it was not my fault that I didn't like dogs. I had been attacked by dogs twice, without even having noticed or shown any fear of them – which is usually the reason for dog attacks.

After the dogs had gone, I relaxed, pulled out my notebook, and began to take shorthand dictation, which I would later transcribe and type in multiple copies and bring back the next day to be checked, signed and sent off. It was such a slow process compared to office efficiency today. God bless the inventor of the computer, the internet and the e-mail system of correspondence today. For the rest of the month, the pattern repeated itself with the exception that on some days I saw his wife in the hallway and exchanged a few words with her. What was more, they had learned to keep the dogs outdoors, away from me.

*****

I worked in that office for two years. Then one day my Dutch-American co-worker, Louisa, who was married to an Iranian, told me about another high-paying job at the prestigious Seven-Year-Plan Organization. She told me that two young Harvard-educated Iranian men who lived in the apartment above theirs were looking for an experienced secretary for their newly-established Economics Department, and suggested that I apply for the position. She arranged an interview during our lunch break.

When I got to the apartment, the two young men were having their lunch and invited me to join them, but having just had my snack, I thanked them and waited. The interview was short. They were impressed by my resume, experience and especially the secretarial diploma from England, and hired me on the spot with a much higher salary.

After discussing it with Seboo and going through the formalities and resigning from my position at Litchfield-Whiting Co., I was about to start the new job when I found out that I was pregnant. In those days home-pregnancy-test kits were not available. So my urine was tested at Tehran University's Medical School laboratory, where my father, Vartges was its head. It was an interesting procedure. They injected a toad with the pregnant woman's urine. If the toad's breasts swelled, it meant that the woman was pregnant. My toad's breasts did swell, making me both happy and frustrated: happy that I was going to be a mother and frustrated because I was about to start an exciting job.

I did start the job at a newly furnished office in the multi-storey building of the Plan Organization. I was the executive secretary to Dr. Khodadad Farman-Farmaian, the CEO of the Economy Department. Every morning, I took a taxi to the office through congested traffic to Jaleh Square at the far east-side of town. The smell of the polished wood in my office nauseated me. I worked alone in a large room and missed the happy atmosphere of my previous office, but in the long run it was worth the change. In addition to my salary from Plan Organization, I also got on the payroll of the affiliated Ford Foundation next door, for which I started working concurrently.

Every morning for eight months I took the elevator up to the office. The conductor who saw me every day, once asked one of our employees, "Tell me, Miss, this Hovanessian, is she a miss or a missus?" He was not a dumb person. He judged from what he had seen. I hadn't gained much weight, it was winter and I was wearing a loose overcoat that concealed my belly.

One month before giving birth, when I told my boss that I was going to resign, he looked at my belly and asked, "Because of this?" I blushed and nodded. "You're doing the right thing," he said. "A baby needs its mother. We'll surely miss you here. But you are welcome back any time you are ready to work." He was a family-friendly person. He had twin girls himself.

I never returned to that office, nor did I see him again. He later became the president of the Plan Organization and an influential person during the reign of the Shah. He was lucky to have fled Iran after the revolution of 1979 and to have settled in England. I didn't have any contact with him until in 2004, a year after the publication of my novel, set in Iran, when he called and congratulated me. He said that he had read the book and had especially liked its first chapter that was set in a Tehran coffeehouse and the intimate conversation of its working-class customers. He said that many incidents had happened throughout his life and if he were a writer, he would write a book about them.

*****

Throughout my pregnancy, I was scared, anxious and nervous, dreading the day of the delivery, because in those days there were no Lamaze classes and no epidural injections to prepare the pregnant woman for the experience and to alleviate her excruciating childbirth pains, during which the baby or the mother sometimes died. That was the reason parents usually didn't decorate a room before the baby's safe arrival. Then one day, walking on the crowded Naderi Avenue, looking for a book store, it suddenly dawned on me that all those people walking in the street, and consequently, all the inhabitants of the globe had been born from a mother. I was ashamed of myself for being such a coward. Then finding the bookstore, I bought a copy of the newly arrived paperback, *Baby & Child Care*, by Dr. Benjamin Spock. It was the book that would help me raise my two children up to their teenage years.

Our son, Aram, was born on March 26, 1959, two weeks ahead of the due date, and five days after the Iranian New Year, Now-Ruz.

I'm glad I resigned from my position and took care of my newborn baby. Although I loved my job, I loved my son even more and wanted to raise him myself. As for my mother, she couldn't help me on a daily basis as she was quite involved in social and community activities. Besides, Vartges was accepted at the Harvard School of Public Health, and four months later, in July 1959, they were going to leave Iran for the United States. On the other hand, about the same time, Seboo resigned from Litchfield-Whiting Co. and started working full time in his own company which had been successful in securing a contract with a Belgian firm to construct a sugar factory in southern Iran. With Seboo spending most of the time away from home, I became a full-time, stay-at-home mom, and loved every stage of it.

Chapter 13

My "Illness"

A few days after Aram's first birthday, I started feeling sick. When it dragged on for a week, I visited our family physician, who after running a few lab tests, diagnosed rheumatic fever and prescribed some pills, along with three weeks of bed-rest. He explained that rheumatic fever is an acute disease that occurs in children and young adults (I was neither). It is characterized by fever, inflammation and pain in the joints (which I didn't have), and if not treated on time, would affect the heart valves.

Since my mother was not there to help, we decided to ask Seboo's younger aunt to move in with us and give us a hand in taking care of the baby, while our maid would do the chores. We asked her, she accepted, and everything went on schedule for a week. I stayed in bed, got fed, took the medicines, and the baby got used to the new situation. There was one problem, however. The aunt didn't live in Tehran. Her family lived in Ghazvin, and having children of her own, she got homesick and suggested that she take the baby along to live with her family for as long as my treatment would take. Since we didn't have any other choice, we agreed reluctantly. I had been to Ghazvin before. A one-time capital of Iran, ninety miles west of Tehran, Ghazvin had a few historical buildings and extensive vineyards.

One morning, Seboo packed everything, including the baby's crib in a rented truck, and drove the two of them to Ghazvin for a tentative period of three weeks. Before leaving, I pressed the baby to my chest and kissed him several times before letting him go. I stayed calm until the maid closed the door then I gave way to a torrent of tears. As I calmed down, I began to console myself by thinking about the grieving mothers whose children had been separated from them by force – during the atrocities of war and genocides – and I thanked God that I was not one of them.

Before going back to bed, I decided to take a shower. Warm water had always relaxed my irritated nerves and lifted my sunken spirit. In the bathroom I slid under the shower, turned the faucet to its fullest force, and let the hot water run down my hair, face and body, washing away the pain and frustration of the moment. However, I wasn't able to fully relax until Seboo returned late that night and reassured me that the baby was happy and in good hands.

Those three weeks felt like three years. Although my friends and relatives visited me frequently and tried to keep my spirit up by bringing flowers, books and magazines, and telling anecdotes and funny stories, I still felt restless and empty inside. Among those visitors, there were also some tactless ones who depressed me by telling inappropriate stories. Once an elderly relative told me about a woman who had rheumatic fever just like me and had died within a year.

After the treatment and a visit to our physician and some lab tests, he said to my relief that I was cured and could go on with my regular life. Then one Friday morning in late April, Seboo drove to Ghazvin again and brought back my baby boy. He was lucky to see him in Ghazvin where he drove every Friday. But I hadn't even had a chance to hear the baby's voice or cry on the telephone. The aunt didn't have a line.

When Aram came home and saw me, he screamed in delight and threw himself into my arms. I hugged, kissed and pressed him hard to my chest, as if I was trying to catch up with lost time. From that day on, he stuck to me, and for many years to come, shuddered when he saw a suitcase.

During my convalescence, my grandmother suffered a stroke, leaving her paralyzed and unable to speak. In those days (1960) there was no cure for the disease, with no physical or speech therapy for the afflicted person – at least not in Iran. The patient suffered in bed for months or years until the day she or he died. Grandma, Mariam, who was 68-years-old and already had a great-grandson, died in late May. I was frustrated for not being able to participate at the funeral of the woman who had done so much for me and whom I loved dearly. Even my mother was not able to come from half a world away to be present at her mother's interment.

In her last letter, mother had informed me that after Vartges' graduation at the end of June, they would board a ship from New York bound for Portsmouth, England then would take a train to London. Since Vartges was still on his sabbatical, they had decided to spend the rest of the summer in England. She had suggested that Aram and I join them in London, where I would have a chance to visit a cardiologist to see if the rheumatic fever had done my heart any damage.

Seboo and I discussed the matter and decided that Aram and I would go to England and he would join us in August. My student passport had expired and I wasn't a student anymore. So we applied for a new one through an agent who got the document in a couple of weeks, and I got a visa at the British embassy. We flew to London by Quantas, with stops in Bagdad and Beirut, during which I lost the baby's milk bottle, got air sick and threw up as the stewardess kindly watched the baby. At Heathrow

Airport, my family was delighted to greet us, especially Aram whom they hadn't seen for a year. We took a taxi to a family-run bed-and-breakfast in Earl's Court, where Aram and I shared a large room with them. The next day, the first thing I did was to make an appointment with a famous cardiologist, recommended by our family physician in Tehran.

A few days later, Vartges and I visited the cardiologist's office in upscale Harley Street. After asking detailed questions and examining me thoroughly, the specialist shook his head and said, "I have good news and bad news for you. The good news is your heart is in wonderful condition. The bad news is I don't see any trace of rheumatic fever, for which you have taken so many unnecessary medicines and gained weight during bed-rest." In the end, he ordered regular exercise and diet, and wished me a good life.

When we left the office, I was both delighted and frustrated, delighted because I was a healthy woman, frustrated because not only had I suffered emotionally, but had also involved Seboo and Aram in it. Who was responsible for all the inconvenience, if not our family physician? In Iran there was no such thing as filing a lawsuit against misdiagnosis by a physician. It didn't exist then, and doesn't exist now. Even if there was, we were not going to take action against our old physician. So I tried to make peace with myself, forget the past, and make the most of my time in London, which I did for a while. Since mother took care of my son, I went out with a couple of friends who lived in London, and saw the recent American movies, among them *The Nun's Story*, with Audrey Hepburn and Peter Finch; *The Apartment*, with Jack Lemmon and Shirley McLain, and *Saturday Night and Sunday Morning*, based on Alan Sillitoe's 1958 novel that I had read back in Tehran.

In mid-August, Seboo joined us in London. Before leaving Tehran, he had gone for a check up and our family physician had noticed a shadow under his heart on his chest x-ray. Knowing that Seboo was going to England, he had suggested that he visit the same cardiologist who had seen me. The cardiologist studied the x-ray. He was concerned about this being something as serious as cancer, a collapsed lung or possibly a benign cyst. He recommended surgery.

The surgery took place a few days later in a hospital in East London by an expert cardiothoracic surgeon, whom the nurses addressed by the title of "Sir" instead of "Doctor." The result was unexciting. There was a hernia, an inborn rupture in his diaphragm, which the surgeon sewed together. The incision extended from the middle of his chest to the middle of his back. After the operation, the surgeon drove me to Knightsbridge in his convertible sports car, giving me information on Seboo's condition. He recommended that I go shopping at Harrod's department store to amuse myself.

I didn't do any shopping that day. I wasn't in the mood. I took the underground train and went straight to the hotel to be with my mother and son. I visited Seboo daily, taking an-hour's train ride back and forth to the hospital, staying with him for a few hours. He remained in the hospital for ten days.

Before Seboo's arrival in London, Vartges and Emil, who had joined us for a couple of weeks, had gone to Germany to buy a car which they planned to drive to Tehran. Mother and Armen stayed with us to fly home together.

The day we were returning to Tehran, a physician friend of Seboo's saw us at the airport, and without knowing about his surgery, slapped him on the back in a friendly gesture, making him cringe with the impact. The man was so embarrassed that he didn't dare speak to us on the plane all the way to Tehran.

The trip to London in 1960 was not as exciting as it was in 1956. Other than a few movies that I saw during the first few weeks, for the rest of the summer I was busy taking care of the baby or being with my sick husband. Before the doctor's decision to do the surgery, we had planned to fly to Edinburgh in Scotland to attend a few concerts at its world-famous annual music festival. But that was not meant to happen at that time or any other time.

Chapter 14

Our New Home and New Baby

In the early spring of 1961, we started construction of a house on a piece of land we had bought a couple of years earlier. It was located in the northern part of Tehran, not far from our rented apartment. When we moved into our new home in the fall of that year, the building was not fully finished, but once we settled in, the workers picked up their pace and soon the construction phase was completed.

The building was three and a half stories high. We lived in the two storey house, which had three bedrooms, a family room, and two bathrooms on the second floor. A balcony in front of the rooms overlooked the back yard that had a lawn, a few rose bushes and an apple tree. On the first floor, there was a modern, state-of-the-art kitchen with cabinets and counters, a breakfast nook, an L-shaped dining and living room, a music room where we had set up a stereo with assortments of LPs from classical to light music, and where Seboo sometimes practiced his violin. The architect had used the latest in acoustic ceiling tiles, folding doors and vinyl tiles, all novelties in those days in Iran. On the third floor, there was a two-bedroom apartment, which we rented to a middle-aged California couple. On the fourth floor there was also a two-roomed half apartment with a toilet and shower and a large terrace, which we had given to Seboo's cousin and his wife to live. What was more, the building had central heating that functioned with gasoline, which a tanker delivered to the house and filled the basement tank. It was a convenient change in our lives. We both had come a long way from our childhood days when we had a coal heater in our homes. Then, when we got married, we bought a kerosene heater with a sophisticated design, which blended with our modern furniture.

After we settled into the house, I learned how to drive and got my license in a couple of months. In February of the following year, we threw two large house-warming parties: one for our immediate families, and one for our friends and Seboo's colleagues.

After grandma's death, my grandpa lived alone, but every Wednesday he came over and stayed with us for lunch and dinner. The rest of the week he spent his days at his other children's homes. He didn't go anywhere else. Once on mother's insistence, he had gone to the Armenian club where one of his acquaintances had upset him by exclaiming, "Haig, are you still alive!" He was seventy two years old. In our house, he felt happy, played with Aram, told him stories, or repaired broken appliance. One of the items that went out of order and he fixed was my grandma's manual sewing machine which he had given me when he was sorting out her belongings. Another item he had given me was a large handicraft brass tray, which is an antique now, and one of few items I brought to America.

*****

On September 1, 1962, we had just gone to bed when a strong earthquake shook our building. I remember the date because we had returned from the birthday and christening party of a close friend's daughter, for whom Seboo had stood as godfather. The details are blurred, but I remember Seboo rushing to Aram's room, scooping him up, running down the stairs into the dark street, climbing in our car, and driving us to an open space, where we waited for a while, then drove back home. Later we found out that the earthquake, although quite strong, hadn't caused any casualties or major damage to the buildings.

Then one week after the incident, the American radio station in Tehran announced that another earthquake was anticipated that night. People panicked and made telephone calls to relatives and friends, informing them about the announcement and the dangers of staying at home. When my mother called and warned me about the earthquake, I laughed and said that I didn't believe it. I dreaded earthquakes, but I also knew that an earthquake couldn't be predicted. But my parents and friends kept calling and begging us to leave the house. I didn't want to hear of it. I had a rough day, I was tired, and I wanted to sleep. I finally gave in to Seboo's insistence and decided to leave the house. I looked in my wardrobe for something appropriate to wear, but having done a large load of laundry that day, with most of the clothes still hung out to dry, I found the wardrobe almost empty, and told Seboo that I didn't have anything to wear. He looked at me with amazement and said, "I didn't know women had a special outfit for earthquakes!" Later he exaggerated and turned that simple statement into an anecdote and told it to our friends, who teased me for a long time to come. When I finally found something to wear, we got into our car and drove toward the nearby Chehel-Metry Boulevard. I had never seen the streets of Tehran so jam-packed with so many automobiles in gridlock. The traffic at that time of night was incredible. In the words of Henry Kissinger who would comment about the Tehran traffic later: "It is not traffic. It is a moving parking lot."

What we saw in the streets of Tehran that night was worth filming. Some people had gathered on the boulevard's middle isle, spread a blanket, placed a samovar and food, and were eating and drinking while waiting for the earthquake to happen. Some women were in their transparent negligees as if they had just emerged from their beds.

After a futile attempt to move, Seboo decided to return home. Up to that point no earthquake had occurred. We turned on the American radio station. There was no sound. Then a few minutes later, someone cleared his throat, and with a husky voice began to apologize for the mistake they had made by misinforming the people of Tehran, terrifying and causing them inconvenience. Seboo and I looked at each other with disbelief. How could the authorities of the American broadcasting radio station make such an error, turning the lives of a city's population upside down, causing numerous accidents and casualties? Once again, it was proven to me that earthquakes couldn't be predicted.

*****

In early April 1963, I found out that I was pregnant again. I had a difficult pregnancy for the first three months, with morning and evening sickness, usually caused by the smell of certain foods, chemical products, or even by the sound of certain tunes.

In the summer, Seboo flew to Germany to buy a car and drive it back home. I was alone in that big house, with a four-year-old boy, and the fear of political unrest that had taken over Tehran in his absence. I had witnessed many clashes between the students and the police during my college years, but this one was quite a different story. It was the result of a simmering hostility that had existed throughout Iran's history between the secular government and the clergy, which was provoked from time to time, giving way to conflicts between the two forces. As a result, troops were mobilized, tanks rolled through the streets, bloody incidents took place, a few clergymen were arrested and imprisoned, shops closed, food became scarce, and a temporary curfew was declared in Tehran. However, I was lucky to have my parents beside me throughout those scary days.

In late summer of that year, my brother, Emil, having graduated from the Architecture Department of Tehran University, and having been accepted at the *Ecole de Beaux Arts* in Paris, flew to France in search of a higher degree. During his three-year stay in Paris, he also worked in the studio of the legendary architect, Corbusier. In one of his letters, he expressed his surprise about an Ethiopian student who could speak Armenian. "Can you believe that a black African speaks our language?" He had met the boy at the *Cite Universite*, where they both lived. Apparently there was an Armenian community in Addis Ababa, among whom that Ethiopian had lived and learned the language.

One morning when my maid came to work, she was shocked and distraught by the news she had heard on the bus radio. John F. Kennedy, the President of the United States had been assassinated. It was the 22nd of November. Once again people's moods went sour in Tehran. Kennedy was highly regarded in Iran.

Later that morning, our door bell rang and when I opened it, I was surprised to see Mrs. Peterson, our Californian tenant standing in front of me. As I invited her in, she burst into tears and between sobs talked about Kennedy's assassination, how he was shot to death as his motorcade was passing through the streets of Dallas, and how the American nation was in shock at the loss of its popular young president. She said that although she and her husband were Republicans and hadn't voted for Kennedy, they had admired him and were overwhelmed by his untimely death. I gave her a cup of coffee and tried to console her by telling her that we all were devastated and saddened by the tragedy.

In late November, Seboo flew to the United States on business and returned a few days before I went into labor. During his trip he had a chance to visit a few prisons, and was especially impressed by a unique prison in Terre Haute, Indiana. The so-called prison was a collection of well-furnished bungalows nestled in a pine and oak forest, with no walls or guarded gates. The inmates, mostly university students, served a prison term for some kind of crime. They were driven daily by the prison bus to the campus to attend classes or study in its library. Seboo was so impressed by the concept that he joked he wouldn't mind being a convict in America to live in that prison, to read and write a book as some of those inmates had been doing.

Ever since I heard about that prison, I always thought that all the prisons in the United States were similar to it, until years later, living in Los Angeles, watching an interview on the *Oprah Winfrey Show*, I saw a young woman confessing to her how she had been repeatedly raped and beaten by a guard while serving a prison term. Then I read a well-researched series of documentary articles in the Los Angeles Times by its correspondent Mark Arax about Corcoran penitentiary in Central Valley, California. In those articles, the writer had exposed the poor living conditions in the facility in graphic detail, the frequent occurrence of violence among the inmates and their unjust treatment by the prison authorities. And I asked myself: is it possible that a period of thirty years would make such a big difference in human character, both in the criminals and the authorities? Or was the prison in Terre Haute for real? Maybe it was a model prison, an experimental concept that could be imitated in other locations.

One night in a heavy snow storm in late December, Seboo drove me to the hospital. This time, unlike my first delivery, the doctor gave me anesthetic. At dawn when the baby was born and the nurse was placing me on the bed in my room, I opened my eyes and unable to think clearly, asked her, "Is it a boy or a girl?" But she didn't answer. Instead, she quickly finished her job and left the room. Then my mother came in, approached my bed and said, "Congratulations, Elma. It's a girl!" I was exhilarated. Now I had a son *and* a daughter. At that moment, another nurse entered with the baby and put her next to me. She was bathed and clothed. She was a tiny cute girl with pink cheeks like a pair of apples, whom we later named, Hoorik which means "little fire" in Armenian, or Hoori, which means "angel" in Persian. As for the nurse who had refused to tell me about the baby's gender, I later learned that she hadn't known how I would react to the news of having a girl, because most Middle-Eastern families had a preference for boys. She didn't want to take the risk of disappointing me.

Before going to the hospital, grandpa, Haig had been admitted to another hospital for a stroke. When my mother came to see me, she said that he was doing well. Then one morning, a friend of mine who was visiting me started to talk about my grandpa and his funeral which she had attended. I was shocked and devastated. I asked her if she was telling the truth. Now it was her turn to be devastated. She blushed and asked, "Didn't you know about it? I'm sorry to be the bearer of bad news." Later I learned that grandpa had died the day after my daughter was born. He had been told about the baby and had blessed the two of us. Sadly, I couldn't go to his funeral.

When we went home with our "bundle of joy," Seboo started to prepare me for the sad news by maneuvering around the subject. He talked about grandpa's illness that had taken for the worst, that the doctors had given up hope for his recovery, and that he was already seventy four years old. When I told him that I already knew, he was surprised then relieved, but wanted to know who had given me the news of a death when I had just given birth to a baby. Naturally, I didn't give away the identity of my friend who had begged me not to tell anybody about the mistake she had made. After all, I didn't want to offend or lose her friendship. I had learned in life how a bit of secrecy, sincerity and mutual trust could go a long way in keeping a friendship alive – a vital element in our community.

Chapter 15

London, Brussels and Beirut

In mid-June 1965, mother and I, with six-year-old Aram and eighteen-month-old Hoori flew to London for the summer, with the plan that Seboo would join us later to spend his vacation there. The furnished house we rented in Wimbledon Park was the same one we had lived in 1956. It was close to the tennis courts and a huge park after which the area was named. At that time, London was the center of fashion, art, and pop music. Those were the days of miniskirts, short, straight hair symbolized by Twiggy, clothes designed by Mary Quant and the music of the Rolling Stones and the Beatles that shocked the older, conservative British generation. Their music blasted out from transistor radios in the parks, in the underground trains and through open windows of the houses we passed by. I got so addicted to the lyrical songs of those four "youth culture" musicians – John Lennon, George Harrison, Paul McCartney and Ringo Star that I bought most of their LPs. They were, *Love Me Do, She Loves You, I Want to Hold Your Hand, Penny Lane, When I'm Sixty Four,* and *Help* (whose recent movie I saw at the Odeon cinema). I also bought Mick Jagger's signature song, *I Can't Get No Satisfaction.*

On certain days, mother and I would take the children to Wimbledon Park, especially on Sunday afternoons where a brass band in traditional uniform played on the bandstand. We would sometimes take the underground train to the huge Kew Gardens with its exotic plants and flowers in bloom, to Battersea Fun Fair or Oxford Street. In those days England was a mecca for shopping. Its clothing was of the latest fashion and of the highest quality (especially its wool and cashmere) with affordable price tags.

In his last letter, Seboo had indicated that on his way to London, he would stop in Brussels for a few days to attend some business meetings. He asked me to join him if my mother would take care of the children. When I asked her, not only did she agree but also reminded me of her motto, "Don't give up a good opportunity if you can afford it." So I bought a one-way ticket to Brussels, took a train at Victoria station, and travelled to the port city of Dover, where I boarded a boat on the turbulent English Channel and sailed to Ostend in Belgium, from where, I took another train to Brussels.

On our way to Brussels, as we passed the towns of Bruges and Ghent, a British fellow-traveler told me about a famous altarpiece in the cathedral of St. Bavo in Ghent. The large folding altarpiece that was placed above and behind the altar was painted by the 15th century Flemish artist, Jan Van Eyck. He recommended that I see both towns, known for their medieval art and architecture. Unfortunately, I didn't see them then or in the future, but I did learn about those works of art years later when I took art history courses in the United States.

Arriving in Brussels, I took a taxi to the hotel where Seboo was staying. He was in the room when I knocked at the door. We were both happy to see each other, and took turns asking questions about the children and overall happenings in Tehran and London while we were away from each other.

Brussels, the capital of Belgium is an international, economic and political center that houses, among other organizations, the European Economic Community (EEC) and the North Atlantic Treaty Organization (NATO). The day I arrived in that busy city, it was a bright sunny day, but the next day it started raining and didn't stop until the day we left. However, those gloomy wet days didn't prevent us from exploring the site of the 1958 World Fair and what was left of it – the famous Atomium, a huge sphere, a symbol of Expo that represented the modern era. We saw the Grand Square surrounded by 15th century buildings, among them, the Hotel de Ville (the town hall) with its perforated spire and the statue of the archangel Michael, the city's patron saint. We liked Belgian and Flemish food, especially assortments of their hors d'oeuvres. Once at a restaurant in the Grand Square, I saw on the menu, a dish called *Carbonate de Flamendre* which was their specialty. It sounded interesting enough to make me order and see what it looked and tasted like. It turned out to be a runny stew with pieces of beef and potato swimming in it, which I hardly finished, while Seboo ate his steak and fries with relish. After that experience, I didn't order a dish that was not familiar to me.

One of the best things to do in that dreary weather was to take refuge in a store or movie theater. We saw *Sandpiper* with Elizabeth Taylor and *My Fair Lady* with Audrey Hepburn and Rex Harrison. I bought the most beautiful children's outfits in bright or pastel colors, mostly appliquéd with shapes of animals or flowers from their stylish stores. I also bought a few examples of famous Belgian lace in the form of runners and small pieces for my living room coffee-table and end-table.

Back in London, after a smooth flight on Sabena Airlines, we found everything in order and resumed our vacation, attending plays and concerts,

With Seboo, Aram and Hoori at our home in Tehran (1964).

especially the summer Proms in the Albert Hall. We also took Aram to the much-talked-about movie, *The Sound of Music*.

One evening, we attended a most interesting concert in Albert Hall. As we took our seats, we were surprised by the sight of six grand pianos on the stage. When the lights went off, someone appeared and after giving an explanation about the presence of half a dozen pianos, gave the audience an account of their cost. I don't remember the brands, but I do remember their astronomic prices. Each cost £25,000, which multiplied by six, would total £150,000. Then six famous pianists, each in the costume of the composer they were personifying came on the stage and introduced themselves as Frederic Chopin, Franz Liszt, and four other composers of that era whose names I don't remember. Then they all left the stage, except for one, who sat at a piano, removed his white gloves and played a couple of pieces. When he left, the next one entered and played another piece. After all six pianists had performed their pieces, they returned to the stage, sat at their pianos and played a piece together. Soon the stage and the hall were vibrating with the music produced on the six grand pianos, dazzling and exhilarating the audience that appreciated and honored their magnificent and disciplined performance with a standing ovation and passionate applause.

The concert we attended that night turned out to be unique, the like of which we neither had attended before, nor would attend in the years to come. I regret that I don't remember the details of the selected pieces and haven't kept the program. The only programs I have treasured and carried to America are those which hold the musicians' autographs.

*****

On our way back to Tehran, we stayed in Beirut for a week to visit Seboo's brother who was a student at the American University of Beirut. My mother didn't go with us, remaining in London with a friend for one more week. We stayed at the Omar Khayyam Hotel in the center of town. With two small children, the best thing to do in the heat of late summer was to spend our time at the beach, and we chose the soft, sandy Mediterranean beach-front of the George V Hotel with its first class services.

Among the worthwhile places we visited was Jaita caves (the Grotto), about ten miles northeast of Beirut, where we were overwhelmed by the illuminated portion of that fantastic cave and its lake as we explored it in a small boat (with our terrified children clinging to our arms). The extremely quiet, hollow space was filled with magnificent multi-colored formations of stalactites and stalagmites, some of them so low that they almost touched our heads. We were told that the grotto was discovered accidentally in the 1830s by an American tourist named Thompson, who during a hunting trip had stopped to rest at the mouth of the cave. Hearing the sound of water from inside, he had sneaked in through its narrow opening where he had found the huge underground lake, then had shot his gun, which had resonated in the hollow dark space. However, it was not until forty years later that it was seriously explored and ranked as the largest cave systems in the continent of Asia, and one of the natural wonders of the world.

One of the delightful things that happened to us in Beirut was to find out that one of Seboo's old friends, Vartan Gregorian and his family were the guests of the hotel. In the evenings, after dinner when we put our children to bed, Vartan and his wife, Claire, Seboo and I would sit on the deck-chairs on the terrace in front of our rooms, and have the most interesting conversations about current affairs, politics, the past, present and our futures. The family had arrived from the United States and was staying at the hotel looking for a furnished house to settle in for a couple of years. Having completed his Ph.D. dissertation and written a book on Afghanistan through a Ford Foundation fellowship, Vartan had obtained another fellowship to write a comprehensive study of Armenian history and culture, including the Armenian Diaspora. The base of his research was in Beirut and Yerevan, the capital of Soviet Armenia. However, before settling in Beirut, Vartan was going to Yerevan for his scholarly research, and his wife with their two little sons were planning to go to Iran to get the children baptized in the Armenian church of Tabriz, Vartan's birth place.

We enjoyed the time spent with them so much that we preferred to stay in the hotel, rather than go out, except for once, and that was to the famous

Casino de Liban which had a fantastic show equivalent of Follies Bergere or Pigalle in Paris. Actually, at that time, Beirut was called the "Little Paris of the Middle East" with its fashionable boutiques and night life.

After we parted, we didn't see them again until twenty years later, when we met Vartan at a concert in Los Angeles and invited him to our place. He had gone to UC Berkeley for an interview for the post of UC president. Although we haven't seen him since, we have followed the chain of his brilliant achievements: his appointment as president of the New York Public Library, dean of Brown University and president of the Carnegie Corporation. Before seeing him again in 2003 at the book-signing of his memoir, *The Road Home* at the Glendale library, I had seen his name engraved on a marble plaque dedicated to the trustees of the Getty Center, where I volunteer.

*****

When we returned to Tehran, our American tenants notified us that they were returning to the United States and would vacate the apartment at the end of the month. We were saddened by their departure, because we knew that we would miss them. They were a conscientious, quiet couple, the kind of tenant every landlord would wish to have. But since they were happy to return to their home and family in California, we wished them bon voyage and good luck in life. After they left, we renovated the place, painted it, replaced the floor tiles with parquet, and decided to move in ourselves. Our two-story house was too big for us and difficult to take care of, even with the help of a full-time maid. Tehran is a dry and dusty city. Carpets had to be vacuumed, floors washed and the furniture dusted on a daily basis. To move heavy items to the upper floor, we hired a man called, Reza, a well-known porter in the area. This wonderful porter, a man of average build, carried our heavy furniture, including the refrigerator, on his back. He rolled up our room-sized Persian carpets by himself and carrying them on his shoulder, climbed the steps to the next floor and put them in their designated spots.

Later that fall, we rented our two-story house to a Persian family, a couple with a little boy who lived there until our relocation to the United States in 1976. Six months after our departure, they too emigrated to the United States, settling in San Francisco. Homa Garemani, who had a graduate degree in German literature from Tehran University, was a writer, who has published a novel in Los Angeles in 2005, called *Fortress of the Golden Dragon*. It is an interesting Persian tale inspired by the 10th century epic of *Shah-Nameh* (Book of Kings) by Fardowsi.

*****

During the two-week Now-Ruz holidays in the spring of 1966, we drove to Isfahan, where we stayed in a hotel for one week, re-visited the mosques in the Grand Square and the *Vank* in New Julfa, met relatives and friends, then drove further south to Shiraz. At that time Seboo's construction company was building dormitories for the University of Shiraz, and had rented a big house for its engineers to live in. The house had several bedrooms and a cook who catered for them and their occasional guests.

In Shiraz, we visited the tombs of Iran's most famous and respected poets, Saadi and Hafez. In Pasargad, we saw the tombs of Cyrus and Darius, carved into a cliff, called Naghshe-Rostam. Most important of all, we visited the ruins of magnificent Persepolis, thirty miles northeast of the town. Persepolis, or Takht-e-Jamshid as it is known to Iranians, was built between 520 and 460 B.C. by the decree of Darius and Xerxes, successors of Cyrus the Great of the Achaemenid Dynasty, but burned and destroyed by Alexander the Great in 330 B.C.

As I looked at the remains of the palace with its monumental stone pillars, lofty gateways and stairways facing west, I asked myself: why would Alexander want to destroy such a majestic monument, which in those days must have taken thousands of human beings to build, using their physical strength and inadequate tools, within a period of more than a half century? How could Alexander the Great, who was a student of the Greek philosopher Aristotle, a worshiper of Cyrus the Great, who respected the religion, culture and identity of the countries he conquered, destroy so much? What was his motivation? Was it impulsive rage, revenge, or a show of prowess? Or had he done it, as the history suggests, "...in a gesture symbolizing the destruction of Persian imperial power...."?

Throughout my visits to those historical spots, Seboo stayed with the children, assuring me that he had other opportunities to see them – but he never did.

The day after we returned to Tehran, my parents told us that they were going to fly to London in a few days. My mother said that she had been diagnosed with cervical cancer, and since radiation therapy was not available in Tehran, she had to go to London for complete treatment. I was devastated and speechless. In those days, the word "cancer" was equivalent to a death sentence. I had nothing to say except to suggest to them that my two brothers move in with us during their absence.

At that time, my brother, Emil, who had returned from France and was employed by an engineering firm, was going steady with a nice Armenian girl, and mother decided to formalize their relationship before their trip. So one day our family, together with the families of my three uncles and two paternal aunts, made a pre-arranged visit to the girl's house with baskets of roses and tulips, boxes of chocolates and bottles of brandy as was the custom. My brother slipped a diamond ring onto his girlfriend's finger, after which we congratulated them and were treated to dinner.

After completing six weeks of radiation therapy in London, but not surgery, mother and Vartges returned to Tehran. Apparently, her cancer had spread and the oncologist had concluded that radiation therapy was a better option than surgery.

In the summer of that year, the Women's Organization of Iran was hosting one of its annual international conferences in Tehran. Having returned from London and gotten herself involved in community activities, mother was selected as a representative of the Armenian Women's Charity Organization to participate in the conferences that were taking place at the Royal Hilton Hotel. Finding the experience very fulfilling, she suggested that I too apply for a volunteering post, and introduced me to an influential member of the organization with whom she had made friends. I was soon invited to work as a hostess who could speak four languages. In reality, I didn't have a responsible job; I was not an interpreter or presenter of women's issues, just a hostess, who had to fulfill the demands of the delegates, like when someone had trouble with her headphone or needed some kind of stationery. In those cases, all I had to do was to refer to the technician, or to order the item through the person in charge. The exciting part of the task, however, was during the breaks and lunch time, when I had a chance to talk to some of the female delegates who had flown in from all over the world – the Americas, Europe, Africa, Asia and Australia.

At the end of their schedule, the delegates were invited to the Armenian Club where they were treated to a buffet lunch in its shady garden on Naderi Avenue. I had never met so many women from exotic countries who wore their ethnic attire, spoke unfamiliar languages, and appreciated the Iranian food with cries of ah and ooh.

The Women's Organization of Iran, besides coordinating local and international conferences related to women's issues, had a much more important role in the Iranian community. It was a network of numerous associations, branches and centers that provided services in child care, family planning, vocational training and teaching language classes. Its sizeable staff of professionals and volunteers rendered their valuable services to underprivileged women in the urban and rural areas of Iran.

In early fall of that year, I was offered the position of secretary/coordinator at one of the branches of this organization. Although I was flattered by the offer, I had to turn it down because of the responsibilities I already had toward my family, especially mother, whose health was deteriorating, and who needed my help. It was one thing to work temporarily for a special event, and quite another to work full time as an office employee. I was glad about making this decision, because in late October, among the week-long festivities of the Crown Prince's birthday, my Uncle Hrand died of a heart attack at the age of forty-nine, leaving his wife and three children alone, together with my devastated sick mother.

One month before Hrand's death, Seboo and I had bought tickets for a trip to Beirut, Rome, Vienna, Frankfurt, Paris and Geneva, and had sent letters to our friends who lived in some of those cities. But after the misfortune we decided to cancel the trip. We didn't want to leave my bereaved mother alone. At her insistence, however, we changed our minds, left the children with her and flew to our destinations.

My mother never ceased to amaze me with the strength that she could find in herself to handle difficult situations like that, even control her feelings regarding her fragile existence. By taking care of my children, apparently she wanted to distract her mind from the loss of her brother and her own fatal disease, and to keep herself busy with them.

Chapter 16

Trip to Europe

Seboo and I started our one-month trip to Europe at the end of November. Except for Beirut, where the weather was mild, the European cities we visited were very cold. We stayed in Beirut for a couple of days to see Seboo's brother at AUB. In Rome, we stayed in an old hotel in Piazza del Popolo, in a room that looked like a football-field with minimal furniture. When we spoke, our voices bounced between its high ceiling and the bare floor. In spite of the two radiators, the room was always cold, and when I wanted to wash my hair, I had to summon all my courage, because drying it was another challenge. The room didn't have any electrical outlet for a hair dryer, so after washing my hair, which I did late at night, I wrapped my head with a towel and went to bed. With all its flaws, we were still happy that the hotel was centrally located and within easy reach of everything we needed.

In the evening of our arrival, we went out to a near-by pizzeria for dinner. On our table there was a carafe of red wine. When we asked why it was there, the waiter laughed and told us that in Italy they drink wine like water, so we'd better try it. The wine was called Lambrusco. It tasted sweet and sour. We drank all the contents of the carafe, fell in love with it, and ordered a refill. Since I was not used to drinking alcoholic beverages, I got dizzy and sleepy to the point that Seboo had to drag me to the hotel, up the stairs, and to our room.

We had a friend whose husband was a medical student at the University of Rome, specializing in cardiology. With their red Volkswagon Beatle, the couple showed us around town, giving us in-depth information about Roman history, its antiquity, as well as contemporary Italian art and architecture. In Villa Borghese we found, among the magnificent works of Roman sculptors, a second-rate statue of Fardowsi, the 10th-century Persian epic poet, donated by the Iranian government. As I looked at it, I recalled a Persian proverb: "This is like sending cumin to Kerman" (a city in Iran which is famous for producing cumin).

For lunch and dinner, our friends took us to small local restaurants and pizzerias. There, we ate the lightest, mildest, and simplest pizzas, which were baked right in front of our eyes in wood-burning ovens, and brought to our table with the cheese still melting and bubbling on the surface. We ate the most delicious *lasagna el forno*, without the heavy tomato sauce they use elsewhere. Lunch or dinner was usually followed by heavenly desserts. One of them, Mont Blanc, was a sponge cake laced with rum, topped with fluffy whipped cream and named after the snow-covered peak of the Alps on the French-Italian border. I haven't eaten anything like that anywhere else, even at the Armenian Club in Tehran which served varieties of international desserts and delicacies.

In Rome, we also had a chance to meet another friend, an opera singer, a soprano, who after graduating from the School of Music in Tehran, had attended Santa Cecilia, the world famous school of music in Rome. She had married an Italian tenor and together they were giving concerts in Italy and other European countries. Sometimes she performed with famous tenors, such as Giuseppe Di Stefano.

One early morning, Seboo and I boarded a bus for a day-long tour of Amalfi, Capri, Sorento, Naples and Pompeii. We stopped in those cities, visiting their landmarks and tourist attractions. We didn't go to the island of Capri, but only saw it from afar. It was out of season and impossible to hire a boat. The ruins of Pompeii, however, were the most impressive of them all. It seemed as if a living town had stopped in its tracks since the year A.D. 79, when Vesuvius had erupted and buried it under thick lava, to be excavated in the year 1700. It was interesting to learn about that ancient city's sewer system, especially the wonderful Roman aqueduct structure which could transport water through a covered passage from a remote source.

We walked in its well-planned, cobble-stoned empty streets as we visualized people walking, and chariots clanking on the stones. We visited the Roman baths and villas and atriums and saw their colorful mosaics and details. In one room we found an empty safe, the valuable contents of which must have been taken by their owners prior to fleeing from the city. In its museum, we saw a charred loaf of bread, a scorched human body bound in chains, primitive kitchen utensils, marble and bronze sculptures preserved from everyday Roman life. We were told that the people of Pompeii had used a special bright red, a *bold* red, I should say, in their art and architecture that was called Pompeian-red, the exact like of which I haven't seen anywhere else.

During our stay in Rome, I bought a stylish evening dress and an expensive *novella* (newly arrived) black leather purse for which we haggled just like we did in Tehran. While shopping and looking everywhere, I finally found a pair of soft leather gloves with cut-out flower design on the wrists, a specialty of Italy, something my mother had asked me to get for her. When we were looking for Via Veneto, a street known for its elegant stores, we stopped an Italian and asked him for directions in English. He thought for a second, gestured the act of walking with his two fingers, then held up his ten fingers and pointed to the end of the street. What he meant was if we walked for ten minutes, we would reach our destination. We thanked him and continued on our way, buying roasted hot chestnuts from a street vendor, munching them like squirrels before getting to our desired spot.

*****

In the snow-covered Vienna, we took tours of its historic palaces, such as the Rocco style Schonbrunn summer palace of the Hapsburgs and the Spanish Riding School, where they trained a special breed of white horses imported from Spain. One of Vienna's landmarks, Saint Stephen's Cathedral, amazed us with the details of its stonework that looked like delicate, exquisite lace, woven from silk thread. In our free time we walked in the city's underground malls, where we ate lunch and dinner with plenty of colorful bell peppers, and for dessert, the well-known Viennese cream or chocolate cakes. One evening, I cried while watching a phenomenal performance of Puccini's *La Boheme* in the world-famous Vienna State Opera House, in the presence of a most sophisticated and elegantly-dressed audience.

*****

We didn't have any friends in Frankfurt, but we did have one in Darmstadt who was studying mechanical engineering. One early morning, we boarded a train in Frankfurt and met him in Darmstadt. As our taxi drove us through the still-lighted streets of frozen Frankfurt to the train station, we saw a large number of people hurrying to work or waiting at the bus-stops in the dark of 6:00 a.m. We then realized why that hard-working nation had succeeded and recovered economically after its defeat in WWII.

After taking a tour of Darmstadt University, our friend drove us to see Manheim and Mainz, where we met another friend from Tehran who was continuing his higher education. We also visited Heidelberg (a picture-perfect university town) along the River Rhine, as well as Wiesbaden, with its numerous casinos. It was unbelievable that we had driven and seen five towns in just one day.

In Frankfurt, we saw Verdi's opera, *Aida,* together with our friend who, after the performance, introduced us to a young Iranian woman, the prima-donna of the opera's ballet group. We invited her and her German husband to dinner and talked about her successful career, which had started in Iran, then continued at the Leningrad Ballet School. Years later we met her in Tehran, where she had opened a ballet school.

From Frankfurt we flew to West Berlin and visited the city's contemporary and ancient buildings. Among them, we saw remnants of WWII destruction, and the bombed-out bulk of the Kaiser Wilhelm Church, standing next to a modern high-rise building. We tried to buy tickets for a concert performed by the Berlin Philharmonic, but were disappointed to find them sold out. It was so cold in the streets of Frankfurt and Berlin that my jaws locked together, preventing me from talking. Thank God for the roaring fires in the lobbies of our hotels where we could sit in armchairs, get warm and relax.

One day we boarded a tour bus to see East Berlin. At Checkpoint Charlie, the entrance gate of the Berlin wall, the bus was stopped by the guards and our passports were carefully checked before we were allowed to enter the city.

Once inside the city, we couldn't believe the contrast between the two parts of a metropolis that had been divided by an extended concrete wall after the war. One part was a prosperous modern city with dense traffic and crowded streets, throbbing with life and prosperity; and the other, a forlorn and empty one, devoid of people, with rows of desolate buildings as if it had stopped in its tracks the moment the war had ended. Other than driving us around town, the only site of interest the tour bus took us was a depressing mausoleum that housed the tombs of war heroes. The last place we visited was a center where we spent the rest of the day, walking around, having lunch, buying souvenirs and slides. We were not allowed to leave the tour group.

In late afternoon when we were leaving East Berlin, at Checkpoint Charlie, our bus was checked again – this time more meticulously. While a guard was checking the passports of the passengers inside, two others were holding a huge mirror underneath the vehicle to see if anybody had hidden there to sneak out to the freedom of West Berlin.

*****

From Berlin we flew to Orly Airport in Paris, where we met George, Seboo's friend, who drove us in his Citroen to a small hotel, opposite the Opera Comique where we bought tickets for the performance of Rossini's *Barbier de Seville*, which we attended that same evening. We saw Puccini's *Tosca* at the Paris Opera, and spent most of our time with George, a bachelor who took pleasure in entertaining friends who visited Paris.

One day George drove us to the countryside to see some ancient castles. We were so busy finding places and visiting them that we lost track of time and realized that it was well past lunch time. We started looking for a restaurant and eventually found one in a village which, if I remember correctly, was called Chevreuse. The restaurant was empty except for a few farmers who had gathered in front of the bar and were drinking and arguing boisterously. We sat at a table and when we asked the waiter for their menu, he checked his watch, raised his eyebrows, and said, "You know, it is Sunday. We serve lunch until 2:00 p.m. It is 3:00 p.m. now. Our cook is preparing to leave for Paris, but if you wish, I can bring you some sandwiches." We were so hungry that we couldn't refuse his offer, so Seboo asked for ham-and-cheese for the three of us, and the waiter left to bring the order. After a moment he came back and said, "You know, the cook decided to postpone his plans and to serve you a complete meal." We asked him to thank the cook, and ordered roasted chicken and French fries, with a large bowl of salad.

After a while, during which the waiter brought us some whipped butter and a basket of fresh baguettes, he unloaded on our table a tray of two platters, one a whole roasted chicken on a bed of parsley, the other a larger one full of French-fries, which we thought was too much to eat. But we did eat the whole meal to the last bit and generously tipped the waiter *and* the cook who had changed his plans in order to serve us lunch. It was the kind of graciousness we hadn't experienced in any large city.

We flew from Paris to Geneva where we stayed for only twenty-four hours, then returned to Tehran at the end of December, shortly before Hoori's third birthday.

While in Europe, I had constantly worried about the children, and somehow felt guilty for leaving them with my sick mother. But when we returned to Tehran, to my relief, I found her more refreshed and vigorous than the day I had left her. Apparently, the children had kept her busy, and more importantly, during our absence, she had a surprise visitor. My mother's aunt, grandma's younger sister, who lived in India, and whom mother had never seen, had stopped in Tehran on her way from Calcutta to California. It was then that I realized how all my worries had been baseless and I had tormented myself in vain.

Chapter 17

My Mother's Illness

On October 16, 1967, Iran celebrated the coronation of Mohammad Reza Shah Pahlavi who, in a spectacular ceremony, after crowning himself, crowned his wife, Farah Diba, with a diamond-and-emerald tiara, giving her the title of Shah-Banou. In her memoirs, *An Enduring Love*, she points out that by doing so, "The king made me feel that he was crowning all the women of Iran."

In early December, my brother married his fiancée, for which my parents threw a party at the Armenian Club.

A few months later, in March 1968, mother began suffering shortness of breath and pain in her shoulders. One evening in their house, Vartges found me in the kitchen, and without any preamble, told me that mother's cancer had metastasized and spread into her lungs and rib cage, and she was not going to make it. Agitated, I tried every means in my power to persuade him that he was wrong and other factors might be the reason for her pain. But when he looked deeply into my eyes with a sad expression in his glance, I shuddered at its intensity, and felt a stab of pain in my heart. I stood there transfixed, not knowing what to say or do, as if a momentary shock had paralyzed my brain. To make matters worse, the young male housekeeper, whom mother had trained and taught how to cook, had heard the conversation and burst into tears, imploring, "Sell this house and pay for her treatment! She's too young to die." He was right. In her mid-fifties, mother was still a healthy, dynamic woman, whose gynecologist had assured me that she was going to live a long normal life after her treatment in England. Then why had cancer struck her like a biological terrorist?

I moved into their house with my two children the next day to take care of and to be near her for the rest of her days.

Mother didn't know her cancer had recurred. At least nobody had told her so. The family physician, a colleague of Vartges, had assured her that she was suffering from anemia and arthritis, and with the right nutrition and medication she would pull through in no time. But I knew that deep down she didn't believe him. She was a smart woman and being a physician's wife for almost twenty five years, she was familiar with the symptoms of certain diseases. There were days when she felt much better and optimistic and began planning for the future. She would say, "In spring time I'll plant rose bushes in the front yard," or, "I'll get the bedrooms new curtains when I get well." There were days too when she was down and would speak about death and what we should do after it happened. Once, during one of those spells, she said, "Listen, Elma, if I die, don't grieve for me. I have lived a full happy life. Go on with your own, raise your children, and help your brothers if they need you." She was an amazing woman. She liked to count only her blessings, not the hardships she had gone through after my father's death, and not the fact that she was still too young to die.

One day she told me to go to the bank and bring home her jewelry from the safety deposit box. She wanted to divide it into three parts and give them to me and my two brothers. I tried to dissuade her, assuring her that she was going to get well, and that bringing home the jewelry was not a good idea. "Let's put it this way," she argued, "if I die, you won't have trouble in dividing it. If I *don't* die, you'll give it back to me." Actually, she didn't have much jewelry in that small box other than a couple of gold crosses with their chains, a bracelet, a pair of diamond ear-rings she had inherited from her mother, a couple of emerald and diamond rings from her two marriages, a gray pearl necklace brought to her from Japan by an American friend and a gold Swiss watch Vartges had bought her recently. She divided them up, put them in separate boxes, and told me to place them on the upper shelf of her wardrobe. Later, I heard that she had taken off her wedding ring from her finger and given it to Vartges.

One Friday in early July, all our family was invited to Uncle Hovik's orchard in Karaj and, since mother was feeling a little better, we decided to take her along. We spent a relaxed day with my cousins, swimming in their pool, picking luscious cherries, peaches, pears and apples, and having a delicious lunch of rice and shish-kebab. In the early evening, when everybody was preparing to leave, my uncle's wife, Mary, asked mother and me to stay overnight. It was cool and quiet and mother could sleep comfortably. We decided that Hoori and I would stay, and Seboo and Aram would go home.

We were sleeping in the room next to mother's when we were awakened in the middle of the night by her continuous groans. "Why is grandma crying?" Hoori asked, sitting up straight in her bed, rubbing her eyes. "She's sick, dear. She has pain, but will feel better as soon as I give her some medicine. Go back to sleep," I said and went to mother's room to administer her regular tranquilizer. I sat on the edge of her bed, unable to do anything else, until she was drugged into sleep. I then went back to my bed and slept for a while before I was awakened again by her monotonous moans. As I tiptoed toward the door, still dazed with sleep, Hoori's whispers stopped me at the threshold. "I wish I had brought my doctor's set with me. I'll make grandma well when we go back home." I stared at her and her unusually shining eyes. "The medicine doesn't do her any good. I'm going to become a doctor when I grow up." That little girl who had been exposed to human pain at the age of four was speaking with the voice and determination of an adult so unusual for her age. She seemed to have matured in one night.

My mother died on August 7, 1968 after going through a month of excruciating pain which was alleviated by daily injections of morphine. Two days later, we buried her in the company of a huge crowd of relatives, friends, members of the Women's Charity Organization and the PTA of Armen's high school, with eloquent eulogies rendered by community dignitaries. That was the bitterest day of my life. When they were lowering her coffin into the grave, I felt as if she was not going alone, but was taking along all the happy and sad memories of our lives. I also felt as if a part of me was dying inside, leaving a void in my heart that would never completely be filled.

Throughout my life, I had always wanted to have an intimate talk with her, not necessarily about any serious matter or problem, just a mother-daughter chat, maybe to ask her questions about my father, about the past, or just to open my heart. But somehow it never happened. It seemed that there was no right time or place for it. Then after she got sick and died within a short period of time, I realized what a big opportunity I had missed. Now that I have a married daughter, I try to *make* the time to be alone with her, to tell her tit-bits of my experiences in life, about our large family, and the virtues and vices of its certain members – information that could help her in solving problems that might arise between them. And, what is more, it is a way for her to open her heart and be sincere with me.

My mother died, but the desire to become a doctor didn't die in her granddaughter. It seemed that the pain of losing her grandma obsessed her even more in the years to come. Although Hoori was not capable of saving my mother's life at that time, she did save her father's life when she was in the fourth year of medical school at the University of Southern California. One morning, when Seboo was feeling terribly tired without any reason, she drove him to the emergency room of St. John's Hospital after realizing that his heart rate had dropped drastically. The cardiologist examined and admitted him to the hospital, then decided to put a pacemaker in his chest to regulate his heart beats. If Hoori hadn't acted promptly, we would have been facing a serious problem, not to mention death.

*****

After mother's death, things started to fall apart in our family; the central pillar that was mother wasn't there to hold it together. But life didn't stop. It went on and dragged me along too.

One year after her death, my brother, Armen, who had graduated from Tehran Polytechnic, majoring in electrical engineering, was accepted at the graduate school of Stanford University. He was twenty-two years old. On the day of his departure, Vartges, Seboo and I with other members of the family and a group of Armen's friends went to Mehrabad Airport to bid him farewell and see him off. As the time of his departure approached, my heart began to sink, but I managed to control myself until he disappeared through the door to the customs, then I gave in to a torrent of tears. It seemed to me as if mother had died one more time. And I cried all the way home as Seboo silently drove the car.

After Armen's departure, Vartges came over for dinner once a week, and we visited him on certain occasions. Whenever we were there, I liked to stand in front of the china cabinet and look at mother's collection of fine crystal that ranged from exquisitely carved Czechoslovakian antique vases to the bulky, clear or colored examples of modern French Baccarat and Lalique. I also liked the miniature dolls in their ethnic attire and the tea-spoons with the emblems of the cities she had visited during her trips abroad. Looking at those collections, I could imagine the pleasure she might have felt when buying and treasuring them. I wondered why I hadn't inherited her love and taste of collecting beautiful objects, but realized that the contents of my own collections were just memories of my personal life, notable historical events and incidents that had happened throughout my life and travels, both at home and abroad. And yes, photographs – thousands of them.

Vartges remarried the following year and sold their newly-constructed two-story house, into which my mother had put so much of her good taste and energy when they had returned from England after her treatment. It was painful for us to witness the collapse of our old family and the demise of the home that had once held us together. However, piece by piece, we started letting go of the past and accepting the present, as our family and social life went on quietly with our friends who tried not to leave us alone, and were there whenever we needed them. That fall, we enrolled Hoori at the kindergarten, and bought a piano for nine-year-old Aram to start taking lessons, with the intention of distracting him from the pain of his grandma's loss. In the meantime, I kept myself busy with working for the PTA of Aram's school.

*****

On July 24, 1969, a few days short of the anniversary of my mother's death, our family of four was seated in front of our black-and-white TV set, watching Neil Armstrong, landing on the moon then emerging from the four-legged Lunar Module and hopping in his bulky outfit over the low-gravity moonscape, collecting samples on his way. We had already seen how Apollo XI had lifted off the ground at Cape Canaveral (now Cape Kennedy) in Florida and zoomed in a fiery blaze toward the sky, disappearing into space.

For us, it was odd to see the surface of the moon so bare and chalky. It was not at all like the moon idealized in Persian literature. It was not a paragon of ultimate beauty, to which youthful, charming female faces were likened: "She is as pretty as the moon," or "She looks like the full moon on its fourteenth night." Of the many comments made by famous persons about landing on the moon, I remember two. The one that Armstrong has said: "That's one small step for man, one giant leap for mankind," and the other that the Dalai Lama, Tibet's Buddhist leader has predicted, "Man's limited knowledge will acquire a new dimension of infinite scope." And I secretly hoped that his prediction would include a remedy for the fatal diseases of mankind, and the samples brought to the earth would contain some substance that could help the scientists do some useful experiments with them.

Chapter 18

Trips to America and Europe

During the Now-Ruz holidays of 1970, Seboo suggested that I take a three-week tour of Europe and America, offered by Swiss-Air for the price of $700. The package tour included the round trip plane fare, hotels with breakfast in London and Paris, and sightseeing tours of New York. It was too good an offer to refuse. As for the children, I didn't have to worry. Seboo would take them with his old aunt to the shores of the Caspian Sea in Saghi Calaieh, where we had built a villa on a piece of land a year before.

On my birthday, coinciding with St. Patrick's Day, I flew to New York with a short stop in Geneva. I checked in a hotel in Manhattan with the tour group, but I spent most of the two weeks with friends or distant relatives, citizens of the United States.

One of the friends whose house I stayed in for a couple of days was my close friend, Gladys, with whom I had been classmates in high school and had worked with at the Point IV Organization. She had an American boyfriend then, a shy, handsome guy, who served in the American military base in Tehran. Seboo and I had double-dated with them a few times. Years later, she went to New York to continue her education, and ended up marrying an American lawyer, a distant relative of the Kennedy family, and lived in Brooklyn with their three little sons. While I stayed with them, she took me to see *Fiddler on the Roof,* an Easter performance at the Radio City, and the controversial movie, *Women in Love*, based on a novel by D.H. Lawrence.

While waiting and talking in the movie ticket line, a young black man who was standing with a woman in front of us, turned back and asked, "Excuse me, ladies, what language are you speaking?" And when I said Armenian, he suddenly threw up his arms in delight and said lewdly, "You know, I had made a bet with my girlfriend that if I'm right in my guess about your language, she'll sleep with me tonight." I felt embarrassed. I was a married woman with two children, but had never heard a man talking to me so explicitly about sex. Later when I saw the film, starring Alan Bates and Julie Christie, and its erotic sexual scenes, I was more than sure that the black man was going to reach his goal. Returning home on the subway, Gladys, who had remained silent since the stranger's outburst, said to me, "You know, Elma, this city is turning into a Sodom and Gomorrah."

Four years later a stranger called me in Tehran and said that Gladys had died of breast cancer at the age of forty-two. I was devastated, unable to believe my ears. I checked with one of her relatives who confirmed the sad news. I sent sympathy cards to her husband and mother, and when we came to Los Angeles, every year on Gladys' birthday, on the first of June, I called her mother and talked to her, and kept doing so until her death at the age of over ninety. As for Gladys' husband, he married a school teacher, who took good care of their children, and every year brought them over to Los Angeles to see their maternal grandmother.

I called Armen at Stanford from New York. I didn't have the time to go to California, and he was busy preparing his thesis. During our short conversation, he told me that in summer he was planning to marry his fiancée, Stella, who would join him in London from Tehran. He suggested that all of us go to England for the wedding, and to my delight, he also asked if Seboo would like to be his best man. He was about to obtain his master's degree in electrical engineering, and after their marriage, wanted to continue his education towards a degree called an engineering degree.

On our way back, our tour group stopped in London and Paris for a few days. In London, I saw a matinee play on Shaftsbury Avenue, starring Allan Bates. In Paris I saw a French comedy. In Geneva where we had a long stop, we took a sightseeing tour of the city.

On the flight to Tehran, I was already planning for our next trip to London, and Armen's upcoming wedding. I was also exploring the possibility of going there early in the summer and registering the children at a summer school. In Tehran, for the last few years, it had become a trend among the upper middle class families to send their children to British or Swiss summer schools to brush up on their language skills and gain exposure to Western culture.

Back in Tehran, Seboo and I discussed the matter and decided that at the end of the school year, I would take the children, Aram eleven and Hoori six, to a summer school in England for a period of one month. In the meantime, I would spend the time with my close friend, Anoush, who would join me in London the following week. So I investigated and contacted a boarding school in Bexhill in the south of England, and sent them the required deposit. Via mail, they informed me that the driver of the school car would meet us at Heathrow Airport, but they would send me another letter with more detailed information. It was important for me to get the letter before our departure. I waited for it up to the last day, but it didn't arrive. I didn't have the school's phone number and it was not so easy to put through a long distance call from Iran to England. On the other

With my children and sister-in-law, Stella, in Rye, England (1970).

hand, we couldn't postpone our trip because of the summer high season. So we decided to take the chance and fly to London anyway. After all, Armen would be there at the time and would meet and help us at the airport. We boarded an Iran-Air plane bound for London in late June and arrived at Heathrow Airport before noon the same day, local time.

After going through customs, which didn't take long, we walked out to the arrival hall. I looked around and didn't see Armen among the welcoming crowd. We then went out to the street and I didn't see any car with a school placard either. Instead, all I saw was a line of airport buses waiting for passengers for London. I approached one of the drivers, who was leaning against his bus, and showing him the school's address, asked him what was the best way to get there. He threw a brief glance at it, shook his head and said, "Lady, you can't find direct transport to that beach town. You have to catch a train to Rye, the nearest town to Bexhill, but to catch that train you have to go to Victoria Station in the center of London. You're lucky that this bus is going there in ten minutes time." I thought a second then gave the driver the suitcases, and the next thing I knew the children and I were sitting in the bus, traveling at a great speed on the M4 motorway. I hadn't been to London since 1965, and hadn't seen that highway or the high-rise apartment buildings which had sprouted along its sides.

Once at the busy and noisy Victoria station, dragging our suitcases along, I approached an information booth and asked the girl behind it. "Miss, could you tell me how to get to Rye?" "How do you spell it?" the girl asked in a Cockney drawl, looking at me with such astonishment as if I was talking about a remote village in China. "R-y-e," I spelled out slowly. The girl went over a thick directory and said, "The train to Rye leaves from Waterloo station at 2:00 p.m. If you hurry you might catch it."

We took a train to Waterloo, found the platform for the train to Rye, bought the tickets and waited. According to the timetable, the train was due to arrive within half an hour, so I left the children with the luggage and ran over the bridge to a fast-food stall to buy some snacks. Like everywhere in London, there was a long line in front of the stall. Luckily, it moved forward fast enough and I was able to buy two *Wimpies* (hamburgers) and two small cartons of milk.

As soon as I ran back and handed the food to the children, a train arrived. There was no signboard to show the list of stations that the train would stop at. The loudspeaker announced some unfamiliar names in a blurred voice, among which I didn't hear "Rye." I looked around and, not seeing a station attendant, approached a man who was entering the train and asked if he knew if the train was going to Rye, but he shook his head and said that he hadn't a clue. Then before I could make sure that it was the right train for us to board, the doors hissed closed and it pulled out of the station.

As the platform emptied, I spotted a station attendant whom I hadn't seen before. I walked toward him and asked, "Excuse me, sir, was that train going to Rye?"

"It sure was, ma'am," he sneered. "But why were you asking a passenger about it?"

"Because nobody else was here to ask," I retorted. "But if you saw me asking a passenger, why on earth didn't you come to my help?"

"Look, ma'am, it was *you* who needed help," he said and shook his head. "Never mind, another train will arrive in an hour."

"Is it a direct trip to Rye?" I asked.

"No, ma'am, you'll have to change at Ashford station." He grinned and strode away. I stifled a scream that had been developing in my throat since we had left the airport.

An hour later after the platform had filled with passengers, the train arrived and I was able to board it with the help of a male passenger. Later I learned that the train to Ashford was originally leaving from Charing Cross station every hour and only had a short stop at Waterloo.

A few minutes after we had made ourselves comfortable on the seats and the train had pulled out of the station, I heard the regular breathing of my children. I couldn't afford to doze off myself and miss the Ashford station, so I looked out the window and relaxed with the peaceful scenery that passed by us. I saw woolly sheep grazing in green pastures, apple and pear orchards, then the back yards of rustic cottages, facing the railroad tracks, with people lying lazily on their deck-chairs, watching the passing train as their children waved to us. I checked my watch and asked the woman sitting across from me, reading a newspaper, "Excuse me, ma'am, do you know how many stations are left before Ashford?"

The woman looked at me absent mindedly, thought a little then said, "I'm sorry, I don't know. Actually, this is my first trip to the south."

I decided not to ask anybody for directions anymore. So far they had only confused and frustrated me with their ignorance or misinformation. I stood up, pulled the suitcases as close to the door as possible and shook the children awake. I'm glad I did, because the next stop was Ashford, quite a large station and junction, where the station attendant was announcing through the loudspeaker in a monotonous tone: "Change here for Folkstone and Rye. Hurry up! Take platform No. 4 for Folkstone and No. 3 for Rye." We managed to board the train and arrive in Rye in a short time. The few passengers who had gotten off had already left in private cars.

I caught sight of a telephone in the street, installed on the wall, above which was written in large letters TAXI. I approached it and lifted the receiver. This time I was not surprised at the line being dead, because I had come to the conclusion that the sunny day in England was *not* my lucky day. I didn't see anybody to ask. I just didn't know what to do.

As I was standing there figuring out my next move, I noticed a barefoot, unkempt hippy young man leaning against a wall, eyeing us with curiosity. Reluctantly, I walked toward him, and showing the school's address, asked him how could we get there. He cast a glance at it, gave it back to me and said, "This is Rye. The school is in Bexhill. It is a fifteen-minute ride by bus which leaves every half hour." It was impossible for us to start another trip, no matter how short, so I asked the young man if he knew any hotel in the neighborhood.

"Yes," he said, pointing to a sign around the corner of that short street. "It's a small bed-and-breakfast with a pub. I can help you with the luggage if you wish."

I followed him as he led the way. When he put down the suitcases in front of the reception desk of the Cinque Ports Hotel, I tipped and thanked him, feeling ashamed for misjudging the young man because of his shabby appearance.

Before going to our room, I ordered some sandwiches and a pot of tea. It was a small room on the ground floor with three beds barely fitting in it. After we ate our snacks and the children took their baths and crawled into their beds, I went to the hallway, asked the receptionist for a telephone directory, and called the principal of the boarding school.

"Good evening, Mrs. Hovanessian," he said cheerfully. "Where on earth are you?" I said I was in Rye.

"How did you get there, and when did you get to London? Our driver has been waiting for you at the airport parking lot. How could you miss him? The car had a large yellow placard carrying the school's name. I had given a detailed explanation about it in my last letter." He kept talking, without giving me a chance to answer. Finally, I told him that I hadn't received his letter nor had I seen the school car, but had gone through a hell of a time getting to Rye. He said he was sorry for all the trouble. Still, I had to pay the amount of ten pounds for transportation. He said he would send the car next morning to pick us up and drive us to the school, but he would *not charge* me for that.

I made a second call to Armen, who was delighted to hear my voice. He and his fiancée, Stella, had also been in the airport and somehow had missed us. They promised to visit us the following Saturday if I would still be in Rye. I said I would let them know as soon as I made my plans.

Back in the room I found the children asleep. I filled the tub with hot water and lay in it, soaking and relaxing as I thought about our incredible journey of that day. Later in bed, I wasn't able to sleep. It wasn't just the fatigue but a kind of depressing disappointment that had began to set in, especially since that phone conversation with the principal of the school. How inconsiderate of him to claim those ten pounds over the phone. Couldn't he wait until the next morning when we would meet? And why did he charge that much? With that amount of money I could stay at the Cinque Ports Hotel for a whole week.

Sometimes there are moments in life when you find yourself defeated, frustrated and angry as a result of a mishap, an argument, or simply an injustice done to you. Yet you can't do anything about it, but forget and make peace with yourself. That was exactly what I did. I tried to look at the bright side of the whole experience. After all, I had met different people along the way and had learned certain things about human nature. What was more, I had taken my children to a peaceful town – a unique place that was not in my itinerary – but I would enjoy and remember it for the rest of my life.

The next morning, I woke up with the golden rays of sun on my face. I looked at my watch. It was 6:30 a.m. We had slept for ten hours. At that time the children woke up and Aram started to nag about going to boarding school. "Can't we stay here for only a couple of days then go back to

London?" he implored. "I don't want to go to school again." I convinced him that four weeks was nothing compared to nine months of school, which would pass before he knew it. Hoori didn't complain. She accepted the fact and looked forward to a new experience. It was I who worried for her. After all, she was six years old and it was the first time she would be away from home, and what was more worrisome, they both knew very little English.

The school car arrived after we had breakfast at the cafeteria. I took the children's suitcase and climbed into the car. We drove through a countryside paradise, with thatched rustic cottages covered with climbing red roses. It was a breath-taking scene, the like of which I hadn't seen anywhere else.

At the school, the children were delighted to meet two Persian brothers about their ages. They had just arrived from London. Their young mother looked like a hippy. She was wearing a long, printed floppy dress. She was barefoot, and had long unkempt hair. That Persian woman hadn't lost much time in adapting to the fashion trends of the hippies. That was the fashion I later saw among the British youth in London, a dress style that the older generation found decadent. But what puzzled me most was that I couldn't tell the difference between male and female. They all looked alike with their long hair, flat chests, and unisex garments.

After the children settled in their room, I met the principal, Mr. Moor. He assured me they would be well-cared for, and asked me one more time for the ten pounds which I reluctantly paid in cash, and he thanked me with a broad smile. Then after telling the children that I would visit them every afternoon for the rest of the week, I took the bus to Rye. I had made up my mind to stay there until the next Sunday.

Back in Rye, I didn't go to the hotel, but walked the 13th century narrow and steep cobble-stoned Mermaid and Lion streets, with their timber-framed Georgian houses, family-owned teahouses, candy stores, Boots (drugstore), bed-and-breakfast inns, a branch of W.H. Smith (a stationary/bookstore chain in England) and the 15th century Mermaid Inn. I entered a Norman style parish church, whose massive tower had a 16th century clock with two golden cherubs striking the hours. The church was empty but a sign indicated that a mass would be held in the early evening, which I decided to attend. After leaving the children behind, I felt depressed and needed some spiritual support.

I entered a candy store and asked a saleswoman if there were any other worthwhile places to see. "Of course," she said and pointed to an 18th century house across the street where Henry James, the American philosopher-author, had been living and writing during the final years of his life. She told me about other writers' and artists' houses which I later visited.

Those visits set a trend for me to look for other writers' and artists' houses wherever I traveled in the future. Among them, I have seen Earnest Hemingway's house in Key-West, Florida; Robert Frost's in Sugar Hill, Vermont; Frieda Kahlo's in Mexico City and Diego Rivera's in picturesque Juan Juato, Mexico, all of which have filled me with insights about the characters of those writers and artists.

Being a curious person, I read and learned from a tourist handbook much about Sussex and its history. I found out that every town, village and beach had a tale to tell. Some of those quiet resort coastlines had been very active, sending fleets of warships to Europe during WWII. From among them, the most important was the D-Day-invasion-fleet carrying thousands of Allied troops, brought together for intensive training before embarking on the warships for Normandy. However, after the war, those beaches had been cleared of land mines and war equipment, and had gone back to their peaceful role of holiday resorts.

I spent the rest of the week in that charming town, taking the bus to the nearby picturesque and quaint town of Winchelsea which I learned had almost become submerged in a vicious storm in 1287, but later had got back much of its land. It was rebuilt and became an important port and a military stronghold, defending its coasts from the Spanish and French invaders. On my way to Brighton, I got off at Burwash to find Kipling's home. Those places were so ancient and quiet that you thought time had stood still. In Brighton, I found its beach swarming with people, swimming in the sea or basking in the sunshine.

In the British Isles, where the sky is mostly overcast with frequent rainfall, sunshine means a great deal to its inhabitants. Having lived in that country for a couple of years as a student, vacationer, and a temporary resident, I have seen how the Britons can make the most of the sun whenever it shines in the sky. I remember one day in a hotel room in summer time hearing hurried footsteps in the hallway. When I came out, I saw men and women running toward the stairs. Panicked myself, I stopped one woman and asked what was going on. She looked at me and said with a surprised tone, "Don't you see? It's a sunny day."

Armen and Stella arrived from London late in the morning on the next Saturday. After almost a year, I was happy to see my brother, with whom I had so much to talk about. After having coffee and cheesecake at a pastry shop in Lion street, we took the bus to Bexhill to pick up the children and spend the day together.

Bexhill is a popular resort and unlike its neighboring sleepy towns is an active, modern one, with wide promenades and shops running along its crowded sandy beaches, where we all went for a leisurely walk and window shopping. All along the walk, Hoori complained of a loose front tooth that had been bothering her for a while. I touched the tooth and finding it ready to fall, twisted and forcefully pulled it out. I hadn't extracted a tooth before, but at that moment I used my common sense and did what was expected of me. Although it hurt a little, she was happy that the ordeal was over and she wouldn't have to struggle with it anymore. We didn't have the Tooth Fairy custom in Iran, but in order to distract her from the pain, I took them to a toy shop and bought a small Lego set for her and a toy car for Aram. After they played on the beach, we took a bus and rode a few miles inland to the market town of Battle where the battle of Hastings had taken place in 1066. We walked around the town, and had "high tea" at a typical English tea house, where they served us a pot of tea and an assortment of sandwiches, scones and cookies.

At the next table, a British family (a mother, father and their seven children) were waiting for their order to arrive. But as soon as the waitress placed a platter of sandwiches on the table, seven little hands wiped out the platter in a second. Their father called the waitress and asked for more. The woman nodded and disappeared through a door then came back with another full platter. The arms reached out for the sandwiches, and cleared the platter again. Their embarrassed father called the waitress and ordered some more. This time, the young waitress put her hands on her sides, apologized and told him that since it was the end of the day, the tea house was out of food and about to close. I looked at the disappointed faces of the children, then at the leftover sandwiches on our table, and asked the father if they would like to have them. He smiled, nodded and accepted our half-full platter with appreciation.

The sun was setting gorgeously when we took the bus back to Bexhill and returned the children to their school, with the promise of visiting them every Sunday before the end of the month. Back in Rye, Armen and Stella caught the train to London, hoping to see me there the next day.

*****

When I arrived in London the next morning, I took a taxi to the Mount Royal Hotel in Marble Arch where my friend Anoush and I had reserved a room. I was delighted to see her waiting in the lobby. After we checked in and went to our room, we sat down and talked for a long time, giving each other an account of what we had done during the past few weeks.

Anoush, with whom I had been classmates only in the twelfth grade, was a graduate of the Women's College in North Carolina and had completed her education at Columbia University in New York. Although she had majored in physics, she never practiced it in her lifetime. Instead, she worked as a manager at her father's paint factory in Tehran. Despite her charm and popularity, she still hadn't married, but recently was dating a widower, who was a biochemistry professor at the University of Tehran. Anoush and I had so much in common. We both were bookworms and discussed books with each other whenever we had a chance. We also liked to see plays and good movies, so we didn't lose any time in London, the city that had so much to offer. We saw the magnificent performance of the Bolshoi Ballet at the Festival Hall, and the newly staged modern musicals, *Hair, Godspell, Showboat, Oh, Calcutta!* (a musical sculpture), and *Hadrian the Great*. We also saw matinee movies, among them the controversial *The Go Between*, based on a novel by D.H. Lawrence.

After Anoush left for Paris to visit a relative, I moved to the old bed-and-breakfast in Earl's Court where I had lived with my mother in the summer of 1960. The next week, Seboo arrived in London, followed by Vartges and Stella's mother, but other members of the two families hadn't been able to make the trip. As for the children, we brought them to London at the end of the fourth week. Although they hadn't learned much English, they had learned how to live and cope with other children, including some vicious ones who had taunted them and ransacked their belongings.

The wedding ceremony was performed at the Armenian Church near High Street Kensington. Seboo was the best man, and Hoori the sole bridesmaid who held the tail of the bride's dress. As I focused my camera on the couple, I couldn't help admiring them through the view finder. The bride in her white lace dress and a tulle veil over her long hair looked absolutely beautiful. The groom in his dark suit looked handsome and so young. After all, he was twenty-three years old. I wished our mother were alive and could see her youngest son's happiest day.

After the church ceremony, we went to the newly opened Intercontinental Hotel in Earl's Court, where we had a full-course dinner with wine and a wedding cake in its stylishly decorated restaurant. It was a good wedding, but not a typical Armenian one, with the requisite loud music, a big crowd, and dancing until dawn.

The next morning the newly-weds left for Kent, another beautiful part of south-eastern England, for their honeymoon. Two days later, Seboo and I took the children to Devon and Cornwall in the southwest of the British Isles, where we explored the gorgeous landscape and relaxed on its sandy beaches. On a trip to the port of Plymouth we took a look inside a naval ship and a claustrophobic submarine.

In mid-September everybody in the wedding group returned home, with the newly-weds returning to Palo Alto in the United States.

While in London, I bought a mink bolero, the fashion of the day, which I wore at dinner parties in Tehran. Buying a piece of fur without having any knowledge and experience, or an expert friend's advice, was not an easy task. Nonetheless, we did succeed in buying one after visiting several specialty stores, asking questions, studying different kinds of furs, comparing their quality, appearance, consistency and prices. That piece of fur that cost us £150 was a soft, thick mink bolero: a short jacket, the color of a lustrous pearl, which I received in the plane on the flight to Tehran. The reason the store hadn't given it to me was because they didn't charge sales tax to a foreign customer who was going to take the merchandise out of England. So they handed it to me when they made sure that I was leaving the country. That mink bolero turned out to be a good buy because after using it for thirty nine years, it still is as lustrous and pretty as the day I bought it. In London in those days, there were plenty of fur stores and fur sections in the department stores, with a wide selection of coats, stoles, boleros and hats. However, that was not the case when I visited London in 1999. The only fur I saw in a few department stores were fake, tinted ones in bright pink, violet, green and the like. Wearing genuine animal fur was banned. There was a rumor that if a woman dared to wear a fur coat in the street, it would be slashed by the blade of someone who belonged to the "Animal Protection Association."

Chapter 19

London: 1971-72

The summer of 1970 had been so pleasant and educational that we decided to go back to England the next year, enroll the children at a British school, live there for a whole year, and perhaps consider residing there on a permanent basis. So in spring of 1971, we began to downsize our apartment, leaving the minimum basics for Seboo who would need them while staying in Tehran. We had decided that he would accompany us to London, stay for a month, go back, and return for the Christmas Holidays. Now that his engineering company was doing well, with two sugar factories in southern Iran and the dormitories of Shiraz University under construction, he could afford a month's vacation.

We rented a furnished apartment in Ealing Broadway, and as soon as the schools closed in Tehran, we packed four suitcases and flew to London by KLM, staying overnight in a hotel in Amsterdam. The next afternoon, when we boarded the plane for London, Aram realized that his two gold rings were missing. Apparently, he had left them on the washstand near the soap bar in the hotel room. That year, Aram had graduated from elementary school and had received many gifts from our friends and relatives. I wrote a postcard to the hotel's management from the plane and mailed it the moment we arrived at Heathrow Airport, but never got a response.

The first thing we did in London was to enroll the children at different schools: Hoori at Montpellier Elementary in second grade, and Aram at Twyford High School in seventh grade. Everything was going right according to our plans, except that I wasn't happy in the apartment we had rented. The landlady who lived on the first floor was fastidious and demanding. The only kind of heating system that the building had was a couple of coin-operated built-in-the-wall gas heaters, which didn't do an adequate job of heating the rooms, even in the cold of mid-summer that sometimes occurred in London. We didn't have a telephone and were not allowed to use hers, even for emergencies. So Seboo and I went to a real estate agency in the area and asked for a one-or-two-bedroom apartment. They gave us a few addresses in the neighborhood, but the owners were not interested in discussing rental as soon as they found out we had children.

One day, returning from one of those house-hunting excursions, we saw a rental sign on the lawn of a duplex on Crofton Road. We rang the bell, and a middle-aged blond woman opened the door. We asked about the rental, and she took us in and showed us around a one-bedroom furnished apartment in the right wing, with an identical one on the left where she lived with her husband. It was a small but convenient and manageable place and I loved it the moment I saw it. The bedroom had two twin-size beds and a queen-size hide-a-bed in the combined living-dining room. To use the bathroom, we had to pass through the living room and the narrow kitchen which had an outlet to a little back yard. It was within easy reach of the market, the schools and public transportation. What was more, it had central heating.

Outside, we told the woman that we had two children. She looked at us and said apologetically, "Please don't take it personally, but I prefer to rent the place to adults only." Then she pointed to the second floor windows and said, "In fact, a week ago I rented it to four bachelors from New Zealand. They're such nice people." Then noticing our disappointment, she added, "The problem is my husband is an irritable man, who gets easily annoyed by noise."

The woman's approach to the subject of children was the mildest one we had encountered that far. So Seboo didn't lose the opportunity and said quickly, "We understand you very well, ma'am. You have every right not to rent us your place but believe me, our children are well-behaved and will be in school most of the time. However, there's one other thing you should know. They play the piano. *That* might bother your husband." With the mention of piano, a miracle happened. The woman's face that had been serious all along, split into a broad smile and she said wistfully, "You know, my two children used to play the piano, but now that they've grown and gone away, I miss the sound of it very much." The next thing we knew, she called her Sri-Lankan husband, introduced us, and we all agreed on the amount of the deposit and the rent. Later when I thought about that conversation, I realized how a little reasoning, sincerity (and a bit of luck) could go a long way.

When we moved and settled in the apartment, there were two more things to be done: first, to provide a piano for the children; second, to find a teacher. In Tehran the children had been taking piano lessons; Aram since 1968 and Hoori two years later. When we did some research, we found out that buying a used piano would be much cheaper than renting one for twelve months. So we looked at the classified section of the London Times and, after visiting a few homes in the neighborhood, bought an old upright, whose owner delivered it in his pickup truck. We called a piano tuner who turned out to be a blind man, whom I met at Ealing Broadway station and led him to our residence. As for a piano teacher, we found one through Montpellier School.

*****

After Seboo left for Tehran and the children started school, I registered at Chiswick Polytechnic for an English literature course, starting the routine of our year-long stay in London. I loved my female professors, especially the one who taught Shakespeare, with whom I made friends. Sometimes after class we went to a matinee play, like *King Lear* or *The Merchant of Venice*. When I didn't have a class, I took a bus and explored the city and its whereabouts, making sure to be home before the children arrived.

In the evenings, the children did their homework, practiced the piano then watched the BBC programs for children. Later, I watched *Coronation Street* on the ITV channel, a serial drama that dealt with the daily lives of ordinary British people, with its distinctive, addictive theme-tune pulling me to the TV from wherever I was in the house.

On Saturday mornings, I worked with the children on Farsi, Armenian (and Arabic with Aram) to keep them fresh for their next year's classes, in case we returned to Tehran.

On Sunday evenings, we all watched *On the Buses*, a favorite comedy sitcom, starring Reg Varney as Stan Butcher, the driver of the No. 11 double-decker bus, who spent more time drinking tea with his dysfunctional family than driving the bus. Then we watched "*Top of the Pops*," the twenty most popular records on the best-seller list in the United Kingdom.

In early October, I was constantly asked by my British acquaintances, "Don't you miss the celebration of the 2,500[th] anniversary of the Persian Empire?" No, I didn't miss it because I was currently seeing a telecast of the ceremonies that were taking place among the ruins of historic Persepolis, in the presence of foreign kings, queens, princes and princesses, heads of states, and thousands of foreign and Iranian dignitaries. There, Mohammad Reza Shah, in an eloquent speech associated his monarchy with the past glories of the ancient Persian kings: Cyrus the Great, Darius and Xerxes.

Later, I read in a book by one of Iran's cabinet ministers that on October 12, 1972, at the opening of the celebration of the 2500th anniversary of the Persian Empire in Naghsheh Rostam, near Persepolis, the Shah had stood in front of the tomb of Cyrus the Great and addressed the founder of the Persian Empire, concluding his speech like this: "Cyrus, sleep peacefully. We are awake and vigilant in guarding your majestic eternal legacy…" Then after the speech, a magnificent wreath was laid at the foot of the tomb, followed by a 101 gun-salute and a spectacular sound-and-light show. Cyrus the Great was an exemplary ruler in history, who after conquering a country gave freedom to its people and respected their identity, culture and religion, and whose human rights decree is preserved in the British Museum.

After the formal ceremony, the guests were treated to a sumptuous dinner prepared by French caterers who had been flown in from Paris. Some of the delicacies included caviar, quail's eggs and peacock, stuffed with *pate de foie gras* (goose liver). The ceremony that was telecast worldwide was heard and seen by millions of people around the globe.

In London in those days, I constantly saw various cynical remarks about that historic event in the British papers. One of them was a caricature of Princess Ann who had attended the ceremony with her father, Prince Philip. She had a sandwich in her hand and, showing it to her mother, Queen Elizabeth II, was saying, "Mother, I have brought you a peacock sandwich from Persia!" Then I heard some jokes made by Iranians about the Shah's address to Cyrus: One day the prime minister of the time, Amir-Abbas Hoveyda, paid a tribute to the tomb and repeated the Shah's address: "Cyrus, sleep peacefully. We are awake…" Cyrus then lifted his head and retorted, "You, for one, can shut your mouth!"

*****

I felt happy in our apartment except for certain nights when my sleep was disturbed by the high-volume of music played by the second floor tenants. Once I complained to the landlady and found out that she and her husband too were frustrated by the unruly behavior of the four bachelors from New Zealand who liked to drink, sing and play the music aloud. Not that I didn't like to hear the sentimental, romantic song of *Precious Moments*, or the Beatle's *Yesterday, Michelle* and their other songs, but I could do without the screaming vocals and the thunder of bass and drum that took on momentum at four in the morning. Not knowing how to solve the problem, I went to the nearby Boots (drugstore) and asked if they had anything to help cut down the loud noises. The white-haired pharmacist smiled and asked, "Noisy neighbors, huh?" Then he gave me a small plastic box, on the cover of which was written: Sleep better naturally by reducing harmful noises. I looked inside and saw six pairs of pink wax ear-plugs covered with fuzzy cotton wool. I thanked the man, paid for it and left, hoping that they would do the trick.

Believe it or not, those tiny soft ear plugs worked magic for me. Not only did they help me sleep throughout the noisy London nights, they also helped me cut down the noise level in planes, noisy hotels, at wedding parties, and stays in hospitals. As for the fun-loving bachelors, one day when nobody was at home, they sneaked out of their apartment without paying their pending rents *and* the money they owed to the milkman who used to leave two bottles of milk in front of their door.

Before going to England, Aram could speak a little English, thanks to the classes he had taken in Tehran, but Hoori knew very little. However, by the Christmas holidays, when her father came back to London she was so fluent in the language that she insisted on speaking English with him. She even spoke English in her dreams. In late December of that year, we celebrated Hoori's eighth birthday by ourselves, a low-key event, unlike her birthday parties in Tehran with the children of our relatives and friends. Here in London, she still didn't have any close friends to invite.

Aram developed a high fever, sore throat and a severe cough the day before Christmas. We thought it was a simple cold and treated him with aspirin, cough medicine and home remedies, and decided if necessary to call a doctor at the end of the three-day holidays. On Christmas Day an Armenian couple visited us with gifts for the children. When they found out that Aram had a fever, they advised us to call the area's family physician. When I phoned the office and didn't get an answer, I left a message with the answering service. Half an hour later, a young physician knocked at our door. He asked a few questions, examined Aram, and said, "It's the bug," which we later learned was the flu virus. "It's an epidemic and is all over the town. It's a serious disease and many patients have died of it." He gave us samples of medication for twenty-four hours until we could go to central London, to one of the few pharmacies open for emergencies. We offered him tea, but he refused, saying that he was in a hurry to see other patients.

Early the next morning, Seboo left home to buy the prescribed medication and brought it home in the evening, just when the samples were finished. During the holidays, most of the trains had modified their schedules. Aram recovered from that dangerous flu, thanks to our guests, whom I called and thanked for their timely advice. They were the same couple that had rented my parents a room when mother was undergoing treatment for cancer. They belonged to the third generation of Armenians in England whose ancestors had fled from New Julfa to India during the Afghan invasion of Persia, then had moved to England.

After the holidays, Seboo left for Tehran, planning to return in April.

Chapter 20

Spain, Italy and Greece

On their way from the United States to Tehran in March, Armen and Stella stopped in London for two weeks, spending a wonderful time with us, going to plays, musical shows and concerts. Armen had graduated from Stanford University with a master's degree in electrical engineering, followed by a higher degree, called an engineering degree. He was heading to Tehran with hopes and plans of finding a job and starting a family. Soon after they left, my friend Anoush arrived from Tehran and stayed with us for a week. All the time that she was there she tried to talk me into returning to Tehran, counting all the blessings and privileges that we had back there: a good job, a comfortable house, caring relatives, a close friendly circle and an active social life – important elements that she had noticed we were missing in London.

Before going to England, Seboo and I had discussed the possibility of a permanent sojourn there. We had decided that after living there for one year, if everything went according to our plans, we would liquidate our possessions in Tehran, buy a house in London and settle there. However, after doing some research and gathering some experience, we realized that being a non-British subject, Seboo's chances of finding a job in his field of engineering were minimal. It was also next to impossible for the children to be accepted at a prestigious university, especially in the field of medicine, in which Aram was much interested. In those days priority was given to British subjects, citizens of the United Kingdom and the Commonwealth. If a few spots remained for other nationalities, they naturally took in the top ones – for which I doubted if our children would have a chance. So Anoush's suggestion about returning to Tehran made sense, and I decided to discuss the matter with Seboo on his return.

After Anoush's departure, we had a schedule for a field trip to Stratford-on-Avon, Shakespeare's birth place, arranged by Chiswick Polytechnic for the students of our class and their family members. On the morning of the field trip, we woke up to pelting rain, which made me wonder whether we should forego the trip. But one glance at my excited children who were up and getting ready for the adventure was enough to make me put my hesitation aside and get ready myself. After all, there was always the umbrella to protect us while walking to the underground station.

When we got to the gates of the college where we were supposed to board a bus, to our surprise we found it already filled. The downpour hadn't been a problem for anyone. Fortunately, a friend of mine had thoughtfully saved us seats. As the bus started to move, my friend nudged my arm to take a look at the next seat. I turned my head and saw a young girl in a bizarre outfit. Being the hippy era, I was not much surprised at her choice of style; a pitch black pantyhose, a fringed mini lavender skirt and a dark green turtleneck sweater. But when my friend made a funny remark about the girl, the girl turned and stared at us for a second, then asked in Armenian, "Are you Armenian by any chance?" I nodded, blushing, but soon realized that she wouldn't have understood the remarks. The Armenian she spoke was Western, the dialect of the people who came from Turkish Armenia or the Middle East; whereas the one we spoke was Eastern, the dialect spoken in Iran and Soviet Armenia. We introduced ourselves and soon made friends with her. She was from Khartoum in Sudan, whose ancestors had fled to that African country after the Genocide of 1915, then relocated to England and became British subjects. She lived in London with her family and was a student at Chiswick Polytechnic. We found her a charming girl and invited her to join us throughout the excursion.

When we arrived in Stratford, the rain had stopped and the bright sun was shining in the sky making every flower, plant and tree glisten with color. As we got off the bus, our guide gathered the students in a group and leading us toward Shakespeare's house, explained that Stratford-on-Avon was positioned at a spot where an ancient Roman road ended. A borough of Warwickshire and a market town for centuries, Stratford had become a major tourist center because of its special association with Shakespeare's birthplace.

Shakespeare was born in 1564 in a half-timbered house in Henley Street. He attended the local grammar school, and at eighteen, married a girl named Anne Hathaway. By 1592 he had reached the apex of his career as an actor and playwright, living in London with fame and prosperity as a member of London's Lord Chamberlain Theater Company. In 1597 he returned from London to his home town, where he died in 1616 and was buried in the parish church of Holy Trinity. The house was pulled down in 1759, but the house next to it, called Nash's House, was later used as a museum, housing Shakespearean mementos.

After making our way through the front yard of the museum, with its shrubs of mauve, blue and white rhododendrons, and seeing the well-kept personal and historic items inside, our guide took us to a set of much newer buildings. The buildings near the Avon River, known as the Shakespeare

Center, housed a library, art gallery (opened in 1881) and the Royal Shakespeare Theater (opened in 1932), where his plays were produced annually, from March to October during a festival. That evening, they were presenting *A Midsummer Night's Dream*, which unfortunately, we were not scheduled to attend. So after having a late lunch on the terrace of a quaint restaurant, we went to a gift shop to buy some souvenirs. The shop was crowded with a group of Japanese tourists busy buying some imitations of Shakespearean relics. As soon as they left, the salesgirl, who was putting our purchases in a bag, whispered to us, "You know, I didn't have the heart to tell them that the plaster busts of Shakespeare they just bought were made in Japan!"

The visit to charming Stratford-on-Avon and Shakespeare's house, with the Japanese- made souvenirs, information and photos that I had taken was another addition to my list of the houses of artists-and-writers, which I had started to collect on my trip to England in 1970.

On our way back to London, our bus made a brief stop at the church of Blaydon for a visit to Winston Churchill's grave. Among his family graves, we started looking for a stately tombstone in the churchyard, maybe with a mini monument, or a marble bust with an elaborate epitaph suitable for a person of his rank. Instead, we found a modest gravestone which was only inscribed: "Winston Churchill, born November 30, 1874, died January 24, 1965."

We were all amazed at the simplicity of the gravestone that didn't carry any prominent inscription to epitomize that great statesman who had been the prime minister of the United Kingdom from 1940 to 1945 and from 1951 to 1955, and had led Britain from near defeat to victory during WWII, and at whose funeral the entire world had paid tribute. But we were told that it had been Churchill's own wish to have an ordinary tombstone like an ordinary person.

*****

Spain

When Seboo returned to London during the Easter vacation with plans to stay until September, the four of us took a two-week tour of Barcelona, a surface trip that we started at Victoria Station. We traveled by train to Dover, where we boarded a ship crossing the English Channel and sailed to Calais in France. It took us two more train trips to get to our destination: one to Paris and one to Barcelona. In the latter train we slept on berths and arrived in Barcelona at noon the next day, on Good Friday.

We stayed at Hotel Paris, a bed-and-breakfast, run by a Catalonian family. It was located on a narrow street, off the lively Las Ramblas, a broad pedestrian-only promenade, flanked by two narrow traffic lanes. We were urged to go out and see the Good Friday procession that afternoon. Outside in the streets, we saw a large crowd of Spaniards who were observing and commemorating the event by walking and carrying the crucifix of Jesus Christ, the image of Virgin Mary surrounded by white flowers and related paraphernalia. It was a scene whose re-enactment we would witness years later in Patzcuaro, Mexico.

Walking in the nearby street, we passed the windows of a few pastry and confectioner's shops where we saw pastries, chocolates and candies, specifically created and designed for Easter. I remember a huge castle made of chocolate and colorful Easter eggs made of marzipan. Among them I saw something similar to the Armenian traditional *nazook* – a sweet round pastry like a loaf of thick bread – which my mother used to bake for the occasion, with the difference that they had put a couple of whole eggs on top of the dough that had cooked and cracked in the oven.

On Easter morning, we took a tour of the thousand-year-old Benedictine Monastery that was the sanctuary of Our Lady of Monserrat. There, high in the mountains, after waiting in a long line of worshipers, we kissed the hand of the Black Virgin, a statue carved in black stone, dating back to the 12th or 13th century. In the basilica we listened to the hymn of Monserrat and other ecclesiastical songs sung by the Esconalia Boys' Choir, a choir that was founded in the 13th century. Then we visited the monastery's art gallery where we saw art works by Italian and Spanish artists such as Caravaggio and El Greco, with modern ones like Picasso and Miro. On our way back, we stopped at one of the best wineries in Catalonia, where we were offered samples of a variety of wines. We bought two bottles of the kind we had liked. In those days the price of alcoholic drinks in Spain was almost equal to the price of water. I don't remember the price of wine, but I do remember the price of a large bottle of whisky that we bought for one English pound.

Late that afternoon, back in Barcelona, we danced in the town-square to a live band, together with the locals. We Armenians are fun loving people. Give us some lively, rhythmic music, and we will jump to our feet in an instant.

We took local tours of the city and its environs during the day and explored every corner of that lovely city. We saw the Santa Maria, one of Christopher Columbus' three ships anchored in the harbor, not far from our hotel. It was empty, except for some thick heavy ropes that were coiled in a corner and smelled of decaying wood. Thirty years later when my daughter's family visited Barcelona, the ship wasn't there any more. I remember hearing that it had caught fire and burnt.

One of the notable places we visited in Barcelona was Mont-Juic, the Jewish Mountain, or the Hill of the Jews, which we climbed using a funicular, a cable railway. We found beautiful gardens on top of the hill overlooking the Mediterranean, with well-tended flowers, where people were roaming and enjoying the fresh air and quiet. In the past, markets and a Jewish cemetery had existed there, and some of its gravestones were preserved in its museum. In its soccer stadium, the soccer-loving Spaniards gathered to watch the games and encourage their champions.

We also visited the Picasso museum in Barcelona where we saw his early Blue Period paintings, some of them done at the age of nine. Among his works, I noticed a few small souvenir albums belonging to his classmates, in which he had drawn an image, written a few words of wisdom, and signed. I remembered that I too had a souvenir album in elementary school which I gave to my friends to draw and write in it.

Most nights we stayed in the hotel, and while the children slept, we sat with the owner's family in the hallway and got involved in their discussions. The father was a French-educated Spaniard with conservative political views. He was in the habit of starting in English, then switching to French when he got excited. I understood French and liked to listen to his genuine, refined accent, but Seboo politely reminded him to switch back to English. In contrast, his son and daughter who were university students had more liberal political views. They opposed him and bitterly criticized the despotic policies of their leader, General Franco. When we showed surprise at the low prices of alcoholic beverages in their country, the son laughed and said, "Franco has made the purchase of alcohol easy, so that people can drink and drown their frustrations in it!"

*****

Italy

When you live in Europe, it is very easy and inexpensive to travel to other countries on the continent. So we tried to make the most of the opportunity while we lived in England. Those were the peaceful days of the pre-hijacking, pre-terrorism era when the mere thought of them didn't steal the joy out of our trips, but allowed us to savor them with peace of mind. So in May, Seboo and I took a one-week tour of Italy, leaving the children with my sister-in-law's sister who was studying in London. We were delighted when she made the offer, saying that it would be a change for her to spend a week with our children, away from the strict discipline of the boarding house where she was living at the time.

From London we flew to Milan, boarded a bus at the airport and drove to Florence, Venice and Rome, staying in each city for one or two days and traveling to the nearby towns of Pisa, Siena and their nearby villages. During the day we explored ancient and contemporary art and architecture, enjoyed the delicious Italian cuisine, and in the evenings listened to the best vocalists at the opera, or attended pop or classical concerts. On the whole we indulged ourselves in that lively country and its rich culture, regretting that we had to leave when the time came.

Our fellow-travelers were mostly British, Irish and Scottish citizens, some of whom we had made friends with during the trip. One morning in St. Marcus Squaree, in Venice, it started to rain so hard that in a few minutes our shoes were filled with water and we were soaked from head to toe. I turned to the woman next to me and said, "I haven't seen this kind of rain in my life." She laughed and replied, "Then you should come to Scotland!" When we returned to England and set foot on the ground at Gatwick Airport, one of our fellow travelers, a huge Scotsman, a highlander, perhaps, sighed noisily with relief and exclaimed, "At last, back to the center of civilization!"

*****

One gorgeous Saturday in early June, one of my high school friends and a colleague at Point IV, Vivian, who had married a Scot and lived outside London, invited us to her house to spend the day with her family. Since Seboo and Aram wanted to watch a soccer game on TV, they declined the invitation, and only Hoori and I made the one-hour train trip to Burnham. There, we took a taxi to their lush green residential area, not far from the the "village," in the center of which stood a mossy medieval church. Having read in the news that the body of England's former king, Edward VIII, the Duke of Windsor, had been flown from Paris to Windsor Castle for the British people to pay their last tributes, Vivian and I decided to go there. We didn't want to miss that historic event at any cost. So Duncan, Vivian's husband, drove us to the adjacent town of Windsor, then took Hoori and their two daughters to the nearby park to play.

When we arrived at the gates of the castle, an enormous crowd of people were waiting in line to enter it. They had gathered there to see the coffin of their former king, who had reigned over their country from January 20 to December 10, 1936, but had abdicated the throne when the British royal court and parliament had disapproved of his choice in marriage to Mrs. Wallis Warfield, an American divorcee. The couple had married in France and lived there for thirty-five years, without being allowed to visit the British Isles in their lifetime.

Once inside the huge hall of the castle, following a slow-moving line of sniffling mourners, we circled around a table which held a modest coffin, adorned with a wreath of white orchids and roses sent by his wife from Paris. It was ironic that during his exile, the Duke of Windsor had not been allowed to set foot on the soil of his beloved homeland, whereas his seventy-eight-year-old body had been welcomed and honored by the state, his fellow Britons, tourists and foreigners like me. They all were showing him respect for his gallantry, will power, and huge sacrifice in giving up the pompous British throne for a woman he loved.

*****

Seated in our living room one day in late June, Seboo and I discussed the advantages and disadvantages of our stay in England, and with all things considered, came to the conclusion that we would return to Iran at the end of summer, despite the fact that the British Home Office had given us a year's renewable visa which would automatically become permanent at the end of four years. In the meantime, we made a long-term plan of waiting until Aram's graduation from high school in Tehran then consider moving to the United States for the children's higher education. So in early September 1972, we gathered our belongings that had multiplied in one year, said goodbye to England and left for Tehran, with a one-week stop in Athens, Greece.

As I was packing our suitcases the evening before our flight, I noticed a plastic bag of dirty laundry in the wardrobe. I grabbed it immediately and hurried to the nearby Laundromat. I knew that it was open until midnight, but when I got there, I found it empty. I pushed the coin in the slot, filled the machine with hot water, put the clothes inside, and sat on a chair with a magazine. At that time in England, "Decimal" currency had replaced pounds, shillings and pence, but those machines still worked with the old coins.

When the machine stopped and I took the clothes out to throw in the dryer, I heard the sound of a tiny metallic object falling inside the washing machine. When I peered down, I saw a ring and took it out. The metal was a piece of thick solid gold that glittered under the ceiling lamp. For a second I was confused. What was I going to do with it? The attendant was not there, nor was anybody else to discuss the matter with. Then, I thought: this is your lucky day, actually Aram's happy day. Maybe this is a replacement for his two gold rings that he left in the hotel in Amsterdam one year ago. Take it home and surprise him.

*****

Greece

On the plane to Athens, we met a Greek-Armenian who lived in Canada and was on his way to visit his parents, survivors of the 1915 Genocide. He gave us useful information about the city and told us where to put our extra luggage for storage and gave us the name of a hotel that was affordable and centrally located.

The hotel overlooked a square, which was transformed into an out-door restaurant in the evenings, and where tables were set and people dined and danced to a live band, with the children playing around them. We spent most of our evenings in that square.

Instead of taking any sight-seeing tours, we made a list of a few historic landmarks, hired a taxi and went there on our own. One of those ancient places we explored was the Acropolis, the higher city, which rose in bright colors above the olive groves and rooftops of the houses. There, we saw the majestic Doric temple of the Parthenon, famous for its numerous sculptures (some of which I had seen in London's British Museum). It was known especially for the ivory-and-gold statue of Athena Parthenon which is said to have survived until the second century A.D. At the Acropolis Museum we saw the marble relief of Nike, the goddess of victory, fastening her sandal at the temple of Athena Nike.

We took a taxi to the docks on the last morning in Athens and boarded a small boat bound for one of the Greek islands in the Mediterranean. After an hour of sailing on the calm blue waters, enjoying a view of the white houses along the way, we arrived on the shores of the island. Not knowing where to go, we approached the first of the waiting taxis, climbed in, and asked the driver in English to take us to the most popular beach on the island. The middle-aged bearded man stared at us blankly. It was apparent that he hadn't understood a word of what we had said. In Athens, the people we had met had spoken English. I tried French then Farsi. Seboo tried Turkish, but the expression on the driver's face didn't change. Frustrated, we started speaking in Armenian. Then something amazing happened. The driver threw up his arms and exclaimed in Armenian, "Why didn't you tell me you are Armenian! Greek is the only other language I can speak. Now, tell me where do you want me to take you?" And when he knew that we were tourists and wanted to spend a leisurely day on the beach, he said, "I will take you to the best spot on the island, where you can swim and eat the most delicious Greek food."

He talked about himself and his parents, who had been driven from their homeland in Van, victims of the 1915 Genocide that had annihilated 1.5 million Armenians in Western Armenia, scattering what was left of them all over the globe. He was another example of those refugees, whom I had met throughout my life, both at home and abroad.

We enjoyed our day on the beach, swimming in the warm waters of the Mediterranean Sea, sunbathing on its soft sands, and having a hearty Greek lunch at a restaurant. However, in the evening on our way back to Athens, we all were silent, submerged in our thoughts. I guess each one of us was thinking about our flight to Tehran the next day and what was awaiting us after a year of absence.

Chapter 21

Home, Sweet Home

In the early morning of our arrival in Tehran, I was awakened by the sweet voice of a street vendor who was praising his wares: "I have fresh loaves of bread for your breakfast. O people of Allah, come and take away these *Barbari* breads that are just out of the oven!" The voice was familiar. It belonged to a villager in shabby clothes, who pushed his creaky cart every morning, singing invitingly, his eyes closed, his hand pressed on his right ear, savoring the quality of his voice that rang in the morning air. Still dazed with sleep and jet lag, I listened to him with nostalgia and satisfaction and my heart swelled with joy as I remembered that I was at home, lying in my own bed, in my home town. That song and another one that followed, sung by a fruit vendor, made me realize how much I had missed those little human touches that had spiced the routine of my life and with which I had grown up. I suppose when you live in one place for a long time, you take everything for granted until you stay away from them for a while.

Having arrived late the night before, Seboo and the kids were still asleep, but once awake, I was too excited to go back to sleep. So I got up, dressed, went to the kitchen, filled the kettle with water and put it on the stove. I opened the door to the balcony and stepped out. I breathed a lungful of the crisp air, looked at the bluish Alborz mountain range in the north, and thought to myself: this is home, our sweet home – with all its advantages and disadvantages.

It was strange. No matter how much I enjoyed traveling abroad, seeing interesting places, learning things and having fun, returning home to our family and friends, to the familiar sights and sounds, and even smells was a pleasure that I wouldn't change for the world. That one year in England, however, was a period of time that would become a turning point, a milestone in our family's life, the fond memories of which we would cherish for ever. Later, England became a foothold, a base for us where we would sometimes spend part of our summer vacations, benefit from its cultural life, and travel to other countries on the continent of Europe.

But now, back at home, we had to deal with a lot of work, starting with the children's registration at different schools, cleaning and painting the house, buying new appliances and furniture to replace the old ones that we had sold before leaving Iran.

We enrolled Hoori at the same Armenian elementary school she had left at the end of the first grade. But we had difficulty in getting Aram into Alborz High School, which accepted students in the seventh grade only. Since Seboo had graduated from the same school and had even taught a few mathematical subjects in its classes, he decided to talk with the principal personally. At a meeting in his office, Dr. Mojtahedee agreed to admit the son of his old student in the ninth grade, on one condition that he attend eighth grade elsewhere. So we enrolled Aram at the Armenian Koushesh High School for that academic year.

In 1940, when the legendary Dr. Jordan, the founder and the principal of the American College retired and left Iran after forty-two years, the government bought the premises from its American owners and renamed it Alborz High School. The school had three principals between 1940 and 1944 before Dr. Mojtahedee took over. The new principal who had obtained his doctorate degree in mathematical sciences from the University of Sorbonne was also a skillful administrator. During his thirty plus years of tenure – known by some as the Golden Age of Alborz – he had turned the school into a top tier institution. Its students passed the national final exams and were accepted at universities by scoring high at the entrance exams (concourse). And what was more important, the school's high standards were well recognized by major universities worldwide.

When in London, Hoori had sent a birthday card to her teacher, Mrs. Kate Mead, followed a few months later by a Christmas card. In return, in late December, Hoori received a beautiful musical card from Mrs. Mead on her ninth birthday. I wrote her a thank-you letter, giving an account of our lives in Tehran, to which Hoori added a few lines. Thus, a regular correspondence was established between Kate Mead and me. She was originally from Australia and had a British husband but no children. Even now, over thirty years later, with them living in Hong Kong, and us in California, we have kept our ties by sending each other Christmas cards every year and keeping each other posted about our family lives. When my novel was published in 2003, she bought one copy for herself and a few copies for her friends and the library of Hong Kong University, where she and her husband, Graham, were teaching.

The winter of 1972 passed uneventfully. Aram took a bus to his school, and Hoori's school minibus picked her up at 7:30 a.m. and brought her back home at 4:30 p.m. Aram struggled throughout his heavy curriculum, while Hoori became a member of her school's boy-and-girl-scout organization. They both went on with their piano lessons and took part in the piano recital given by the Armenian piano-teachers' best students. In their spare time, however, they relaxed with American children's programs shown on Iranian TV, which ranged from *The Flintstones, Gentle Bear, Flipper* and *Get Smart* to *Bonanza* and *Gunsmoke*. In the meantime, I volunteered at Hoori's school PTA and took French courses at the Franco-Persian Institute, polishing up the language I had previously taken at Tehran University. I watched *Dr. Kildare, the Fugitive* and *Peyton Place* in the evenings, all of them dubbed into Farsi. The last two dramas were so popular in Tehran that the cultural societies avoided scheduling events on the nights they were screened.

*****

Seboo had organized a surprise birthday party for me in March. Since I hadn't made any plans for that evening, he told me he had reserved a table at a newly-opened Greek restaurant for us to spend a romantic night together. He suggested that I go to the hairdresser, and chose for me one of the dresses that I had purchased in London to wear.

The restaurant was almost empty when we walked in. A formally-dressed waiter approached us and wanted to show us to a table, but when Seboo whispered something in his ear, the waiter nodded and told us to follow him. Suddenly, I saw a long table in the dim light of the hall, around which many of our friends were seated. When I saw them smiling and greeting us, I was truly surprised. I didn't have the faintest clue about the arrangement. How Seboo had managed to keep it secret from me was quite a wonder. I usually don't like surprise parties, neither thrown for me, nor for others, but this one was very special. To spend a pleasant evening with my friends with whom I had so much in common was a dream, and I thanked Seboo for his thoughtfulness.

Among those friends was a violinist, who later became the conductor and music director of the Reno Chamber Orchestra. Another was a director who directed classical and contemporary plays both in English and Farsi at the Iran-American Cultural Center and the City Theater. He had collaborated in London with the famous British director Peter Brook, and had participated at the annual Art Festival in Shiraz. Among the group were two pianists, one of whom was a teacher at the Tehran School of Music, who gave our children piano lessons. There was also an electrical engineer who was also a talented caricaturist, who later had an exhibition at an art gallery in Los Angeles. And of course, there was Anoush, who had helped Seboo organize the party.

With that group we gathered once a month at the home of one of us to have dinner, discuss art, music, plays, movies, literature – and yes, politics.

That evening, we had the most delicious Greek dinner with the best Iranian wine of those days, *Chateau Sardasht,* followed by a birthday cake. We talked, joked and danced the Armenian and Greek circle dances to the music of a live band. My birthday celebration turned out to be one of my life's unforgettable events.

In the summer of that year, we spent most of our time in our villa near the Caspian Sea, inviting relatives or friends to stay with us to swim in the sea, bask in the sunshine on the warm sandy beach, and to eat beluga caviar and barbecued sturgeon fish, fresh and plentiful from the sea.

In the fall of the same year, we learned that the renowned pianist Albert Ferber had accepted an invitation to perform at Tehran University. While in London, we had been introduced to him by our children's piano teacher, who had invited the pianist as a judge to a student recital. Mr. Ferber was a handsome, middle-aged Swiss who traveled around the world performing at concerts. We were so thrilled with his trip to Tehran that we notified and urged our friends and relatives to attend the event. That night, he played some pieces from Beethoven, Schubert, Chopin and Debussy to a full house. At the end of the concert we went backstage and introduced ourselves. He was astonished, delighted and relieved to have found acquaintances in that unfamiliar surrounding. We invited him to dinner, together with some of our friends, and had a great time with him playing some popular pieces on the piano. Then one night, he invited us to a dinner party at the Swiss embassy. After he left, we regularly exchanged Christmas cards, even after we settled in the United States.

*****

Right after the schools closed in Tehran in mid-June 1974, the children and I flew to London again to spend the summer vacation, with the prospect of Seboo joining us in mid-July. Our itinerary this time was Tehran-London-Cairo-Tehran. We had planned to spend a week in Cairo on our way back to Tehran. As for our residence in London, through our regular correspondence with Mrs. Mead, we had agreed to rent their house for the months of July and August, as they were planning on going to Canada.

Since Montpellier, Hoori's old school wouldn't close until the end of June, I agreed with Mrs. Mead's suggestion that Hoori stay with her family to attend the school, to brush up her English, and be with her old classmates. As for Aram and me, we stayed at a bed-and-breakfast hotel in Holland Park, making arrangements for Hoori to join us on the weekends. The small hotel that belonged to an Iranian friend was a two-story terraced house with a railed flight of stairs in front, the like of which I see on PBS's British sitcom, *As Time Goes By,* with Judi Dench and Geoffrey Palmer.

Aram attended an English language class during the week, while I either shopped, went to the library or to a matinee play. On Saturdays we went to a movie or an amusement park. On Sundays we attended the Armenian Church, where we met a few friends who either were visitors from Tehran or just lived in London. We sometimes went for lunch with them at a close-by Persian restaurant which served rice and kebab to its customers.

On the first of July, we took a taxi and moved into the Meads' house on Croft Road, Ealing Broadway, in the same neighborhood we had lived two years before. A week later Seboo arrived from Tehran, and we spent an excellent summer vacation together. We bought tickets for concerts at the Festival Hall and Albert Hall, and made short one-day trips to Brighton and other seaside resorts.

Among the short trips that I made in England, a trip to the 2000-year-old city of Bath with my friend, Vivian, has made a deep impression on me. I had chosen that Saturday because there was going to be a soccer game on TV between a British and a German team, and Seboo and Aram wouldn't want to miss it for the world. Even Hoori who was a fan of the legendary George Best, Manchester United's striker, the blue-eyed, dark-haired British idol – the David Beckham of yesterday – insisted on staying at home. Aram was so fond of soccer that the previous week he had persuaded us to allow him to attend a soccer game by himself at Wembley Stadium (the site of London's Olympics in 1949), scaring us to death by not returning on time. It turned out that he had taken the bus to the stadium on early Saturday afternoon, but hadn't realized that in the evening, the bus to Ealing Broadway wouldn't stop at the same stop. He had waited and waited before asking someone, who had told him to walk to the next stop half a mile away.

On Saturday morning, I took the train from Ealing Broadway to Burnham, where I met Vivian, and we boarded a train bound for the inland spa town of Bath. After passing several little towns and villages and changing trains at Reading, we got off at our destination and walked to a nearby café, had a cup of coffee, then stopped at a travel agency to buy tickets for a sightseeing tour.

After a week of downcast and rainy days in London, it was a gorgeous sunny day, full of colors in Bath. As the double-decker tour bus passed through the city, we indulged in the beauty of its bright greenery that glistened on both sides of the Avon River, with classical 18th-century red-brick buildings still standing among them. As we visited the steamy indoor hot springs and its huge pool, I was amazed how those mineral springs

In London with Hoori (Summer, 1974).

which had attracted the ancient Romans 2000 years before, motivating them to found a city, had been transformed into such an elegant health resort by the Britons. Many writers, including Jane Austen, had written novels about the resort, depicting late 18th-century life of upscale English society outside London.

After seeing a few old residences-turned-museums, we were driven to Claverton Manor, two miles out of Bath, where we visited the American Museum in Britain, with its fascinating collection of Americana. That collection of objects relating to American history, folklore and geography motivated me to see more of them in the United States.

We shopped at the numerous boutiques and souvenir shops when the tour ended, then entered a coffee shop and had typical English fare: fish and chips with a dash of vinegar, a glass of apple-cider, and ice cream with fresh strawberries for dessert. An hour later, after we paid the bill, I reminded Vivian that we had a long way to go and it was time to leave, but she looked at the bright sun in the blue sky and laughed. "You want to go home this early? The sun won't set until 10:00 p.m. and I'm not tired at all. Are you?" I *was* tired but agreed to spend an additional hour back in the main street. If she was enjoying her time so much why hold her back from it? After all, we might not have a chance to visit Bath again.

After spending another hour buying more souvenirs, we headed for the train station. Since I wasn't familiar with names of the area, I left it to Vivian to take over and lead the way. Trains that stopped at the station, each headed for a different destination, their names showing on an electric board overhead. As soon as the second train arrived, Vivian told me to get in. The train was crowded and we barely found two seats far apart from each other. When it started moving, making several stops along the way, I noticed that none of those names seemed similar to the ones we had passed in the morning. I panicked and looked at Vivian to get her attention, but I found her fast asleep, her head down on her chest. I turned to the woman next to me and asked if she knew if the train was headed for Reading, but she shrugged and stood up to leave. We had reached a station where almost all of the passengers had left, leaving only the two of us in the car. But before I could get to Vivian and shake her awake, the train started to move again. One station later, the train came to its final destination.

We got off and stood on the platform without knowing where we were. We looked around. There was nobody there, except for a station-attendant whom we asked for directions to Reading. He pointed to the other side of the platform to a standing train and said, "Take that train and get off at the first station, then take the train for Reading." To get to the opposite platform, we had to climb a flight of stairs, cross the bridge and climb down another flight of stairs, which we did at a run. But before we could enter the train, the doors closed and we stood there breathless and disappointed. We saw another station attendant and asked him about the next train. He said that the next one would arrive in an hour.

I looked around. There was no one else besides us, and to make matters worse, the man disappeared after a while. Since the weather was turning cold, we went to the waiting room and sat on a bench. All that time, Vivian hadn't said a word, and I was too angry (at her *and* the situation) to initiate a conversation. But as the time of the train's arrival drew nearer and people started to fill the platform, I told her that from that moment on *I* was going to figure out how to get back to Burnham.

When the train arrived, the car which stopped in front of us was a dining-car. Vivian warned me against entering it, because if we did we would be fined. Passengers in the dining car had to pay an extra fee in advance. I didn't pay attention and climbed aboard. I couldn't risk another wrong move and miss the train one more time. I kept walking toward the end of the moving car that led to the next one. I jumped the distance between the two cars and entered the regular car, with a frightened Vivian following me. There, we found some seats and from sheer exhaustion collapsed on them, giving vent to a torrent of laughter, much to the astonishment of a few uptight old British ladies.

We didn't have to wait long in Reading to catch a train to Burnham. It was a busy junction and trains arrived and departed constantly. In Burnham, I said goodbye to Vivian and took another train to Ealing Broadway. That trip to Bath had taken me thirteen hours. However, when I got home and found everything in order, I relaxed. Later when I thought about Bath, I realized what a wonderful day I had spent there, in spite of some frustrations. I also realized how much my friend and I differed in character. Whereas I had been nervous and worried for God knows what (maybe for not getting home on time), Vivian had been relaxed, savoring every moment of her day. And I remembered Eleanor Roosevelt, who said: "Yesterday is history. Tomorrow is mystery. Today is a gift, that's why they call it the present."

That summer in London, we watched on TV President Nixon's impeachment, his resignation over Watergate and his family's departure from Washington, a sad historical event we wouldn't be able to watch on Iranian TV.

Chapter 22

Egypt

At Heathrow Airport, we boarded a plane bound for Cairo in early September 1974. It was just one year after the Arab-Israeli war of 1973. Anwar Sadat was Egypt's president, having succeeded Gamal Abdel Nasser in 1970 shortly after his death. Sadat was known for his participation in the efforts to find a final solution to the problems of the Middle-East. What was more, his strained political relationship with Iran had just started to thaw.

When we arrived and checked in the hotel where we previously had booked a room, a middle-aged Egyptian, a handsome man with steel-gray hair and blue eyes approached us in the lobby, and politely asked if we would like to have a private guide and a driver with his car. He told us his fee, and we hired him.

Returning from breakfast at the nearby Sheraton on the bank of the Nile the next morning, where we would have our lunches or dinners in the days to come, we found the guide and the driver waiting in the lobby. And thus, for one whole week that Egyptian, who had been an official guide with the Ministry of Tourism, and who could speak English and French fluently, showed us places in Cairo that other tourists could hardly visit.

In the Egyptian Museum of Cairo, he showed us the incredibly magnificent remainders and treasures of an ancient civilization. Among them was the golden mask of the 14th century B.C. Egyptian king, Tutankhamen, whose intact tomb had been discovered in 1922. We saw rows and rows of hand-carved sarcophagi, funerary objects, and yes, mummies, some of them five thousand years old. What amazed us most were the wheat seeds, preserved so well in the tombs of the pharaohs that if they were planted, they would sprout and produce fresh grain.

In the days that followed, the guide took us from one historic ruin to another. We saw Memphis and the colossal statues of some pharaohs and the enigmatic mighty sphinx, *Abolhol* – as known to the Arab world – a figure in Egyptian mythology, having the body of a lion and the head of a man, with its weather-beaten, mutilated face, believed to belong to the pharaoh, Chephren.

We saw the stepped pyramid of Saqqara and the three pyramids of Giza which were considered funerary edifices, built with the purpose of bringing the Egyptian rulers closer to heaven. Unfortunately, I don't have a pleasant memory about a visit inside a pyramid, which we entered through a small entrance, climbing a steep, narrow staircase toward a flat surface and a king's tomb. Once there, I suddenly panicked and headed back down, pushing aside those who were climbing up. I categorically refused to continue the ascent to a higher level where a queen's tomb was situated. Being a claustrophobic, I couldn't stand small spaces and low ceilings closing in on me. Sometimes when I think of dying and being placed six-feet under the earth, I thank God that my body will be free of its senses.

One night, the guide took us to the legendary show of Light and Sound at the site of the pyramids and sphinx. As we passed the streets to our destination, we noticed throngs of people walking on the lighted pavements, with some sitting in the cafés, drinking, eating or smoking. We saw a colorful, vibrant life bubbling in the elegant gardens and restaurants along the banks of the Nile, with people enjoying the cool of the night after having shielded themselves indoors against the intense heat of the day.

When we arrived at the site of the show, it had just started. We saw a huge crowd of tourists seated on rows and rows of chairs watching and listening to the mysterious voice of a man telling the timeless tale of the sphinx and pyramids, with mellow music in the background, as projectors cast their powerful lights on them.

We sailed on the Nile on the little *feluccas* (boats) through the heart of Cairo where we saw a blend of Eastern and Western architecture along the river banks. We visited the Al-Azhar mosque and the 1000-year-old university. While we walked in the streets, we were amazed at the well-arranged urban traffic of Meidan-al-Tahrir, with its congested junction of bus-stops, tramways and trolley-buses. There, poor people in rags were trying to squeeze into a crowded bus, sometimes hanging from its open windows, traveling between the air and the ground. We visited the Khan-al-Khalili oriental bazaar and bought leather goods, souvenirs, and the extract of their symbolic flower, the lotus, to later dilute with alcohol and use as a perfume. I also bought two cotton tablecloths; one dark green with exquisite yellow embroidery, and one peach, with fringed borders. After paying for the merchandise, we were graciously treated to cold lemonade.

On our way to the hotel, walking under the scorching sun, we stopped at an open market and bought three kilos (seven pounds) of their best mangos. They were so cheap that we couldn't turn a blind eye to them. In Tehran, tropical fruit was rare and expensive, so, if we could find one single mango in a grocery store, it would be wrapped in golden paper and placed on the top shelf. In our hotel room, we rolled up our sleeves and began peeling, cutting and eating the succulent fruit, with its abundant juice running down our arms and elbows. We didn't finish them all, but ate enough to run a high fever in the evening. We actually never found out the reason for the fever that afflicted all four of us. Was it the mango that hadn't agreed with our systems? Was it heat exhaustion? Or was it the combination of both? Whatever the reason, we had to get well. The next day, we were scheduled to visit Alexandria, the city my father had fallen in love with on his way to America in 1926.

That night we had difficulty sleeping, not only because of the fever, but also because of a wedding party that was going on in the courtyard down below, with a belly dancer entertaining the noisy guests.

Fortunately, in the morning, Seboo and I didn't have fever, but Aram and Hoori still had some low grade fever. We just didn't know what to do: go to Alexandria or not? The final decision was mine, and it was not an easy one to make. I felt like I was caught between a rock and a hard place. On the one hand, I felt tired and wished to go back to sleep; on the other hand, I didn't want to miss the chance of visiting Alexandria, a city that had inspired my father, and had become my obsession to see. Only God knew if we would be able to make another trip to Egypt. After some discussion, we decided to go, especially when we saw the children's excitement. We thought that if it came to the worst, the guide would know better where to take us. So I prepared a handbag with all the necessary items, took my camera and went downstairs to the lobby where the guide, the driver and his daughter were waiting for us.

The car which had taken us around for the past few days was an old Dodge with ample seating and no seat-belts to limit our space. The four of us sat in the back, with the guide, the driver and his eight-year-old daughter in front. The guide had asked us, with embarrassment, the day before if we would allow the driver to bring his daughter along. She hadn't been to Alexandria before and was eager to see it. Since there was enough room in the car we didn't object to his request and let the girl have the day of her life. Before entering the Cairo-Alexandria expressway, we stopped at a roadside café and, after having a simple breakfast of tea, bread and cheese, started our journey to the northwest of Cairo, to the Mediterranean Sea and the western edge of the Nile Delta.

We arrived in Alexandria around noon. *Eskandarieh* – as it is known to the Arab world – Egypt's second largest port city, with a population of two million. It has been the country's capital from its founding by Alexander the Great between 332 B.C. and A.D. 642 until the Arab conquest. In its long-past glorious days, the Pearl of the Mediterranean has witnessed many historic events, such as the coronation of Mark Anthony as the Emperor of Rome, in the presence of Egypt's Queen Cleopatra. During the 1952

Egyptian Revolution, the city had bidden farewell to the deposed King Farouk, as his yacht had steamed out of the harbor. Now Alexandria was a popular seaside resort because of its temperate weather, mild water temperature and soft, sugar-white sands that stretched along the Mediterranean Sea for many miles.

The driver took us straight to the magnificent Muntazah palace on the coast, at the end of Al-Jaysh Street, which served as a museum and was open to the public. Before starting our exploration inside, we went to a huge terrace in front of the building where we were fascinated by what we saw in the distance. A narrow strip of land, running from the terrace through the calm blue sea, connected the palace with a lush green islet about a quarter of a mile away. Inside the palace, we visited Princess Fawzieh's rooms. She was King Farouk's sister and the first wife of Iran's Mohammad-Reza Shah, whose wedding parade I had seen from our balcony when I was a child. There, we saw her toys, dresses, furniture and crib, with a chamber pot underneath it. We also saw the well-kept personal items of the members of the deposed royal family and numerous valuable gifts that Reza-Shah the Great had presented to King Farouk when the Egyptian princess had become his daughter-in-law. I would have liked to take pictures of those rooms, but the security guard at the entrance hadn't allowed me to take my camera inside the palace. He had taken it from me in exchange for a token. Later, when I got the camera back and tried to take pictures, its shutter didn't click. Mysteriously, something had gone wrong with its mechanism. But I didn't mind and bought a few ready-made slides from the gift shop.

Once out of the palace, we decided to go to the beach. When Hoori saw the blue sea, the white sands and the colorful umbrellas all along the shore line, she begged us to let her go into the water. When I touched her forehead I found out with relief that she didn't have a fever and nor did Aram. They changed into their swimsuits (which I had secretly taken along in case they were able to swim) in a cabin and ran into the water, with the driver's daughter following them. They didn't know each other's language, but they did know how to swim together.

We sat in the nearby café with bottles of cold lemonade as the guide filled us in with interesting information about the city. He told us about the Pharos, the great lighthouse of Alexandria and one of the seven wonders of the ancient world, which had been built in 280 B.C. and had lasted until the 12th century serving as a model for other lighthouses around the globe. He told us about the destruction of its great library of 500,000 volumes, burnt in A.D. 391 during a civil war, and about the days when Alexandria was famous for its multinational population, when it was a cultural, intellectual and economic metropolis.

After a lunch of rice and kebab at a restaurant in town, the guide took us to the library of the University of Alexandria, which housed 1,200,000 volumes. He also took us to the Greco-Roman museum, where we saw a rich collection of antiquities. This was followed by a visit to the Roman catacombs in the old part of the city. We saw another Meidan-al-Tahrir, a square that carried the same name as the one in Cairo, but with a very different plan. We passed by the residence of Princess Fawzieh who lived there peacefully, even after the revolution of 1952 and the expulsion of her brother, King Farouk.

Before leaving the town in late afternoon, we made a short trip to the harbor at my request. As we arrived there and the guide began to give us information about the port's history and its important role in the country's economy, my mind drifted away. As I looked at the setting sun and the silhouettes of the anchored ships, I thought about my father and wondered what it would be like if he woke up from his 38-year-slumber, like Rip Van Winkle, and saw me, a grown woman, standing in the same harbor from where he had sailed to New York in January 1926. I remembered a photograph of him standing on the deck of a ship with a few of his fellow-travelers, next to a coil of thick ropes.

At the beginning of our trip to Egypt, we had planned to go to Luxor, Karnak, and the Valley of the Kings and the Queens, but at that point, we all were so tired and exhausted by the intense heat that we decided against it and left Cairo two days later. The guide and the driver volunteered to take us to the airport where they got emotional when we bid them farewell. At the airport, a stern security guard, who was checking my handbag, changed her negative attitude after she found out I was from Iran. She asked me to give her greetings to Tehran where she had once spent a lovely vacation with Iranian friends.

Back in Tehran, I wrote a favorable article in the English-language paper *Keyhan International* about Egypt and the Egyptian people, which ended like this: "Perhaps this is a suitable occasion to express our thanks and gratitude for the warm and friendly attitude of those Egyptians we came in contact with, whom we found so close to us emotionally, and yet so remote geographically."

Chapter 23

Trip to Paris and Guests from Bangkok

As we returned to the routine of our lives back in Tehran, Seboo and his partners sold their construction company and he found employment with a prominent engineering firm.

In late January 1975, the company he worked for was sending him to Paris for a ten-day assignment. Since it was close to our eighteenth wedding anniversary, he suggested that I go with him. Like every mother, I first hesitated with the question of what to do with the children, but then remembering my mother's advice of not giving up a good opportunity, started thinking about it and came up with the idea of asking Mrs. Ojik for help. Mrs. Ojik was my sister-in-law's mother and had always been kind and considerate toward me, especially after my mother's death. She had told me to count on her whenever I needed her help, mainly in taking care of the children. So, I asked her and she gladly agreed to move in with them during our absence.

We stayed at a hotel in the heart of Paris. While Seboo went to work during the day, I took the metro and went around town, saw places and shopped. In the evenings, after dinner, we went to a musical show, a night-club, a concert or the opera.

We celebrated our wedding anniversary with our friend, George, at La Boheme, a "characteristic" restaurant (as he liked to define) in Montmartre, a quarter that is considered the mecca for French and foreign artists. George and I ordered raw oysters on crushed ice with buttered brown bread, and Seboo ordered steak-and-fries from the menu, accompanied by a large basket of raw vegetables: lettuce, cucumber, tomato, avocado, artichoke, asparagus, endive, and mushrooms, with a variety of dressings (without mayonnaise), a kind of do-it-yourself salad. Then a tray arrived with an assortment of cheeses: peppered Boursin, Chevre, Brie and Camambert.

We had just finished our meal when we heard an Armenian conversation from the next table. Two young men in old-fashioned suits were speaking Eastern Armenian, like us, but with the distinctive accent of Soviet Armenia. Seboo attracted their attention with a joke, then introduced us and invited them over to our table. The couple who seemed surprised to meet Armenians in Monmartre, smiled at us, then one of them pulled out a round watch from his breast pocket, checked it and apologized, saying that as much as they wanted to join us, they couldn't, because they were expected at the hotel within an hour. Right then, the waiter brought us a cake with lighted candles, accompanied by a middle-aged man with an accordion, who began playing and singing, "Happy anniversary." The two men exchanged glances, hesitated, whispered to each other then nodded their acceptance of the invitation, but on one condition that they would leave in half an hour. Seboo ordered five cups of espresso with a bottle of their best cognac, and told the guests that we were going to celebrate the occasion together.

Meeting Armenians from the Soviet Union in those days was an exceptional event. To us they were like an endangered species. Once you met them, you didn't want to let them go. You wanted to know about their situation under the Soviet regime, about their families, or if they knew any of your relatives there. They were artists from Yerevan who had been sent by their government to Paris for a short period of time to get acquainted with old and contemporary French art. Their hours were restricted and they were always under the supervision of a secret police agent, with no right to stay out after a certain hour. But they did stay with us long after their curfew hour. They drank the whole bottle of cognac, filling and raising their goblets in honor of our anniversary every time.

When they got tipsy, they told us what it was like to live under the Soviet regime (with its advantages and disadvantages) then told us anecdotes about their government, laughed with us, and sang popular old French and Russian songs played on the accordion. They didn't check their watches even once. After we separated at 2:00 a.m., we never knew what happened to them. Were they punished for disobeying the Soviet rules, or were they able to get away with it? Our paths never crossed again. As for George, we only saw him again in Los Angeles the following year when he was visiting some of his relatives. A few years later, we heard that he had died of a massive heart attack.

*****

In the summer of 1975, Seboo's stepbrother, Bobby, who worked for the United Nations in Bangkok, Thailand, came to Tehran with his American wife, Bonnie, to spend their two-week annual vacation with our family. We were all excited, especially the children. Since we didn't have an extra room for overnight guests, we had prepared the children's bedroom for them, while putting folding beds in our bedroom for the children.

The four of us drove to Mehrabad Airport to meet and bring them home on the night they were supposed to arrive. We got there a little early and waited in the hall. The plane from Bangkok arrived on time and the passengers filed out into the hall after going through the customs, but Bobby and Bonnie were not among them. We asked the airport authorities for the list of the passengers, and strangely enough, we found their names on the list. We asked if there would be another flight from Bangkok, and they said not that night. Frustrated and disappointed, we returned home and went to bed. It was 1:00 a.m.

Early the next morning, our door bell rang. I woke up and looked at the bedside clock. It showed 5:00 a.m. I answered the door through the intercom. In response, I heard Bobby's cheerful voice who chirped, "Open the door. We're late, but finally here." I pressed the button and got dressed as they climbed the three flights of stairs and entered the apartment. At that point everybody was up and dressed. After hugging and kissing, Seboo put their suitcases in their room, and I invited them to the dining room for breakfast. As they drank the hot coffee and relaxed, they told us that they had missed the plane and had to wait at the airport for a few hours. The reason they hadn't made it to the airport on time had been the chaos of heavy traffic in town, caused by an influx of Vietnamese refugees in Bangkok.

They gave us some information about the fall of Vietnam in April of that year, with details about those historic moments. They told us how the tanks of the North Vietnamese army had rolled into Saigon, smashing through the gates of the presidential palace, and how, in a heroic airlift, hundreds of American helicopters had evacuated about 6000 Americans and 50,000 South Vietnamese, with thousands more fighting their way to the American embassy complex, scrambling and clinging to the last helicopter that was waiting on its rooftop. Most of the Vietnamese who were left behind had headed toward the neighboring country of Thailand, filling the capital and their refugee camps in thousands. Bobby and Bonnie were worried about a few American and Vietnamese friends they had in Saigon. Had they been air-lifted by a U.S. rescue helicopter, or had they been trapped within the anarchy that had followed after the invasion? They talked and talked, pouring out their anger and frustration until they were exhausted and wanted to go to bed. It was 7:00 a.m. We thought they would sleep for a few hours, but they slept until 5:00 p.m., leaving us in a limbo, not knowing whether to take a nap or wait for them. After all, the night before we hadn't slept for more than four hours. By the time they woke up, took shower and came for dinner, it was 9:00 p.m.

Those two weeks passed quickly. They met our relatives and friends, and we met their American friends who worked in Tehran for various organizations. We loaded our Volvo one early morning and drove to our villa on the Caspian shore, crossing the asphalt road to the north, passing by the Karaj River and the newly-built Karaj Dam where Seboo had worked for a year. Arriving at the foothills of the Alborz Mountains, we drove through a long lighted tunnel then descended into a green valley, a dense virgin forest, and the cultivated lands of the Caspian shore, with its fragrant citrus orchards and fertile rice paddies, where women were working, bent over the fields.

At our resort home, we had the best time on the soft sands of the beach and in the warm water of the sea. (The Caspian is the world's largest lake, almost an inland sea.) We also spent many hours on our quiet veranda, talking and discussing subjects ranging from their experiences in Southeast Asia to world politics and the future of our families (they didn't have children). We also talked about a more important subject: the future of Iran and the foreign meddling into its politics, the worrying signs of national divisions, the Shah's shaky situation – whose well-kept secret of suffering from cancer had started to leak out of the royal court – and to top them all: the lack of an experienced successor to the throne.

Bonnie and I had so much in common. We both were freelance writers. Whereas she contributed to an English language publication in Bangkok, I did the same in Tehran. Before she had met Bobby, I knew her from the Ford Foundation, where we both worked in adjacent offices at the Plan Organization. Sometimes in the early evenings, the two of us would sit on the deckchairs and indulge ourselves in conversations about literature, creative writing, books and movies, as we would watch the globe of a burning sun sinking below the sea horizon. Talking with her was the highlight of my days, and those little moments enriched my life for a long time to come. I didn't have many friends who shared my particular interests and I missed my college days and its atmosphere.

*****

As a result of our conversations with Bobby and Bonnie and their frightening description of devastated, anarchic Vietnam, Seboo and I put the matter into balance with the questionable situation of the ailing Shah – who despite U.S. support was in a vulnerable position. We knew that the United States didn't want to lose its friendship with Iran, because to lose Iran was to lose the key to the Middle East. The question was how long could it support Iran in a crisis? We had been considering relocation to Canada or America for a long time. So we pushed our hesitations aside and decided to make a trip in January 1976 to the east coast of Canada and the west coast of the United States to do some research toward our goal. We made arrangements with Mrs. Ojik for the children's care, bought tickets for Toronto and Los Angeles, with a one-week stop in London on our way back to Tehran.

In the meantime, we made a three-day trip to the holy city of Mashhad in the province of Khorasan in north-eastern Iran in the fall of 1975, where Seboo and his colleague, Kambiz, had to make a business trip. Kambiz's wife, Shahnaz, also joined us and thoughtfully took an extra chador for me to cover myself with when visiting the Shrine of Imam Reza. I thought if we were going to leave the country, it was the last chance for us to see the most sacred Islamic city in Iran, especially that we had visited a Christian site of pilgrimage: the semi-ruined cathedral of Thadeh, in the province of Azerbaijan, where St. Thaddeus, one of the Christ's twelve apostles, was martyred while spreading the gospel.

We flew to Mashhad and stayed at the Hyatt-Omar Khayyam Hotel, where an international radiology conference was taking place, with delegates from various countries of the world. We enjoyed the hotel's luxurious comfortable rooms, fine French cuisine and danced in the evenings to the Italian band at its night-club.

One day when our husbands were busy with a business meeting, Shahnaz and I walked to the sacred site of *Astane-Ghodse-Razavi*, where the shrine of Imam Reza, the Shiites' most revered and martyred eighth imam was situated. The 9th century site of the shrine is considered a phenomenon of ancient Persian architecture, with its blue and gold domed mosques, minarets and exquisite tile work. The site also houses an Islamic studies center with a huge collection of Korans.

Being an Armenian, I wasn't used to wearing a chador, much less a slippery crepe-de-chine one that Shahnaz had chosen for me. To make matters worse, I had hidden a heavy Zeiss-Ikon camera under the voluminous chador. It was strictly forbidden to take photos of the mosques, either outside or inside. Call me stupid or reckless, but I did surreptitiously shoot pictures precisely of those glittering gold and blue-tiled domes without being caught. Sometimes a picture taken under tremendous pressure turns out to be your best shot – mine was one of them. To prove my point, I was reading an article in the Smithsonian magazine recently about an English photojournalist named Bert Hardy who had shot the fabulous *Operatic Entrance*, a scene of Queen Elizabeth II's entrance to the Paris Opera for a performance of the ballet *Le Chevalier et la Demoiselle*. There were twenty French and only two British journalists allowed to enter the building to take pictures, and Bert Hardy was not one of those two. However, he managed to sneak in and capture that historic moment in twenty separate shots, later connecting them together into a spectacular masterpiece of photography. It was not an easy job, considering the fact that in those days cameras were bulky and heavy.

Once in front of the entrance, we removed our shoes and, giving them to an attendant in exchange for a token, entered the mosque. We walked toward a monument surrounded by intricate bars that enclosed a black-draped casket. A dense crowd of men and chador-clad women were pushing from behind, trying to reach out and touch the bars. Those who had succeeded in grasping a bar were desperately clinging to it as if it was their last hope. They all seemed to have a problem or grief and were expressing them by performing the centuries-old sacred ritual, walking around the shrine of Imam Reza seven times, unleashing their emotions by sobbing and praying with all the devotion they could muster. I was trying to reach out to a bar and whisper my prayers, but it was impossible to get there, even to concentrate, because I had to follow Shahnaz step by step. I couldn't afford to lose her in that crowd. After all, she was the one who was holding the tokens for our shoes. I was also having difficulty keeping the chador over my head with one hand, and the heavy camera with the other. But I learned it the hard way, when someone punched me in the back and hissed, "Cover your hair, woman! Don't profane this sacred place with your impertinence!"

Fortunately, we both were able to pray in our own language in a holy place, where visiting it was the lifelong dream of every Moslem Iranian. At the end, we inched our way out, feeling peaceful and spiritually satisfied. Outside in the huge courtyard and then in the street, life was going on with men and women walking about in regular attire or covered with chadors.

On our way back to the hotel, we entered two different shops; one to buy saffron, the other to buy turquoise, two trademarks of the province of Khorasan. Saffron, the most expensive spice in the world, was cultivated by the Arabs in Spain in 961. It is believed to be a native to the Mediterranean area, Asia Minor, Iran and Kashmir. The golden-red flower is a bulbous perennial of the iris family, with a strong aroma and bitter taste. To produce saffron, stigmas (part of a flower that receives the pollen) are handpicked, spread on trays and dried over charcoal fires. In Iran, we used water-soluble saffron for flavoring rice, chicken and stews, as well as in pastries, desserts and glazes. So we bought lots of saffron (at a much lower price than in Tehran) for ourselves and for souvenirs, especially packaged for the purpose.

We then entered a shop that was selling a variety of turquoises, ranging from loose gemstones to those mounted in gold rings, or on decorative plates inlaid with the light-blue stones of the same size. They say that the best turquoise in the world comes from Neyshabur, a city west of Mashhad.

So we got busy examining and admiring a wide assortment of the turquoises displayed on the counter. I chose two gorgeous sky-blue pieces that I later gave to a jeweler in Tehran who mounted them in two thick gold rings: one for me and one for my daughter, Hoori.

Back at home, when I thought about Mashhad and the contrast of its two life-styles, I couldn't believe in their peaceful co-existence. How was it that the mullahs and fanatic worshippers – who couldn't tolerate a bare-headed woman on the premises of the holy shrine of Imam Reza – could tolerate the existence of a close-by western style hotel, with its foreign and upscale Iranian guests, drinking and dancing until dawn?

Chapter 24

Trip to Canada and America

On January 9, 1976, three days after Armenian Christmas, we started our forty-five-day trip to Canada and the United States, flying straight to Toronto via London. We were headed for Canada in January to see what it would be like to live there in winter.

We found it as we had expected. It had snowed heavily in Toronto. We also found some remnants of Christmas, like decorative wreaths on the doors and flashing lighted trees in the windows. We stayed at a hotel in down town and took sight-seeing tours around the city. We met a couple of friends who were Canadian citizens, got some information about their daily lives, employment opportunities, and the chances of getting acceptance at universities. On a snow-covered highway on a trip to Niagara Falls, we saw the gigantic waterfall, bordered by ice and icicles, with its dormant surroundings buried under the snow. It was also amazing to see dazzling poinsettias behind the glass walls of a huge greenhouse and the contrast of their cream, pink and blood-red colors against the immaculate white of the snow.

After a five-day stay we left Toronto early one morning for Los Angeles. Although it was a sunny day, the town was still covered with snow. When we climbed the stairs into the Air Canada airplane, I had a wool dress on, with a fur coat and boots. Six hours later at Los Angeles Airport and out in the street, I started to perspire and had to remove my coat. The thermometer showed ninety-five degrees. When we got to the Surf-Rider Hotel at the edge of the Pacific Ocean, we saw a huge crowd of people stretched out on the sandy beach or swimming in the water. We later learned that the temperature in Los Angeles that day had been at a record high. We asked ourselves: with this gorgeous weather in Southern California, who wants to live in frozen Toronto?

Later, we met some relatives and friends, among them, Seboo's stepmother and stepbrother, Shahen, his wife Cathy and two children who had been living in Los Angeles since the late 1960s. After visiting Disneyland, Universal Studios, San Diego, La Jolla and the world-famous Hotel Del Coronado, we flew to San Francisco. There we rented a car, visited Berkeley and Stanford and gathered valuable information for our children's future education. Those were the days of the hippies and barefoot students in rags, wandering in and out of the campus, smoking pot. After seeing the city and meeting with friends, we drove to Lake Tahoe, Reno, Carson City and Virginia City.

On our way back to Los Angeles, we passed through Seventeen-Mile-Drive and stopped at Monterey-Bay and Carmel-by-the-Sea. With its white sandy beaches and dark pine trees bending along the shimmering Pacific coastline, Carmel had a kind of timeless charm and unique beauty that I hadn't seen anywhere else. Strolling through its narrow, steep streets, with its elegant boutiques, fine restaurants, classical and contemporary art galleries and captivating seascape, I couldn't imagine that one day, twenty-nine years later, I would be invited by its hundred-year-old Harrison Memorial Library to present my novel on Iran. There, among the distinguished audience, I found some retired scholars and professors from the American University of Beirut, as well as diplomats from Washington D.C., who mostly had served in Iran in the 1960s.

When we visited UCLA in Los Angeles, we somehow found its atmosphere the most pleasant of all. The diverse student body, mostly in blue jeans, looked happy, roaming about the campus under the sunny sky, where we didn't see any sign of bare-foot hippies or drug addicts. As a whole, we found ourselves more inclined toward Southern California than the Bay Area. One thing that was important for us was the Armenian community which we found in Glendale, Pasadena, the San Fernando Valley, and Montebello, with their own Armenian schools, churches and cultural centers, where we attended some of their events.

While in Los Angeles, Seboo's younger brother, Rubik took a one-week vacation and came to see us. The previous year, after getting his master's degree in geophysics from the University of Kansas, he had been hired by the Chevron Oil Company and was living in Houston, Texas. One bright sunny day when he had driven us to see the Beverley Hills and Bel Air residential areas, I fell in love with a unique country-style road, alongside which Chinese magnolias had bloomed luxuriantly in white, pink, mauve and purple. One thing that made an impression on me was the sight of bare sycamores, with their thick white trunks bent to the ground, and their crooked white branches shooting up toward the blue sky like streaks of lightning. As the road turned and twisted toward the top of the hill, I saw a beautiful red-brick house with cream-contoured windows, in front of which we stopped to take some pictures.

On our way back to Tehran, we stayed in London for a few days, and saw *Volpone* at the Olivier Theater. *Volpone* is a 17th century bitterly satirical comedy, written by Ben Johnson, which was performed by the legendary actors, Paul Scofield and John Guilgud. That night, as we were entering the theater, Prince Charles arrived with a ravishing blond young lady, in a wonderful purple vintage automobile, with the royal crest on its door. The purple color reminded me once again of my father's trademark paint that he had formulated for the Shah of Iran. Later when I studied the subject, I found out that the color was associated with monarchy, and in the Roman republic it was used by the royalty as a means of distinction from the common people.

*****

When we returned to Tehran in late February, Seboo and I discussed the cities we had visited. After considering our options and comparing them with one another, we finally chose Los Angeles over Toronto and San Francisco. Toronto with its cold, long winters was out of the question. As for San Francisco, the main reason we wanted to live there was that the company Seboo was working for had headquarters there, and it would be an easy move for him from the Tehran office. But the fact was we preferred to live in Los Angeles to be close to a few of our relatives and friends. What was more, it was the home of UCLA, the university we wished for our children to attend. As for Seboo's job, he could work in San Francisco part time, or he could find another job in Los Angeles. He talked to his boss, and after some deliberation, the company accepted his terms of part time employment in San Francisco. So we started planning our move to the United States.

Actually, our plans were for the following year when Aram would graduate from twelfth grade, but the counselors of a West Los Angeles high school had advised us that the sooner he started his schooling in the United States the better the chances of acceptance he would have at UCLA. As for emigration, one lawyer in Los Angeles had suggested that we apply for residency when we entered the United States. Seboo still had his business visa for re-entering the country, but my visitor's visa would expire the following month. So one morning I walked to the American consulate, a few blocks away from our house and filled out the necessary forms. When the person in charge asked me the reason for the second trip, I said, "My husband and I want to take our children to America to experience the bicentennial celebration." The man was impressed by my reasoning and gave me and the children a new visa, with the time limit of August 31st. That was the last date we could enter the country.

That date set a deadline for us to expedite the liquidation of our properties and possessions. Through a real estate agent, we put our house on the market and began sorting out our belongings, ranging from household items to clothes, books, albums and whatnots. The difficult part was to decide what to take, what to sell and what to give away. The engineering firm Seboo was working for sent him to San Francisco on business for a period of two weeks in June. At the airport, I told him that if he decided to visit Los Angeles, *not* to buy a house there, and definitely *not* a two-story one – with which I didn't have a good experience.

Two weeks later, one early morning when I had just woken up, the phone rang. It was Seboo. I thought he was calling from the airport, but he was calling from Los Angeles. He told me he had made an offer on a two-story house in West Los Angeles and it had been accepted. It was in the same area as his stepmother and stepbrother lived. It was in a peaceful neighborhood, near a park and had good public schools. I got so angry at the news that I wanted to scream, but I didn't until I put down the receiver. I have told this story many times, and have got various reactions to it. But my granddaughter, Teleen, is the one who truly has liked it and laughs from the bottom of her heart every time she asks me to repeat it.

*****

Long before selling the house in Tehran, we sold our household items through an ad that we placed in two English-language newspapers: *Keyhan International* and *Tehran Journal,* mostly with foreign clients in mind.

In those days Iran was at the height of its prosperity economically. Since the OPEC embargo that had quadrupled the price of oil in 1973, the unemployment rate had dropped to almost zero, to the point that Americans, Canadians, Europeans and Asians were arriving in Iran in search of employment. So when we placed the ad in the morning papers, foreign buyers started calling the same day asking for our address.

On the itemized sale list, there were large items, like whole bedroom sets, dining and living room furniture and kitchen appliances; there were also smaller items like dinnerware, crystal, silverware, books, L.P. records, etc. In the meantime, we despatched our Persian carpets, most of our valuable Armenian, Farsi and English books, and some other necessary items through a shipping company whose workers came over one day, packed everything in cardboard boxes and took them away in a truck.

Since Seboo was at work all day long, I was in charge of the business. As I presented the items, talked, haggled and sold them to customers, I learned a great deal about salesmanship and got acquainted with the nature and attitudes of people from different nationalities.

I sold our contemporary custom-made cream-colored wooden bedroom set to a Canadian who had come to Tehran with his family to start a job. I sold our Danish teak dining room and living room furniture to a British man who said, "I have an empty house and I need to fill it." Then there was that young Indian couple who bought our Magic Chef gas-stove, along with some children's bedding and toys. I still remember the pregnant Indian lady, in a blue Sari, and the piece of advice she gave me. When she saw an ivory statuette among the small items displayed on the dining table, she took it in her hands and looking at it with appreciation and nostalgia, said to me, "If I were you, lady, I wouldn't sell this precious item to anybody. This is the four-armed Shiva, one of the principal deities of Hinduism. Take it along on your trip and keep it in your new home in America." I thanked her and did exactly what she had said. Later I remembered that the statuette was a wedding gift sent to me by my grandmother's sister from Calcutta. That statuette of Shiva, exquisitely carved from a piece of ivory has been sitting in my china cabinet since settling in Los Angeles, with other mementos given by our relatives and friends in Tehran.

Among the potential buyers who visited our house, there were also Iranian housewives who were very fond of foreign-made merchandise offered by departing Americans, or Iranians, and didn't care about the prices. Money was no object for a rich Iranian woman if she set her heart on an item, which she would later brag about to her friends.

However, some of those visitors and especially our relatives reacted with surprise and disapproval to our intention of leaving Iran. "Are you crazy?" one of my friends reproached me. "What more do you want from life? You live in a comfortable house. Seboo has a well-paid job. You have an easy life with a full-time maid. You are surrounded by good friends and relatives. You travel all the time to Europe and wherever you wish. Come on! Stop dreaming! Be a little rational!" Then again, one of my mother's friends said to me, "It's a pity that you guys don't have any parents to show you the way. You make plans on impulse and carry them out right away." Maybe she did care for us, but she didn't know that it was not an impulse, it had been in my mind since the time my father had planned to take his family to the United States, a wish that had been cut short by his untimely death. Then Uncle Johnny reminded me of an English proverb, "A rolling stone doesn't gather moss." He was also referring to our one-year stay in England.

Uncle Johnny believed in the omnipotent power of the Persian kingdom and its rich history that spanned more than 2500 years. He tried to convince me that what we were doing was wrong, and by leaving Iran we were turning our faces from our hard-earned blessings. He said, "What are you afraid of, that the king will die? Suppose he does. He has a son who is already eighteen years old and studies in the United States. Besides, there are a number of educated, old-hand politicians around the Shah who have always helped him during this country's crises. Believe me, Elma, nothing is going to happen to Iran. It has survived many political and bloody conflicts in the course of its turbulent history but has always maintained its identity. You're forgetting that the Shah's foreign allies are supporting him since they brought him back to his throne in 1953. They also appreciate him for the widespread reforms that he has implemented through his White Revolution in the underdeveloped villages, with improvements in education, health care and mechanized agriculture."

Then my father Vartges, who was one of the strong pillars of the Armenian community and wasn't much in favor of our plans, said to me, "You know, Elma, you're a sensible woman, and I hope that you are doing the right thing. But remember that we Armenians have a history deeply rooted in this country, with our ancestors buried here and our youngsters looking forward to a bright future. You're leaving behind a wonderful community that has flourished and refined throughout the past centuries, while contributing to this country culturally and financially. You are trading the blessings of the present with a vague future you still don't know much about. Think about it, and don't make hasty decisions that you might regret later!"

I did think about it. They were both telling the truth and were right to be angry with me, because I knew they cared for the welfare of my family. However, the more I thought about it, the more confused and frustrated I became.

On the other hand, there were individuals who not only approved of our decision, but also encouraged us in carrying it out. They were mostly among the younger generation who, on their parents' insistence, had reluctantly returned from abroad after obtaining a university degree, but were planning to go back to Europe or America after saving some money. Among them were a young man and his fiancée, who had just returned from Germany after graduating from a university and was trying to furnish a temporary home with some of our second-hand furniture. The man, who was not very optimistic about the future of Iran, said to me, "Listen, lady, you're doing the right thing by going away. Our country, huge as it seems with its extensive wealth and gushing oil wells doesn't have enough power to stand on its own feet. In an unstable country like this I won't feel secure enough to raise a family. As soon as I save some money, I too am intending to leave."

Another customer, a young American woman who had married an Iranian chemical engineer in San Francisco and had been offered a good position at NIOC in Tehran, complained to me about another issue. She said, "I hate to admit it, but I don't like the snobbish mentality of this community. I have difficulty surviving in the circle of those upper-middle class women who spend enormous amounts of money on their designer clothes, hair styles, jewelry and furs, and throw lavish dinner parties. The most embarrassing part is that if you don't follow their examples, they brand you as a 'miser,' a word they commonly use to humiliate someone who isn't a big spender like them. It seems that these people are spoiled by the excessive wealth that has poured into this country since the increase of oil price in 1973. As my father would say, more cash than sense!" I couldn't have agreed more. That was a large part of the reason we were moving away from Iran.

Then the wife of my eldest uncle, Mary, who had sent two of her sons to Berkeley in the United States, said to me, "You have made the right decision. Since you're going to send your children abroad, you better live close to them. All the years my sons were away, I worried for them and constantly waited for the arrival of their letters. I don't recommend that kind of life for you!"

With all those contradictory opinions and advice, I didn't know what to do. I felt like a tiger, with a boa constrictor coiling around my chest, suffocating me slowly. While my heart pleaded with me to stay, my mind urged me to leave. However, after some serious thinking and consulting, Seboo and I put our hesitation aside and kept working toward our goal. Right or wrong, we were ready to take the risk. Besides, we were not going to burn our bridges after us. We were leaving behind our friends and relatives, with a villa still standing in the Caspian Sea resort. If worse came to worst, we could always come back and jump start our lives one more time. We had the experience, and *yes*, we were still young.

One thing that consoled us was the fact that my brother, Armen, his wife and one-year-old son were also preparing to go to the United States, but under completely different circumstances. The University of Aryamehr (now called, Sharif), where Armen had been teaching computer science since his return from Stanford, was sending him to the University of California in Santa Cruz to work toward his Ph.D. My other brother, Emil, who worked with Seboo at the same engineering firm, had just divorced his wife, and decided to join us later in Los Angeles.

As for selling our house, the real estate agent who had the listing had not brought a single customer during those six months. Every time Seboo called him, he assured him that he was "working" on it. So we started looking for a customer ourselves and found one, and just three days before our departure were able to sell it, do all the transactions and hand it over to the new owners. In Iran, since properties are sold for cash and at the full amount, it becomes the buyer's possession the moment he pays the seller the money at the notary public, where the two parties sign the legal papers.

Now, with our house and belongings sold, I started to realize with sadness that the end of our lives in Iran had arrived and we had to say goodbye to everybody and everything that were so dear to us. A week before our departure, Seboo and I visited the Armenian cemetery, and laid bouquets of gladioli (my mother's favorite) on our parents' graves.

For the final three nights, we stayed with Vartges' family with four packed, swollen suitcases. Then after a short stop in London, we flew to Los Angeles, to a new life and a new future. It was an amazing coincidence. When we arrived in the United States on August 6, 1976, the country was celebrating the bicentennial of its independence, whereas fifty years earlier, when my father had traveled there as a student, the country had been celebrating its 150th anniversary in 1926.

Part IV

The United States

1976-2009

Chapter 25

Los Angeles

The day after we moved into our four-bedroom house on St. Susan Place in Mar Vista, we found a basket of pink roses on our doorstep. It was sent by the Wilsons across the cul-de-sac who later came over personally to welcome us to the neighborhood. They gave us an extra key to their front door to borrow anything we needed while they were away at work. And with that gracious gesture, a wonderful friendship blossomed between us and Dwight and Prudence Wilson which flourished after a trip to Hawaii.

After settling down, one of the first things we did was to enroll Aram at Venice High and Hoori at Daniel Webster Junior High, and to buy a bicycle for each to ride to their schools. We also bought a used Steinway piano and found a teacher through UCLA. Then with the first things done, we visited the immigration lawyer we had seen before, filled in an application for a U.S. residency permit, gave him the required documents and photos, and were told to wait for an invitation to an interview.

A few months later, we were summoned for an interview at the Immigration and Nationalization Office in downtown Los Angeles. The officer who interviewed us individually was impressed by our family, welcomed us to the United States as residents, and complimented us by saying, "I wish all the people who came to this country were educated and refined people like you." He assured us that we would receive our green cards within a few months. However, that was not meant to happen. We waited not for a few months, but for three years, and when we didn't receive them, we filled in new applications and attached new photos to them. At that point, Aram was nearly twenty one and had to apply separately. Then a year later, one day in 1980, we found the long-awaited cards in our mail box. We noticed with amazement that the photos were the ones we had attached to our first application. It meant that our green cards had been ready on time, but nobody had bothered to open our files to see the green cards and send them to us. That negligence had cost us a lot of money and many problems throughout those four years of waiting, including the period of Carter presidency, the takeover of the American embassy in Tehran by the Islamic militia in November 4, 1979, and its negative impact on our pending visa situation.

*****

While we were living in St. Susan Place and looking for a one-story house in the vicinity of UCLA, one rainy morning in May the broker took us to a flooded road to the top of a hill in Bel Air and showed us a well-planned, three-bedroom contemporary house with a manageable back yard, the owners of which were desperate to sell and move to Oregon. We were told that in the disastrous fire of 1961, a substantial part of Bel Air's elegant houses had burnt down, but had been replaced by new ones. As we were leaving and walking toward our car, I noticed on the opposite side the familiar red-brick house, with its cream-contoured windows, in front of which we had taken a few pictures before. I was amazed at this trick of fate and how it had taken us to the same area, to a house close to the one I had liked. Throughout those two years we had seen scores of properties, some of which Seboo was ready to buy, but I had resisted and talked him out of doing so. It seemed that I was destined to find the house of my taste and in my desired area. So we made an offer, and the owners accepted. We moved in after a month and have been living happily in it since July 1978.

The house on St. Susan Place, in which we lived for about two years, turned out to be a good investment. In that cul-de-sac, which was close to a recreational park, we socialized with some of our neighbors whose children befriended Aram and Hoori.

One morning, two gentlemen from the ABC TV channel knocked at our door and asked for our permission to film a pilot sitcom from the house, which was ideal for filming. They paid us a small sum for the "inconvenience," and later, allowed us to visit the studio and watch the process of filming. However, after showing a few episodes on TV, and not getting high enough ratings, they called off the project. Then after moving to Bel Air, we rented the house to three families in succession, before renting it to the Kenyan consulate, whose four families of consuls lived there for sixteen years. We finally sold the property in 2001 after the Kenyan government closed the consulate for lack of funds.

*****

We started our trips to various parts of the United States in the summer of 1977, first by driving to Fresno and Yosemite, up to Reno, Sacramento, San Francisco, Portland and Seattle. In San Francisco, where Seboo worked for two days a week, we stayed at a suite in Holiday Inn for $40 a day. We had already been to the town on our first visit, but this time we had a chance to see more interesting places and travel on its fully-automatic subway, the fantastic BART, the rapid transit system that runs deep under the Bay and functions with a minimum of personnel. The newly built Hyatt Regency Hotel amazed us with its modern architecture, stylish furniture, indoor plants, appropriate illuminations, and delightful glass elevators that zoomed to the highest floors and the rooftop bar and restaurant.

On our way to Oregon, after driving for hours and passing through a dense forest on a two lane road, we finally saw a sign at a small village, called Leggett. Since it was close to midnight and we were out of gas, Seboo decided to stop and fill the tank, and maybe spend the night there if we could find a room at a motel. Up to that point, the motels we had passed by had the sign of "No vacancies." As we approached a one-pump filling station, I saw a few idle men, seated cross-legged on the ground, smoking cigarettes and eyeing us with curiosity. I asked one of them, "Sir, where is downtown Leggett?" He guffawed and pointing to the ground, said, "Ma'am, you're right in the middle of it." I looked around, and all I saw was a post office with a couple of rooms perched on the top. So Seboo drove the car back to the main road, continued for an hour until we arrived at a motel with the promising sign of "Vacancies," where we were welcomed to its rural setting by the proprietor, a friendly middle-aged woman. However, the memory of Leggett has stuck in my mind to this day, even though I have been to other places less friendly than that.

In the fall of 1977, Uncle Johnny and his wife visited Los Angeles. During their one month stay, Uncle Johnny had liked Southern California so much, with its mild weather, natural beauty, and the freeway system, that he even explored the possibility of moving his own family there. He was especially attracted to Hollywood, the center of movie industry. A movie lover, he had made a number of documentary films in Iran and had invented a liquid coating and a special device to cover the film sound track. On his first feature film, *The White Gloves*, the sound was recorded for the first time on the sound track, synchronizing it with the movie scenes. The invention was an unprecedented achievement in Iran in the late 1950s, and is documented in *The Armenians and the Iranian Cinema*, published by the Museum of Iranian Cinema.

The day Seboo and I drove them to LAX to take a flight to Tehran, while waiting for them to board the plane, an elderly woman approached us with a basket of red roses and offered them to Seboo, who paid for one and gave it to Uncle Johnny. (I don't know why he didn't give it to his wife.) That was the last time we saw them.

One year later, in the fall of 1978 when the riots and turmoil of the pre-revolution had reached their apex in Tehran, with fires engulfing buildings and piles of tires burning in the streets, Uncle Johnny, a sensitive man who was suffering from congestive heart failure, had a heart attack and died in a hospital amid the chaos of the approaching revolution, surrounded by the members of his family. He was in his early sixties.

My family kept the news of his death a secret from me, until one day when I received a basket of white roses from a friend, with a sympathy card attached to it. There is no need to say how upset I was to find out about Uncle Johnny's untimely death, a man who with his caring and easy-going nature had always been there when my brother and I needed him. As I looked at those white roses, I remembered the single red rose Seboo had given him at the airport. It was so ironic. It seemed that by giving him the flower, we had paid Uncle Johnny our last tribute.

On November 3, 1979, Seboo and I, with the Wilsons began a two-week trip to Hawaii. First we flew to Hilo on the east of Big Island, rented a car and drove to the Kona Coast on the west, where we stayed for a few days. On our way, we saw the tropical jungle and the lava desert with its rock formations of shiny black lava, covered with an explosion of bright, colorful bougainvilleas. Kona with its ocean front hotel, the bending palm trees, gorgeous sunsets, and abundance of varieties of orchids are things that I remember. We flew to the beach Island of Maui, then to Kauai, the garden of the Hawaiian Islands, with its huge botanical garden and bamboo and fern forests. We stayed at the Sheraton-Kauai Hotel, a collection of numerous bungalows on the shore of the Pacific Ocean which were wiped out by a vicious hurricane some years later. Toward the end of our trip, we flew to Honolulu on the island of Oahu, where we visited Coco Head, with its ragged, cliff-edged sea shore and high surf, and enjoyed the magnificent rainbows. We paid our tribute to Pearl Harbor by taking a boat ride to the Arizona Monument.

Our memorable trip to Hawaii set a firm foundation to our new-found friendship. Dwight with his easy-going nature was a knowledgeable, retired military man, a third cousin of Winston Churchill, who liked to travel and spend time with his friends. Prudence was an accountant who in her younger days had been a model in her home town in the Mid-West.

On the first day of our trip to Kona, something happened back in Iran that made a long-term impact on us and the lives of Iranians in America. On the morning of November 4th (Prudence's birthday), we read in the newspaper that the Iranian Islamic militia had occupied the U.S. embassy in Tehran, taking its American employees hostage. Seboo and I laughed at the news and didn't take it seriously. Knowing the Persians as a gentle, hospitable people, we didn't believe that the takeover would last for long and that the hostages would be released quickly. But that was not the case. The take-over known as the "Hostage Crisis," dragged on for 444 days, until January 1980, the day of Ronald Reagan's presidential inauguration, when it was suddenly announced on TV that all the fifty-two American hostages had been released and sent to the United States.

*****

If I wanted to give an account of our thirty-something years in America, I would have to write another book. Instead, I would like to concentrate on a summary of our family's activities, like education, travel and volunteering. I would also like to give a little information about the lives of my father, our brothers and the Iranians who relocated to Los Angeles after the Islamic Revolution of 1979.

As for our children, Aram, after graduating from Venice High, and Hoori from University High, both attended UCLA, then medical schools, with medical residencies in Chicago and Fresno respectively. Aram, a family physician, works at the Glendale branch of Keiser Permanente Health Center. Hoori, an emergency room physician, works at the Presbyterian Inter-Community Hospital in Whittier. She has published articles in medical journals and authored book chapters in emergency medicine text books.

Seboo and I also continued our education by taking courses at Santa Monica College and UCLA. Seboo later transferred to CSUN (California State University at Northridge), and obtained a master's degree in sociology. I took courses in liberal arts, without having the goal of obtaining a degree. Instead, I started a novel on which I worked at an "advanced creative writing" workshop, which after finishing, took me years to get published. In the meantime, both of us worked as English/Armenian/ Farsi translators for an interpreting agency, especially after the influx of Iranian refugees who poured in Los Angeles after the Islamic Revolution in Iran. With that influx also came some of our friends and relatives, whom we helped to adjust and find their way around the Los Angeles megalopolis.

Having arrived in the New World from an ancient country, with thousands of years of history, I wished to travel and see its modern architecture, sophisticated technology and unique natural beauty. So we fitted our trips in between our college attendance and work schedules.

Although I was fascinated by the fabulous engineering of the California freeway system, with its numerous bridges crisscrossing midway between the earth and sky, carrying hundreds of vehicles at the same time, I dreaded to drive on it. Then once, seated next to Seboo, looking at other drivers on the freeway, I saw a teenager in a convertible speeding in the fast lane, her hair waving in the wind, with music blasting from her radio. I also saw an elderly woman in a Volvo, driving slowly, squinting ahead, as she concentrated on the road. It was then that I asked myself: if a teenager and an elderly lady can drive on a freeway, why can't you? The next day, I entered Freeway 405 South, stayed in the slow lane and drove to the nearby Fox Hills shopping mall. By that first step, not only my fear was gone, but I also found my self-confidence and felt happy and carefree whenever I drove on a freeway. Nonetheless, on long trips, I didn't volunteer to drive, as long as Seboo was happy to do so. And thus, we continued our trips to various U.S. states and cities.

We visited Sedona in northwestern Arizona and saw the magnificent Grand Canyon, with its timeless layers of rocks. We watched their colors changing from orange and russet to pink and cream as the sun and clouds passed overhead.

I have traveled to Tucson several times and stayed with my cousin's family, and once have given a book-talk at the University of Arizona.

In Phoenix, I stayed with my friend, Emma, a classmate at the ballet school. She had immigrated to the United States almost thirty years before, and with whom I had corresponded for the first few years. Her family had just moved from New York and lived in a big house in the suburbs of Phoenix. I found her phone number through a mutual friend and called her. She invited me over to spend a week with her family, which I gladly accepted. She showed me the modern city and its contemporary architecture, then drove me to the contrasting quaint Indian Reservation.

One evening, the couple took me to a concert by the cellist, Yo-Yo Ma at the hall of their historic San Carlos Hotel in downtown Phoenix, and introduced me to him at the end. At that time Emma was serving on the board of the Phoenix Symphony. She has served on the boards of numerous social, cultural and charity societies ever since, and has received many achievement awards and medals of honor from various foundations. More importantly, the couple has donated $1 million to Arizona State University to fund the expansion of international programs at the university's Russian and Eastern European Studies Center which has been renamed The Melikian Center. Emma, a determined young girl, had made her childhood dreams come true in America, and had made it in a big way. I wish my high school friends who criticized her for not having attended a regular school in Tehran knew about her college education, her happy marriage, and her becoming a Phoenix civic leader and philanthropist.

In Bryce Canyon and Zion National Parks in Utah, we were awed by the monumental rock formations shaped like columns, spires and gateways, with various tones of red, orange and peach. Bryce Canyon looked more like a series of amphitheaters than a canyon. The naturally carved walls of Zion Park carried numerous fossils, showing evidence of the life of its prehistoric inhabitants.

We visited the Temple Square in Salt Lake City, Utah, the world capital of the Church of Jesus Christ of Latter Day Saints, with its Mormon Temple, the Seagull Monument and the Tabernacle with its perfect acoustics, where the sound of a pin dropping on the floor could be heard. Later that year, I watched the Christmas performance of the Tabernacle choir on TV, and enjoyed a few Armenian ecclesiastical songs among them.

We admired the wonderful geysers in Yellowstone Park in Wyoming, especially the famous Old Faithful which periodically sent a column of hot water and steam into the crispy air.

Seboo and I spent a leisurely time with our musician friend, Vahe Khochaian in Reno, Nevada, who conducted the Reno Chamber Orchestra at that time. We saw the Hara's automobile museum and a newly-built modern library, with glass walls, indoor plants and an attractive children's section.

We flew to Houston, Texas in December 1978, where Seboo's brother, Rubik worked for Standard Oil Company. He took us to the Johnson Space Center, from where the flights of the space shuttles are controlled. He also took us to the shores of Gulf of Mexico, in Galveston, and on a forty-mile-long bridge over Lake Pancho Train. On our way to Louisiana, we crossed numerous swamps over the Passage Superiors. In historic New Orleans, we walked in the cobble-stoned, narrow streets of the French Quarter, fringed by old French style lamp posts, gift shops and cafés, at one of which we ate the finest raw oysters. Then we took a tour of the Mississippi River on a steamer, called the President.

In the summer of 1982, Seboo, Hoori and I drove to Denver, the city, Rubik had been transferred to. We drove along the Colorado River on desolate roads with no sign of apparent life, except for rabbits. Driving on one of those roads for hours, bored and anxious about running out of gas, we suddenly noticed a single-pump gas station on the edge of the road, and happily asked the man in charge to fill the tank. Since it was quite late and the dark was setting in, Seboo asked him if there was a motel in the area. The man shook his head and pointed to a cottage behind the station, close to a pasture where a few sheep were grazing. He said he had a room with a bath and could rent it to us. Having no other choice, we stayed the night and had dinner that the man's wife brought for us.

The next morning when we wanted to get into our car, we were stunned by what we saw in front of us. Our gold-color Chrysler, including its windows, had turned completely black. When the man saw our astonishment, he laughed and said, "Don't freak out. Your car is covered by large black flies. There are plenty of them because of the cattle. All you have to do is drive the car." Still, it was not an easy task to approach the car and open the door, which would instantly be filled with flies. Nonetheless, Seboo got in, opened all the windows, drove it around the area, and when he got rid of them, returned to pick us up. What was more frustrating, however, was that after driving a couple of miles, we came across a motel and a diner. Somehow, the experience reminded me of Leggett and its unfriendly people.

During an excursion to the Cave of the Wings near the outskirts of Denver, the guide turned off his flashlight; it was so dark in the cave that I thought I had gone blind. But amazingly, a baby who was in its mother's arms didn't make a single sound during the entire blackout.

In Newport, Rhode Island, in the summer of 1981 we saw the most magnificent old mansions with modern living facilities, one of which had been used as a setting for the movie, *The Great Gatsby*.

In New York, Boston and Washington, D.C. which we have visited several times, spending our time with friends, we have seen their numerous museums and art galleries, and have attended concerts and plays.

In 1985, during the presidency of Mikhail Gorbachev, Seboo and I made a three-week trip to the Soviet Union. The board of trustees of the University of Lavern, California, of which Seboo was a member, was invited by the Soviet Armenian Government to visit the country. We traveled to Moscow, Yerevan and Leningrad, with an overnight stop at Helsinki.

We attended a fantastic performance of *Ivan the Terrible* at the Bolshoi Theater in Moscow. In Leningrad, the Hermitage Museum fascinated us with its grandeur.

We saw a spectacular production of *Anoush* opera in Yerevan. Most important of all, I met Aunt Mary's three adult children whom I hadn't seen for forty eight years. Unfortunately, Aunt Mary, her husband and their eldest daughter were no longer alive, but we spent some time with the rest of my cousins and their families. We learned that during WWII they had had a difficult life, with shortages of housing, food, clothing and other basic necessities. Their family of six had lived in a two-room apartment, waiting for their entire life for a governmental housing complex to be constructed. By the time their new apartment was ready, the children had grown and gone, and their ailing, old parents had died shortly after moving in.

However, the couple had been lucky that their elder son hadn't been recruited and sent to the war because of having maintained his Iranian nationality. But those of his friends who had gone to the front had never returned.

During Aram's medical residency at Cook County Hospital in Chicago in the late 1980s, I visited him a few times. Chicago with its old and contemporary architecture, concerts and art exhibits became my favorite city in the United States. On a visit to the Art Institute of Chicago, I saw a landmark exhibition of a collection of works by French Impressionists, including Monet, Pissarro, Renoir and Degas, which were brought in from the museums of all over the world.

One memorable pastime I had in Chicago was to watch a new daytime show on TV, the *Oprah Winfrey Show*. From the first program, I was attracted to the strong personality of that young lady and her natural ability of handling a new kind of show that dealt with a group of women and their family problems. I was sure that she was going to succeed in her career, which she did – and she did it in a big way. Throughout the years, she improved so much that she was called by some pundits the "Queen of daytime television." Then one morning many years later, walking in our neighborhood on Stone Canyon, I saw Oprah walking with two bodyguards, and joined them in walking and talking. That was the day after the Academy Awards ceremony, for which she had flown to Los Angeles and was staying at the nearby Bel Air Hotel.

Once, Aram and I drove along Lake Michigan to Detroit, where in the late twenties, my father had spent a few years of his life. At the Henry Ford museum, I saw something that I hadn't seen anywhere else before – the last breaths of Henry Ford and Thomas Edison, preserved in tiny glass containers.

In 1987 we stayed with my cousin's family in Fort Lauderdale, Florida. One of our friends who lived in Boca Raton drove us south to Key West on a scary strip of two-lane highway across the Gulf of Mexico, at the end of which we saw a sign that read, "Ninety miles to Cuba." We visited Earnest Hemingway's home where he had written *The Old Man and the Sea*, a 1951 novella that I had translated for an Armenian monthly magazine back in Tehran in my post-college years.

Seboo and I traveled to Costa del Sol in Spain in 1989, where his stepbrother, Bobby, had a villa. He had lost his wife, Bonnie, a few months before and had brought her ashes along to spread at a chosen spot. After seeing the small towns of Costa del Sol, we took a tour of Seville and Cordoba, where we admired the intricate Moorish architecture. At the top

At Arshile Gorky's gravesite in Connecticut, with the
novelist Jack Karapetian and his wife (1989).

of the Rock of Gibraltar we saw the Barbary apes, a symbol of the "British
presence" and a huge lighted cave that served as a restaurant. The sight of
the Strait of Gibraltar in the distance reminded me of my father's trip to
America and the ship that had carried him, passing from the Mediterranean
Sea to the Atlantic Ocean.

From Costa del Sol we flew to Nice in France where we stayed with
Anoush and her husband, Alex. They had relocated to France after the
Islamic Revolution of Iran in 1979. They drove us along the French Riviera
to the coastal towns of Cannes, Juan Les Pins, San Paul de Vance (with its
narrow alleys filled with art galleries), San Rafael and Monte Carlo.
Spending a few days with the couple was one of the highlights of our trip.

As you might have noticed, during most of our trips, we have stayed with
a friend's or a relative's family, whose company not only has been a pleasure,
but has also kept our friendship alive. In return, we have enjoyed hosting
them at our home whenever they have visited Los Angeles.

On our way back home, we had to visit yet another friend in the United
States. After flying to New York and spending a few days with Bobby, we
drove to Connecticut to Jack Karapetian's residence. Jack was a well-known
Armenian novelist who lived with his wife in a rural area near Washington
Depot. Their yellowish-brown teak wood cottage built in the middle of a

seventeen-acre area of forest and pasture was an ideal setting for a writer. Once, walking on the country road, Jack asked me if I would write a review of a newly published novel for the *Armenian Review*, which I gladly agreed to do.

At our request, the couple drove us to Sherman to pay tribute to the grave of Arshile Gorky, the renowned Armenian-American abstract expressionist painter who had died early in life. I had studied his art at the art history class and had seen his paintings in the Museum of Modern Art in New York. He was buried in a churchyard, but his grave was so overgrown with moss and weeds that we had to remove them to read his name on it. I don't cry easily, but I cried that afternoon. It was so sad to see the grave of an artist of his high caliber, who had contributed so much to the world of art, with his paintings selling for millions of dollars, being so much forgotten and abandoned.

In early March of every year, between 1990-1994, when our daughter, Hoori, was doing her residency in emergency medicine in Fresno, we would drive along the "blossom trail," a long country road that would take us through miles and miles of orchards, with blooming peach, almond, nectarine and pistachio trees in white and pink. One of the slides that I had taken of a pistachio orchard was once selected and shown on TV by Channel 5 at the end of its nightly news.

In early October 1995, in Vermont and New Hampshire, we were fascinated by their famous fall foliage and the incredibly beautiful assortments of colors, spectacles of nature, that I have preserved in pictures. One of those pictures has been shown at the Underground Exhibit of the Getty Center and mentioned about in the View Section of the Los Angeles Times.

*****

While studying at Santa Monica College we made two trips to Mexico, arranged by the Art History class, with the theme of "Art and Architecture in Mexico." The first trip was in 1988 to Guadalajara, where Seboo and I flew with a group of students headed by our art history professor, Jim Urmston. We spent a wonderful, informative nine-day spring break there, exploring the periods of indigenous Indian, Spanish colonial, and Mexican modern and contemporary art and architecture. We visited Morella, San Miguel de Allende and the picturesque, hilly city of Guan Juato, where we saw Mexico's famous muralist, Diego Rivera's apartment, in which he had spent his childhood. We also attended a concert at Guan Juato's opera house, dedicated to the late Henryk Szeryng. Szeryng, a renowned Polish

With Anoush in Nice, France (1989).

violinist, who had spent most of his life in Mexico and was granted Mexican citizenship, was revered by the Mexicans for his contributions to their culture in the fields of music and education.

In Patzcuaro, south of Guadelajara, a graceful town of cobble-stoned streets, white houses and large plazas, we bought some silver and leather items at the weekly outdoor market. On Good-Friday, we came across a massive procession by the native Indians who carried crucifixes on their shoulders. On a boat ride on Lake Patzcuaro to the little mountain island of Junitrio, fishermen threw their nets over the water, expertly giving them the form of a huge butterfly, a beautiful show for which they gathered money from the spectators. Patzcuaro became more memorable for me when I read in Frida Kahlo's biography, the Mexican surrealist painter, that she and her husband, Diego Rivera, had visited it in 1939, together with the French surrealist poet, Andre Breton and his wife, and Leon Trotsky and his wife. Trotsky was a Russian revolutionary and an opponent of Stalin, who lived in exile in Mexico from 1929 until his assassination in 1940. The three famous couples had spent some leisurely time exploring the little villages around the lake during the day, and having serious discussions about art, literature and politics in the evenings.

We made a similar trip to Mexico City with my daughter, Hoori, on the next trip in 1990. There, on a heavily scheduled daily program, we visited museums and art galleries, cathedrals and churches, with paintings and murals by Rivera, Orozco and Siqueros, two other Mexican muralists. In

Coyoacan, when visiting Frida Kahlo's residence-turned-museum, I was hoping to find all of her paintings together, but except for a few, I saw a number of wooden sculptures, mostly of a squatting woman caught in the act of child birth. Apparently, those sculptures were a reflection of Frida's obsession with having a child she never had. I saw a huge portrait of Mao Tse Tung and a bust of Stalin in that house, which gave me a hint about Frida's involvement in politics.

To the north of Mexico City we saw the pre-Colombian pyramidal structures of Teotihuacan, "The City of the Gods," the Pyramids of the Sun and the Moon with the residential complexes along a broad central avenue, known as the Avenue of the Dead.

One evening our group attended the Ballet Folklorico de Mexico at the Palacio de Bellas Artes (a Hollywood style production). In Puebla, a city that took our breaths away with its beautiful jacarandas and corals in a riot of light blue and coral red, we visited its cathedral and the Halifax library that housed valuable ancient books in Spanish, Latin, Greek and Hebrew, many of them over 500 years old.

The group we traveled with consisted not only of students but also a few Santa Monica residents, among them doctors, lawyers and artists, with whom we socialized during lunch and dinner, discussing and exchanging opinions about our new experiences.

*****

While visiting a sick friend at St. John's Hospital in Los Angele in February 1996, I noticed an ad in bold letters that read: "VOLUNTEERS ARE GODSENDS." Since I was considering a volunteer job, I applied for it and, after attending a few lectures and orientation tours of the premises, I started working at the information desk for once a week. Apart from leading the visitors to their desired departments and answering their questions, I was in charge of taking flowers to the patients' rooms, sent by their friends or relatives.

One time, I took a basket of white tulips to the room of an elderly man who was surrounded by flower baskets. The man looked at me angrily and said, "What is this, my funeral?" Another time, when I took flowers for a young woman, she started to cry after reading the card. They were from her parents, who lived in town, but had preferred to send her flowers instead of visiting her personally. In both cases, I felt sorry for them, but couldn't make any comments because I was not supposed to.

During the period of volunteering at St. John's, my daughter Hoori and daughter-in-law, Ninette, gave birth to their baby daughters, Taleen and

Christine – nine days apart – giving me a chance to visit them after the work.

In May of the same year, I also applied to work as a volunteer at the Paul Getty Museum, in Malibu. The interviewers at the museum were known to be very strict and picky. They asked me, "Give us two good reasons why we should take you in." I thought a little and answered, "First, I'm a volunteer at St. John's Hospital and know how to deal with patients and visitors, and second, I know three languages which will come in handy with the multi-national visitors to the museum." My reasoning satisfied them and I was invited to join the Volunteer Service Council after attending their training/ orientation program. They recommended casual clothing and comfortable walking shoes.

I participated in the two-day, eight-hour training sessions, with outdoor sit-down lunches, which they hosted in the Main Peristyle Gardens, alongside the shallow blue-tiled pool. The Getty Villa and its extensive gardens located on the Pacific Coast are modeled after the original Villa Dei Papiri at Herculaneum, a Roman country house, built around 200 to 150 B.C. The Villa that was buried by the eruption of Mount Vesuvius in A.D. 79 was excavated in the 18th century.

At the auditorium, they talked about our duties, the security system, and gave us an overview of the museum and its role in educating students in the fields of art and art history. Outside, they led us to the herb and fruit garden, and the top of a hill where they kept an emergency storage facility in case of an earthquake. They also showed us the grave sites of Mr. Getty and his two sons. At the end of the second session, we were given our badges with our weekly schedules. I was assigned to work on Wednesday mornings at the information desk. I worked at the Getty Villa for a year until it was closed down for renovation.

In the summer of 1997, the volunteers were given another training and orientation tour of the new Getty Center that was built on top of a hill in Brentwood, not far from Malibu. After its opening ceremony and lavish dinner parties in December, Getty Villa volunteers, plus newly recruited ones, started to work at the information desk, audio guide desk, orientation theater, arrival plaza, lower tram, family room (for children), and the galleries of photo and special exhibits. For the first few months, the duty of the volunteers was "to control the crowd," especially at the lower tram, from where throngs of people were led into the three-car tram that took them to the top of the hill and the center of activities. Visitors were fascinated by the driverless, computer-operated tram that glided on a cushion of air generated by electric blowers. My first position was at the information desk, where I

At the Getty Center volunteer lounge, with our
Saturday A2 shift group (2008).

worked with other volunteers. Dressed in beige pants and white shirt, we
constantly answered the questions of groups of visitors who had rushed to
see the much publicized museum.

One of the questions that the visitors would ask was, "Why isn't the
Getty Center like a regular museum?" And we would answer, "That's why it
is called a 'center' and not a 'museum.'" The Getty Center, apart from the
museum, also consists of three other departments: Conservation Institute
(GCI), which focuses on preserving and maintaining historic landmarks
around the world; the Research Institute (GRI), with its rich library of
nearly one million books and periodicals in art history, architecture and
archeology is open to students of all nationalities. The Getty Foundation
supports education through its grants and fellowships to researchers at home
and abroad.

Getty Center has two annual parties: one in September for volunteers
and their spouses, the other in January, the "recognition party," which is
thrown in honor of the volunteers who are recognized for their services of
one, five, ten, fifteen, twenty or twenty-five years.

One of the Center's interesting events is an exhibit of art works provided
by the members of staff, VSA (visitor-services associates), security, docents
and volunteers. The exhibit that is held every two years (a biennale) is called
"Getty Underground" because it is held in the underground corridors of the
building. So far, I have participated in three of them with my photographs
of landscapes.

I like working at the Getty, and enjoy the company of our shift, which is comprised of about twenty-five people, mostly women of different ages, some of whom consider our shift group their second family. At the Getty, I have a chance to see its permanent and changing exhibits, to shop at its gift store, or to roam around its fragrant Central Garden, with its well-tended flowers, exotic plants, dancing fountains and gurgling brooks. To me, the Getty Central Garden, designed by Robert Irwin, is much more than a garden. It is a work of sophisticated art and, as they say, "It is a sculpture in the form of a garden." I like to take along those friends who come from other cities or countries and are eager to visit the famous Getty Center. Sometimes, I also take along my grandchildren who enjoy riding the tram, the family room – with its educational activities, like finding works of art on the computer or doing arts-and-crafts – and the garden where they like to throw coins into the wishing pool. Then, their most favorite spot, the cafeteria where they like to eat, chat and ask questions about the day's experiences.

*****

Throughout the fourteen years of volunteering at the Getty, I have seen many changes and replacements in our shift group because of relocation, old age, death, or simply getting tired of the work.

Similarly, with the passing of the years, our family has noticed gradual changes in Southern California. The Los Angeles of today is not the same city we came to in 1976. Gone are the days when we left our car doors unlocked in the street, when freeways were fun to drive, and when the children rode their bicycles safely to school. We miss the days when it was easy to handle a business over the phone by talking to a human being, instead of a machine. *Attari*, the grocery store on Westwood Boulevard, near UCLA, in West Los Angeles (now home to many Iranians), from where we used to buy certain Iranian food items, doesn't exist any more. Instead, dozens of new grocery stores have sprouted on both sides of the street, offering their customers favorite Iranian fruit, such as sweet lemons, persimmons, pomegranates, tiny seedless grapes, and varieties of fresh herbs. In these shops you can find pastries and sweets, like *baghlava*, rice-cookies and *gaz*, and also Farsi newspapers and magazines, most of them published in the United States. Walking along the street, you will see photocopying centers, flower shops, hairdressers, passport and wedding-photo shops, Persian carpet stores and restaurants.

There are a dozen book stores on Westwood Boulevard that sell Farsi and English books. The largest of them is *Sherkat Ketab* (Book Company) that

Our 45th wedding anniversary, with our children and four
grandchildren: Christine, Taleen, Ara, and Eric (2002).

not only publishes the thick Iranian yellow-pages, but also prints books in
both languages and promotes them through Iranian television and Radio
Iran. The popular radio station that has been functioning for the last ten
years has had a crucial role in calling for peace and unity among outraged
Iranians, when after the disastrous 9/11 incident, Iranian men were
summoned to register with the Immigration and Naturalization Office, but
were detained for visa violations. As a result, thousands of Iranians protested
in front of the Federal Building on Wilshire Boulevard, attracting the
attention and sympathy of the media. One of the popular radio programs
which is on air five days a week for two hours is called *"Secrets and Needs."*
For ten years, Dr. Farhang Holakouee, a sociologist/psychologist has
answered questions from thousands of callers and guided them through
their problems regarding family, marriage and children.

For years, Persian movies, plays and concerts have attracted and
entertained nostalgic Iranian audiences. Similarly, a number of social,
literary and religious societies have consoled and comforted displaced and
frustrated Iranian individuals, regardless of gender and age, including the
U.S. born youth with little knowledge of Farsi. Among them, there is the
popular "Lovers of Molana," which Seboo and I have attended a few times.
At a weekly gathering at a senior center in West Los Angeles, Iranians listen
to Dr. Mohammad Pakravan, a scholar who for over twenty years has read,
interpreted and discussed the lyrical *Ghazals* of Hafez and mystical poems

of Molana with his audience. Shams-eddin-Mohamad Hafez was a 14th century lyric poet whose *Divan* (Collected Poems), a poetical horoscope, has been translated into numerous languages and is frequently used by its readers. Molana Jalal-eddin-Rumi was a gnostic and mystic poet whose, *Masnavi Maanavi*, a masterpiece of Persian literature, has also been translated and widely read in the West. By listening to those poems, you are transported from an ordinary, material life into a more meaningful and profound one, where you can relax, learn, and feel spiritually satisfied.

With all these Iranians and their activities in West Los Angeles and elsewhere in the city, it is not in vain that they call Los Angeles, Irangeles.

Since their arrival in the United States, Iranians have achieved and contributed much in the fields of medicine, engineering, business, journalism, teaching, entrepreneurship, politics and others. Among the university students there are numerous housewives who have balanced their duties as wives and mothers to achieve their goals of obtaining higher degrees. I remember watching a very successful young Iranian businesswoman on the Oprah Winfrey Show who had paid $20 million just to make a trip on a Russian spaceship. However, not all of them have had the chance or the good fortune to succeed in their new country. There are many who haven't been able to make it in life, a sad example of which I saw in the movie, *House of Sand and Fog*. It was a story in which a former Iranian colonel has to work as a trash collector in order to make the both ends meet. Then after being faced with a series of misfortunes, including his son's murder, out of despair, he poisons his wife, then suffocates himself with a plastic bag. In the movie, the role of the colonel's wife was played by an Iranian actress who was nominated for that year's best supporting actress in the Academy Awards.

*****

As for our family, despite frustrations and disappointments, in the long run, we still are happy living in the United States and are counting our blessings. We haven't lost our roots, have kept our ties with the old country and have been concerned about the fate of the nation in times of crisis. When Seboo traveled to Tehran in 2004 to see some of his friends, he visited my childhood residence on Naderi Avenue, where he took a few pictures of the apartment, with the dilapidated old balcony and the sign of "Alborz Laboratory" still standing. Strangely, that side of the avenue had been left untouched, whereas on the other side, old buildings had been razed and new ones were built. As I looked at the photos, I thought about the balcony that had stood the test of time for more than half a century. It had witnessed many historical events since the 1930s and throughout the years leading to the late 1970s – the period of time before and after the Iranian Islamic Revolution.

Here in the United States, Seboo and I are happy that our children have made it in life, both in their education and careers and especially in their personal family lives. Aram married Ninette, the daughter of an Iranian-Armenian couple and old friends, who has a master's degree in aerospace engineering from UCLA. She used to work for Boeing, North America, even after the birth of their daughter, Christine, but resigned after the birth of their son, Eric. Then a few years later when the children were grown up and attending school, she took a job with Teledyne Technologies Corporation.

Hoori married Vache, the son of an Armenian couple from Syria. He has an MBA from UC Berkeley, and works for the Los Angeles County Employees Retirement Association. They too have a daughter, Taleen, and a son, Ara. Hoori has kept working all along as Seboo and I have helped her in raising their children, who have kept us busy and happy. All our grandchildren are doing well at their schools, take piano lessons, and participate in their schools' sports activities and events. And most important of all, Aram and Hoori and their spouses are trying to maintain their children's Armenian identity by educating them in that direction. They send them to Armenian language Saturday school and its cultural events, organized by the Iranian-Armenian Society in Glendale. In order to keep the family relationship tight, we have regularly treated them to dinner at our home every Friday evening since our children's engagements.

In the summer of 2007, Seboo and I planned and made a trip to Yerevan with our children and grandchildren to acquaint them with our Armenian roots and the culture. There, we visited the pagan Temple of the Sun in Garni; the 11th-13th century monastery of Geghart (partly carved out of a solid rock) and its hand-carved *khachkars* (cross stones). We paid our tributes to the Monument of Tsitsernakaberd that commemorates the Genocide of 1915, and the tomb of St. Mesrop Mashtots, the 5th century inventor of the Armenian alphabet, in the village of Oshagan. At *Matenadaran,* a world-class library and research institute, we saw a small part of a large collection of bibles, religious and precious works of art, as well as rare illuminated manuscripts, masterpieces of 14th century Armenian illumination. They were mostly in Armenian and some in foreign languages, with subjects ranging from history, art, literature, philosophy to medicine. We visited the 4th century Echmiadzin Cathedral, the religious center for all Armenians that has stood the test of the country's turbulent history for

With Seboo, Ninette, and grandchildren in the lobby of
Armenia Hotel, Yerevan (2007).

seventeen centuries. We were impressed by the sight of many other
cathedrals and churches in Armenia, some of them a thousand years old,
with the headstones of kings and nobilities surrounding them.

Our grandchildren were very young to fully comprehend what they were
seeing in Armenia. After all, the girls were ten-and-a-half-years old and the
boys nearly nine. But then, wasn't I younger than them when grandpa took
me to the library and museum of the *Vank*, and showed me the ancient
Armenian manuscripts, miniatures and chronicles held there? I didn't
understand them then but the introduction whetted my curiosity to learn
and seek more in the years to come. However, our grandchildren were smart
enough to observe certain things in the daily lives of Armenians, and
expressed their opinions about them. For instance, the boys didn't like the
widespread habit of smoking, the aggressive taxi drivers, and the frenetic
pace of urban traffic (although we seldom saw an accident).

While in Yerevan, I found Aunt Mary's younger son, Mihran, the only
survivor of his brother and sisters. He was a seventy-three-year-old retired
architect who lived alone with the little retirement money he received from
the government. His wife had gone to New York to work for a family friend
and sent a part of her salary to her daughter to pay for her children's tuition.
Their second daughter, a physician, had found a job in Paris, and sent
Mihran the medicines he couldn't afford to buy in Yerevan. Mihran's late

Hoori and Vache's wedding, with our extended family
(September 4, 1994).

Aram and Ninette's wedding, with members of the two families,
the best man and his wife (November 26, 1994).

older brother's wife and their adult children lived in Moscow. His late sister's daughter had married an Italian and lived in Rome. It seemed that after the collapse of the communist regime and the republic's economic crisis, many individuals had left home in search of jobs in America, Russia or other European countries, in order to help their families in Armenia.

In contrast to people emigrating to other countries, there were people who were immigrating and settling in Armenia. I met Uncle Johnny's two daughters and their families who, like other Armenian families, had relocated from Tehran after Armenia's independence from the Soviet Union. The younger daughter had opened a small gift shop, bringing in fancy goods from Iran and the Arab Emirates. Her two sons were attending Yerevan University and helping her at the shop in their spare time. I also met their elder brother whom I hadn't seen for thirty one years. He had especially flown in from Tehran to see me and my family.

*****

In the fall of 1980, Vartges' wife and ten-year-old daughter who had flown to Paris to spend their summer vacation didn't return to Tehran due to the Iran-Iraq war. The war that erupted in September and lasted until July of 1988, forced them to stay in France, changing Vartges' life forever.

Being a diabetic, Vartges had to follow a special diet, but had neglected it completely. He didn't take his medications regularly, and didn't care about his overall health. And to make the matters worse, he was affected by the nerve-racking Iraqi air raids over Tehran, with their alerts, sirens, and missile strikes that would take their toll on his already fragile body and psyche. He had a mild stroke and had to be treated in the hospital then recuperate at one of his friends' home. Fortunately, he partially recovered from the stroke and maintained his good spirits. As the saying goes, "He was bent but not broken." He kept teaching at Tehran University Medical School and headed its laboratory. In the meantime, he continued his volunteer services at the Armenian Free Clinic, the one he had co-founded after WWII. He also counseled and consoled many depressed and despairing individuals who turned to him for emotional support, because he knew quite well what it was like to be left behind and alone by one's family.

A year after the end of the war in July 1988, he left Iran. First, he stopped in Paris to spend a couple of months with his wife and daughter then flew to Los Angeles where he lived with my family and those of my two brothers alternately for a few years. When his health started to deteriorate, we transferred him to a convalescent home where he died in 1993 at the age of seventy six. After his death, he was highly eulogized in Los Angeles and

With my brothers Emil and Armen at aunt Mary's 85th birthday (2002).

especially in Tehran by the Medical School and the Persian and Armenian communities, to which he had rendered his life-long services.

While he was staying with us, I noticed a change of attitude in him. He was not the same happy, easy-going Vartges who liked to crack jokes, tell anecdotes, go out and meet friends. He avoided public places and was cold toward relatives and friends. I don't know what was going on in his mind as he never shared his thoughts with us. Was it his ailment? Was he missing his daughter? Or was he unhappy about his failed second marriage? Whatever the truth, to our family, Vartges was a lion of a man, whose legacy as a family man, physician, professor, author of six medical books, and a person devoted to serving his community will live on in our hearts.

My brother, Emil, still a bachelor, is a self-employed architect who lives in Los Angeles. Armen is a successful computer engineer, who works for Teledyne Technologies Corporation, specializing in aviation electronics. His wife, Stella, is a librarian who works in Glendale. His son, Arby, is a cardiologist who is married with three children. He was the one who woke me up one early morning to let me know about his marriage proposal to his girlfriend in Athens. Armen's daughter, Ani, who recently married a cardiologist, has obtained her Ph.D. in computer engineering at UCLA, where she currently teaches.

Seboo's brother, Rubik, who worked for Standard Oil, is now retired and lives in San Francisco with his wife, Shakeh and daughter, Christine, a Stanford graduate student. Seboo's stepbrother, Bobby, who worked at the United Nations in Bangkok and was later transferred to New York is also

In Fresno, at a family reunion, with Seboo's three brothers
and their wives (2008).

retired and lives there with his second wife, Sonia, whom he married after
Bonnie's death.

Shahen, Seboo's younger stepbrother, who was married and had two
children and five grandchildren, died on New Year's Eve of 2009. He was
the one who had visited us during our honeymoon and brought us Seboo's
wallet. Shahen was a graduate of Baldwin Wallace College in Berea, Ohio,
from where he had obtained a B.Sc. in physics. In 1973 he had established
the Westaire Engineering Company in Los Angeles, where he designed and
manufactured commercial and industrial gravity ventilators and air-
conditioning equipment. Shahen was an energetic, handsome man with a
happy demeanor. He liked to travel and go fishing with his three friends.
Unfortunately, he developed an aggressive form of leukemia in July of 2009
and sought treatment at the Jonsson Cancer Center at UCLA. During his
long-term hospitalization, Seboo visited him regularly and I accmpanied
him occasionally.

On December 19, Seboo, Aram and I visited him at his home and
celebrated his seventy-seventh birthday with his family. He was excited
about his recent achievement: a new environmentally efficient air
conditioner that he had designed and sold to Stanford University for its
School of Management. Three days before his death, Seboo and I visited
him again. He was drugged and unwilling to talk. But when Seboo started

to reminisce about a funny event in the past, he suddenly came back to life and whispered, "This is...good.... This is... so good...." He asked his wife, Cathy, to bring in a few of his Farsi poetry books, and asked me to read a line or two. I chose the *Selected Poems* of Forough Farrokhzad, the famous Iranian poetess. As I leafed through the book and went over the pages, a line caught my attention, and I read it for him aloud: "Remember the flight; the bird is mortal." A smile came over his face, as if those two lines had defined his life. And I chose those two lines for the epigraph of my book.

*****

Although our family lives in west Los Angeles, away from Glendale where a large community of Armenians from Iran, Armenia and the Middle East reside, we often participate in the cultural and social events, organized by their cultural or ethnic societies. We attend church on certain occasions, such as holidays, a baptism, a wedding or a memorial service. We buy books from Armenian bookstores, some of which also publish books in both languages, and present and promote them at their stores or the Glendale public library by informing the community through Armenian papers and periodicals. Like Westwood, there are many ethnic grocery and pastry shops as well as restaurants in Glendale. Like Los Angeles, which is called *Irangeles*, Glendale is known as *Los Armenos*.

Despite all these Armenians and Persians within easy reach, I sometimes yearn for the old country, especially Tehran where I was born and raised. Maybe it is just my youth that I miss, and not the country. Maybe I just like to stroll down the memory lane, remembering the good things that happened so long ago and so far away. Or maybe I enjoy a swift transition to the past through a piece of familiar music or a sweet song, to a "past," that, as William Faulkner has said, "is never dead, and is not even past."

The End

ABOUT THE AUTHOR

Elma Hovanessian was born and raised in Tehran, Iran. A graduate of Tehran University, she majored in English literature and continued her studies in creative writing in London and Los Angeles. She has contributed to English language newspapers and magazines in Iran, the United Kingdom, and the United States. She is the author of Under the Blue Dome, a historical novel set in Iran.